Christian Carl August Gosch, James Hall

Danish Arctic Expeditions

1605 to 1620

Christian Carl August Gosch, James Hall

Danish Arctic Expeditions
1605 to 1620

ISBN/EAN: 9783743323926

Manufactured in Europe, USA, Canada, Australia, Japa

Cover: Foto ©ninafisch / pixelio.de

Manufactured and distributed by brebook publishing software (www.brebook.com)

Christian Carl August Gosch, James Hall

Danish Arctic Expeditions

DANISH
ARCTIC EXPEDITIONS,
1605 TO 1620.

IN TWO BOOKS:

BOOK I.—THE DANISH EXPEDITIONS TO GREENLAND IN 1605, 1606, AND 1607; TO WHICH IS ADDED CAPTAIN JAMES HALL'S VOYAGE TO GREENLAND IN 1612.

BOOK II.—THE EXPEDITION OF CAPTAIN JENS MUNK TO HUDSON'S BAY IN SEARCH OF A NORTH-WEST PASSAGE IN 1619-20.

Edited, with Notes and Introduction,

BY

C. C. A. GOSCH.

BOOK II.

LONDON:
PRINTED FOR THE HAKLUYT SOCIETY.
M.DCCC.XCVII.

CONTENTS OF BOOK II.

PAGE

INTRODUCTION:

   I.—The Life of Jens Munk v

   II.—Bibliography of Early Accounts of Munk's Life and Voyage lv

   III.—Notice of Voyages in Search of a North-West Passage preceding that of Munk . . . lxviii

   IV.—Preliminary Observations on Jens Munk's Expedition to Hudson's Bay xcvii

JENS MUNK'S "NAVIGATIO SEPTENTRIONALIS" . . 1

COMMENTARY TO JENS MUNK'S "NAVIGATIO SEPTENTRIONALIS":

   I. Observations on the Text . . . 60

   II.—Observations on Munk's Map and on the Geographical Results of his Voyage . . . 136

INDEX . . 185

LIST OF MAPS AND ILLUSTRATIONS IN BOOK II.

Munk's representation of his meeting with the Eskimoes, etc.   *Facing* 14
Munk's Map . . . . . *Facing* 21
Munk's representation of his Wintering . . *Facing* 23
Munk's Map with scale of degrees inserted . . *Facing* 151
Track Map showing Munk's Route   *At the end of the volume*

IN THE TEXT.

Map of Port Churchill . . 110

COUNCIL

OF

THE HAKLUYT SOCIETY.

SIR CLEMENTS MARKHAM, K.C.B., F.R.S., *Pres. R.G.S.*, PRESIDENT,
THE RIGHT HON. THE LORD STANLEY OF ALDERLEY, VICE-PRESIDENT.
SIR WILLIAM WHARTON, K.C.B., VICE-PRESIDENT.
C. RAYMOND BEAZLEY, ESQ., M.A.
COLONEL G. EARL CHURCH.
THE RIGHT HON. GEORGE N. CURZON, M.P.
ALBERT GRAY, ESQ.
ALFRED HARMSWORTH, ESQ.
THE RIGHT HON. LORD HAWKESBURY.
EDWARD HEAWOOD, ESQ., M.A.
ADMIRAL SIR ANTHONY H. HOSKINS, G.C.B.
REAR-ADMIRAL ALBERT H. MARKHAM.
A. P. MAUDSLAY, ESQ.
E. DELMAR MORGAN, ESQ.
CAPTAIN NATHAN, R.E.
ADMIRAL SIR E. OMMANNEY, C.B., F.R.S.
CUTHBERT E. PEEK, ESQ.
E. G. RAVENSTEIN, ESQ.
HOWARD SAUNDERS, ESQ.
CHARLES WELCH, ESQ., F.S.A.

WILLIAM FOSTER, ESQ., B.A., *Honorary Secretary.*

DANISH ARCTIC EXPEDITIONS,

1605 TO 1620.

BOOK II.

JENS MUNK'S VOYAGE TO HUDSON'S BAY,

1619 AND 1620.

THE EXPEDITION OF JENS MUNK TO HUDSON'S BAY,

IN SEARCH OF

A NORTH-WEST PASSAGE,

IN

1619-20.

[Translated from Munk's *Navigatio Septentrionalis* (Copenhagen, 1624, 4º)].

INTRODUCTION.

I.—*The Life of Jens Munk.*

HE perilous nature, tragic development, and heroic termination of the voyage of Jens Munk to Hudson's Bay cannot fail to enlist the sympathy of all who read of it, quite apart from the interest attaching to it as a voyage of discovery. All through the events of that expedition, the personality of the leader is conspicuous, and the history of Munk's life altogether is well worthy of notice. He was essentially a self-made man, like so many of those whose names are the best remembered; and his varying fortunes in fighting the battle of life, which began for him when he was a mere boy, present a picture of unusual interest, whether we fix our attention on his personal history or on his public achievements. Nobility of character, unflinching devotion to duty, indomitable courage, and the modesty which charms us most in those who need it

least, always claim admiration, and Munk appears to have been a bright example of each of these qualities. There are few names on the roll of the Danish Navy of which it has better reason to be proud, than that of Munk, the Navigator. Not only amongst the Danish explorers, but amongst those of all the world, he occupies an honourable place. We think ourselves justified, therefore, in submitting to our readers a somewhat fuller account of Munk's life than the object of this volume would in strictness require.[1]

The information now available is not sufficient to clear up all uncertainty concerning Jens Munk's descent and family connections. Still, much more is known of him in these respects than can now be ascertained concerning any of the commanders of the English voyages of the same series, owing to the fact that Munk was the son of a man who in his day was well known in Denmark, though, unfortunately, not altogether favourably. Of Munk's grandfather, it was known that his name was Niels Munk, and that he owned an estate called Hjörne, in

---

[1] The following account, like all other biographies of Munk, is based mainly on one which appeared anonymously in 1723 (see *post*, *Bibliography*, etc.). The author of this states that it is extracted chiefly from Munk's own journals, but partly from other trustworthy sources; and its general agreement with the statements of accredited historians and official documents, in so far as it can be tested by such means, bears witness of its truthfulness. Not a few facts have afterwards come to light in various publications, to which reference will be made in the proper places.

Halland, a province which is now a part of Sweden, but which at that time belonged to Denmark. As he is mentioned in contemporary documents amongst the nobles of Halland, it seems probable that he belonged, though perhaps distantly, to a noble family of the name of Munk, which is now extinct, but which at that time was still flourishing in Denmark. About this, however, nothing further is known. Certain it is that his son, Erik Nielsen Munk—father of our hero, Jens Eriksen Munk[1]—was not considered as of noble birth. This, however, may be reconciled with the foregoing statements concerning Niels Munk by assuming that the wife of the latter, whose descent is not known, was a commoner; for the law of Denmark then required, as a condition of inherited nobility, that both parents should be noble. Erik Munk appears to have been a man of considerable ability, who so distinguished himself, both as a naval commander and in other ways, that in reward for his services he received a patent of nobility in 1580. Unfortunately for his children, his wife was simply the daughter of a surgeon. Jens Munk could not, therefore, claim the status of a nobleman, a circumstance which probably was unfavourable to his advancement later in life.

In other and not less serious respects, Munk's

---

[1] It was customary in Denmark to insert between the Christian name and the family name that of the father, with the addition of *sen* (son) or *datter* (daughter), as the case might be.

start in life was unpropitious. His father had obtained from King Frederick II, not only a patent of nobility, but the grant of certain so-called Crown-fiefs in Norway, the administration of which would legitimately leave him a handsome income. He resided for some years at Barbo, an estate which he acquired near the modern town of Arendal, a part of which—still called Barbo—is built on land once belonging to him. Here his second son, Jens, was born on June 3rd, 1579. But Erik Munk grossly abused the favours bestowed upon him. In the course of a comparatively short time, he accumulated considerable property, but not by lawful means. Loud and many were the complaints of his oppressive exactions and unjust dealings, which involved him in numerous lawsuits. He was accused of maladministration in cutting down Crown forests for his own use, and of otherwise sacrificing the interests of the Crown to his own private ends. In consequence of these charges, he was in 1585 deprived of his fiefs, and commissioners were appointed to investigate his conduct, with the result that in 1586 he was imprisoned in the Castle of Dragsholm, in Seeland (the same where James Bothwell had died in confinement in 1578), and there he remained for the rest of his life. His wife, who had to leave Barbo, went with her children to reside at Frederiksstad, a small town in the province of Smaalenene, where she died in 1623. In 1588, she sent her younger son, Jens—then nine years old—to his father's sister, who had married a wealthy citizen

of Aalborg, in Jutland, Frederik Christensen by
name, who was burgomaster of the town, and also
otherwise a notable man. The boy, however, did
not remain here long, but returned to Norway in
1591. Whether he did so on account of being
by necessity thrown upon his own resources, or
on account of his being naturally of a restless and
adventurous disposition, does not appear; but, at
any rate, from this time, he had to rely upon himself
alone for his maintenance and advancement in the
world. His anonymous biographer tells us that in
that same year he sailed with a Friesland skipper,
named Jacob Gerbrantzon, to England, and thence
to Oporto, where he remained for a year with a
merchant whom he calls Duart Duez, his object
being to learn the Portuguese language. Why he
wished to do so is not stated, but it seems probable
enough that, having heard of the golden chances
offered by the New World, of which the Portuguese
then possessed so large a portion, he wished to
qualify himself to try his fortune there. Very
likely it was with that very object that he had
left Aalborg, where he may probably not have seen
much prospect of advancement for himself, the
penniless son of a disgraced man. At any rate,
after spending a year at Oporto, Munk sailed for
Bahia, in order, by the advice of his host or employer,
to join a brother of the latter who resided there. He
was then only thirteen years of age, and worked his
passage as a cabin boy. He arrived safely, but
only to find that Miguel Duez, with whom he was

to live, had just left Bahia on a visit to Europe. Munk then elected to remain with the skipper, Albert Jansen of Eynkhusen, with whom he had come across from Europe; and, accordingly, he left Bahia again, in order to accompany the latter on his further voyage. But this was not to be.

In those days, trading vessels on long voyages mostly sailed in fleets for mutual protection against freebooters (who then abounded on the high seas), one of the skippers being chosen admiral. In this case, the fleet numbered thirteen sail, four being Dutch and nine Portuguese. The Admiral chosen was Jan van Bossen, of Embden; the Vice-Admiral was Roland of Flushing; and the Rear-Admiral was Albert Jansen, of the *Schoubynacht* (literally, the *Watch-by-night*), with whom Munk was. As ill-luck would have it, they were attacked (apparently not far from Bahia) by a French fleet, commanded by a Count whose name seems to have been accidentally omitted from the biography, the Vice-Admiral being one Ribold of Rochelle. The Frenchmen are described as freebooters, but this does not seem altogether to have been their real character, for it is stated that their intention was to make themselves masters of Baya de todos los Santos (which is the real name of Bahia) an undertaking which would seem to be rather beyond the scope of mere freebooters. The circumstances of the time (to which, however, there does not seem to have been any allusion in Munk's journal) may sufficiently explain the apparent contradiction. In France, civil war was then raging between King Henry III and the so-called *Ligue*, which was supported by King Philip II of Spain, whilst the King of France was especially supported by his Protestant subjects, amongst whose cities Rochelle stood foremost. Remembering, at the same time, that Philip had, eleven years before, obtained possession of Portugal and her dependencies, it appears not improbable that the fleet in question was sent out from Rochelle in order, if possible, to capture Bahia, the principal port of Brazil, even though a certain element of freebooting may have been combined with it.[1]

However this may be, a fight ensued between the trading fleet and the Frenchmen, with the result that the leading Dutch ships were taken or destroyed, Albert Jansen's being burnt, and only seven persons saved, of whom Munk was one. The survivors floated on some wreckage until the battle was over, when they were picked up by the French and landed on a part of the coast where they were in great danger of falling victims to the savage natives. Jens Munk, however, after great hardships, succeeded in reaching Bahia, where he maintained himself for eleven months as a shoemaker's apprentice, after which he lived for six months with a portrait painter. At length, Miguel Duez returned from Europe and at once took Munk

---

[1] An attempt on Bahia had been made by the English in 1588, and another, which was more successful, was made in 1623 by the Dutch, who held possession until 1625.

into his house. With him, he remained between three and four years, until another stirring adventure caused him—unintentionally, as it seems—to return to Europe.

In 1598, two Dutch vessels arrived at Bahia in order to trade; but, as they had not chosen to furnish themselves with a licence for this purpose from the King of Spain, the Spanish authorities decided to seize and confiscate them, according to the usage of those times. In order to effect this, seven vessels, large and small, lying in the harbour, were manned with soldiers at the dead of night, others being posted along the shore to prevent information being given to the Dutchmen on board, and as many of the latter as were on shore were arrested. Nevertheless, Miguel Duez determined to give the Dutchmen warning. Munk's biographer says that, in so doing, he was moved by an honest care for the Dutchmen, which, perhaps, implies that he had business relations with them; but he was probably moved quite as much by the hatred of the patriotic Portuguese against their new Spanish masters. Howbeit, at the request of Duez, Munk swam out to the Dutch vessels in the roadstead and informed them of their danger—in the very nick of time, as it turned out; for no sooner had they cut their cables and set sail, than the Spaniards were upon them. The Dutch, however, succeeded in beating them off and getting away; and Jens Munk (who, under the circumstances, could not have returned to Bahia if he had wished to do so) sailed with them to Amsterdam.

The owners of the Dutch ships showed their gratitude to Munk by liberal presents and offers of employment; and, when he declined the latter, they enabled him to return to Copenhagen, where he is believed to have arrived in the same year (1598), after an absence from Denmark of seven years. Meanwhile his father had died in prison. It does not appear that his cause was ever formally adjudicated upon, presumably because he died before the conclusion of the intricate inquiry and of the complicated lawsuits which arose out of his various transactions. He appears to have tried, but in vain, to appeal to the King's former gracious disposition towards him, and at last, in the year 1594, to have ended his existence by suicide. Owing to this circumstance, all his property, as has been observed,[1] was liable to be forfeited. As a matter of fact, the Crown did retain possession of all his landed property, a very small part of his personal effects being, as a matter of grace, returned to his family in 1598, whilst another portion is believed to have been applied to a public purpose.[2]

Although only nineteen years of age at the time of his arrival at Copenhagen, Jens Munk at once obtained employment as clerk or accountant on

---

[1] According to H. D. Lind, *Kong Christian den Fjerde og hans Mænd paa Bremerholm* (Copenhagen, 1889), p. 193.

[2] Oluf Nielsen, *Kjöbenhavns Historie, etc.* (Copenhagen, 1877), vol. iv, p. 216.

board a vessel in which he made four voyages to Spain. At that period, Danish noblemen engaged not a little in commercial undertakings, for which they enjoyed special privileges; and, in 1601, Munk entered the service of one of these enterprising *seigneurs*, Henrik Ramel by name, a member of the *Rigsraad* (or Council of the Realm), and a great man—the same after whom Hall, in 1605, named a fjord in Greenland "Ramel's Fjord". In his service, Munk made, during four years, fifteen voyages as merchant, mostly to Baltic ports, one to Holland, and one to Spain.

By the end of this time, Munk seems to have acquired sufficient means to commence operations on his own account; and, from 1605, we find him making voyages to different countries in the combined characters of sea-captain and merchant, though at first only as part-owner of ship and cargo. One of these involved him in a lawsuit, of which some record is still extant. It must have been at this time, when he commenced more or less independent voyages, that he had himself enrolled as a citizen of Copenhagen, without which he would not have had a legal status in such undertakings.

At the period in question, the northern seas were attracting considerable attention as a field both of geographical discovery and commercial enterprise. It was then that the expeditions to Greenland treated of in the First Book of this volume were sent out, and both the Danish government and private individuals bestirred themselves in order to secure a share of any advantages that might be reaped in those northern latitudes. Munk, too, soon threw himself into this new line of adventure. It is recorded that in 1608 he sailed to Iceland to fetch home a cargo of sulphur from the rich deposits at Husavik. In the following year, he joined a prominent merchant of Copenhagen, Jens Hvid, in an expedition to Nova Zembla, each sailing in his own vessel. But they never reached their destination at all. Jens Hvid appears to have stopped at some port on the main-land, while Munk attempted to press further on; but he did not get much beyond the island of Kulguew, the coasts of which he explored. His biographer of 1723 states that he reached a latitude of 69° 8′, and that he there took care to observe the magnetic variation, which he found amounted to two points. On the coast of this island, Munk's vessel was caught in the ice and became a wreck, so that he and his crew were obliged to take to their boat, and only after a difficult voyage succeeded in rejoining Hvid. On the return journey, they visited Archangel, and the biographer just mentioned reproduces from Munk's notes some elaborate sailing instructions for the approach to that place. By this unlucky expedition, Munk suffered considerable pecuniary loss; nevertheless, we find him attempting Nova Zembla again in the following year, but it was not on his own account.

The young and active King Christian IV exerted himself in every way, in order to develop the commerce of his subjects, which, on account of the geographical position of Denmark, had to be carried on chiefly by sea. He was himself passionately fond of the sea. Twice he sailed to England to visit his brother-in-law, James I. Almost every year he sailed to Norway, sometimes twice in one year. Once he visited the whole coast of Norway, rounding the North Cape and proceeding as far as Vardöhuus, on which occasion he himself acted as Admiral of his fleet under the name of Captain Christian Frederiksen,[1] no one being allowed to address him otherwise. He afterwards showed himself an able and gallant naval commander, and was emphatically the Sailor King of Denmark. In order to encourage his subjects, he frequently assisted their seafaring ventures with money, ships, and men, and sent out expeditions to explore and open up new fields for enterprise. Acting in this spirit, he despatched two ships in 1610 to Nova Zembla, which had previously been the object of several English and Dutch expeditions (as, for instance, those commanded by Henry Hudson) undertaken partly with a view of trading in these regions, and partly with a view to the discovery of a North-east Passage to India. The ships in question were the *Angelibrand* (which had been to Greenland in 1606 and 1607, under the command of Carsten Richardson) and a pinnace called *Rytteren*. The former was now commanded by Jens Munk, who most likely

---

[1] His father was Frederick II.

was engaged for this service because he had been in those parts before. His mates were Anders Nolk, who had commanded the smallest of the vessels that were sent to Greenland in 1606, and Hans Brock, who was also to act as interpreter, and of whom we shall hear again. The pinnace was commanded by Knud Madsen, he having as mates Anders Oluffsen and Johan Stenge, and as interpreter Niels Munk, Jens Munk's elder brother, who in the instruction is described as "our Russian interpreter".[1] The two vessels were to act independently, but were to keep together as far as possible for mutual assistance. They were instructed to land at Kildin, a trading-place not far from Kola, the goods with which they were to trade, and from thence to proceed to Nova Zembla and to examine the coast from lat. 69° or 70°, as far as lat. 74°, or even 76°, if the ice should permit. If anything in the shape of saleable goods could be obtained, they were to make a cargo. Finally, they were ordered, before returning, to proceed two days' sail into Waygatz Strait, in order to ascertain what conditions it offered for navigation—no doubt with a view to the possibility of finding a North-east Passage to China. Munk, however, was not successful. He brought his vessel home again safe and sound, but with no better cargo than fish, which he had taken on board at Kildin, having been quite unable to reach Nova Zembla on account of the

---

[1] *Norske Register*, 3, fol. 362.

great quantity of drifting ice, and because the crew had neglected to supply themselves with sufficient warm clothing to withstand the cold; nor had his companion been more fortunate.

On the first of March in the following year (1611), on the outbreak of a war with Sweden, Munk obtained a commission as a Captain in the Danish Navy, with a pay of 200 Rixdollars annually, and he soon found opportunity of distinguishing himself. He was at once sent to that division of the fleet which was stationed in the mouth of the Götha Elf, watching the entrance to Gothenburg and the small, but strong, fortress of Elfsborg, which was situated on a rocky island. He was at first to serve as a lieutenant to Admiral Jörgen Daa, who commanded the *Heringsnes;* but, later on, he took command of one of the smaller vessels called *Den Sorte Hund* (*The Black Dog*). Amongst the Danish ships here was also *Den Röde Löve*, which had been to Greenland in 1605 and 1606, commanded this time by the before-mentioned Anders Nolk. On the 23rd May, Munk took part in a naval action; and, a few days after, he captured a Dutch vessel laden with supplies for the fortress, an event which must have been considered of importance, as it is related in Niels Slange's work on the history of Christian IV, though without mention of Munk's name.[1] The Danish Admiral was ordered to capture or destroy

---

[1] *Den storm. Konges Christian den Fierdes . . . Historie* (Copenhagen, 1747, fol.), p. 207.

seven Swedish vessels which were lying under the cannons of the fortress, and this was accordingly attempted on the night of the 27th of November. On this occasion, Jens Munk commanded the leading boat, but the attack did not succeed, because the Danes were discovered too early and compelled by the guns of the fortress to retire, after having set fire to the largest of the Swedish ships, called *Hector*. The Swedes, sallying out from Elfsborg, extinguished the flames, and the Danes had to content themselves with no greater booty than three of the ships' flags, which were afterwards suspended with other trophies in the Church of Our Lady (*Vor Frue Kirke*) at Copenhagen. This account (which is found in the oft-mentioned biography of Munk of 1723) differs from that given in the work of Slange,[1] who refers the attempt to the 27th of December, and says that the Swedes set fire to the *Hector*, that the Danes extinguished it, and that they succeeded in bringing out the Swedish vessels, which they carried with their own fleet to Copenhagen. Some writers even speak of two attacks. But there is no doubt that Slange has made a mistake, and that the ships were not captured in 1611, a fact which testifies to the truthfulness of the biography and of Munk's notes on which it is founded. We learn from this that Munk remained with the fleet before Elfsborg until the severity of the winter compelled them to leave about Christmas. Adverse winds drove them

---

[1] *Op. cit.*, pp. 299-300.

to seek winter-quarters at Kallundborg, instead of at Copenhagen; and, in the month of March, in the following year (1612), Munk was sent to that place in order to refit the vessels that had wintered there, and to repair to Elfsborg with them, taking himself the command of the *Heringsnes*. This he accordingly did, and placed himself under the command of Admiral Daa, who arrived from Copenhagen with other ships, but Munk retained the command of the *Heringsnes*. Soon after, the King arrived in order to reduce the fortress, having with him considerable land forces, amongst which were two regiments of English and Scotch mercenaries. In the operations which followed, Munk played a considerable part. First, he was ordered to cover with his guns the landing of the troops. In the next place, it was Munk who, with his sailors, cut the trenches. After this, he succeeded, under cover of night, in bringing a couple of smaller vessels past the fortress, thereby cutting off the supplies which had been nightly brought to it by water. Niels Slange[1] gives Munk the whole credit of this difficult operation, but the biographer from whom we gather these details modestly says that Munk assisted the Admiral in getting the vessels round. Munk next pushed the trenches close to the walls of the fortress, and assisted in the landing of the siege-guns and the mounting of them in the batteries prepared for them. Finally, he conducted mining operations

---

[1] *Op. cit.*, p. 309.

against the walls. Then he returned to his ordinary duties, and, with his ship, the *Heringsnes*, escorted a Danish fleet of transports laden with necessaries for the army. On the 23rd of May, the fortress surrendered, one of the articles of the capitulation being to the effect that the six vessels which still remained under the walls of the fortress should be handed over to the Danes. The Swedes had scuttled the vessels just before the surrender; but both Slange and Munk's biographer say that the Danes at once raised them, and, after repairing them, sent them to reinforce their own fleet. This event has a special interest in connection with Munk's subsequent expedition to Hudson's Bay, because one of them was called *Lampreten* or *Lamprenen*; and, as there was no other vessel in the Danish Navy of that name, it was doubtless the same which Munk had with him on that voyage. Later in the summer, Jens Munk was placed in command of the transports and victualling ships, and he meditated an important expedition into the interior of Sweden by way of the lakes, when his activity was arrested by the outbreak of a very malignant disease amongst the English soldiers. It proved fatal so quickly that Munk had the greatest difficulty in getting the sick transported to the hospitals at Marstrand, which had to be done by sea. At last, having fallen ill himself, he was compelled to go home on sick-leave, and it was only after the lapse of eighteen weeks that he was restored to health.

After the conclusion of peace, in the early part of 1613, Munk was sent with a fleet to the East Coast of Sweden, in order to fetch home troops, etc.; and, immediately on his return in the month of April, he was entrusted with a charge of quite a different nature, for which his business habits and his knowledge of languages qualified him. A special Embassy was being sent to Spain, and Munk was ordered to accompany it as interpreter and purser. On the 16th of April, the Embassy sailed from Copenhagen in the *Victor* and the *Swedish Hector* (the largest of the vessels taken at Elfsborg, and so-called to distinguish it from an older Danish ship of that name). On the 6th of May, they arrived at Corunna. The Danish Ambassadors, Jacob Ulfeldt and Jonas Carisius, were accompanied by a suite of not less than ten noblemen, amongst whom were several bearers of names which afterwards became historical in Denmark, such as Palle Rosenkrantz and Christen Thomæsen. They were hospitably entertained at Corunna— the ambassadors at the Governor's Palace, the others by the principal inhabitants—until the 24th of May, when orders were received from Madrid, after which they were conducted at the Governor's expense as far as Villafranca, where they arrived on the 31st. From thence to Madrid they travelled at their own expense, and at Villafranca they had to pay custom duties on their luggage, amounting to not less than 8,000 reals. At Madrid they were well received and entertained until the 3rd of July, when the Ambassadors had their Audience of Leave at the Escurial. The party then divided, Jacob Ulfeldt, with two of the suite, returning through France, while the others returned in the ships and arrived at Copenhagen on the 30th of July.

Next year (1614), Munk was again employed in conducting Ambassadors, but this time in a different capacity. Some Russian Ambassadors, who had been in Denmark for many months, desired to return to their home by way of Archangel (Russia possessing at that time no ports on the Baltic); and Munk, who had been there before, as we have told, was commanded to convey them there in his old ship the *Heringsnes*. A number of other persons went by the ship, amongst them Munk's eldest brother, Niels Munk, who, it is stated, was sent to Archangel on the King's service. It was at that time that Christian IV sailed to England on his second visit, so that Munk cannot have accompanied him there.

In 1615, Munk was again afloat on board the *Victor*, this time as lieutenant to his former chief, Admiral Jörgen Daa, who was sent with this ship and another to the North Sea to look after pirates and foreign vessels fishing off the coast of Norway without proper licence. Of the latter, they confiscated several with valuable cargoes: of the former, they captured two, one an Englishman named Thomas Tucker, and the other a certain Mendoses, whose nationality is not mentioned. The pirates were first heard of by the Danish ships at the Færöes, where they had committed many lawless acts, and Tucker, whose ship was wrecked, was taken prisoner on one of the islands. It is related that, when the Danes came upon him and his crew, one half of the latter, who were Irish, escaped, but the other half of the crew, who were English, stood by their captain and shared his fate—that of being hanged—excepting a black man, whose life was spared in consideration of his consenting to act as hangman. Mendoses was not overtaken by the Danes till they arrived at Kildin, or Kjelden, the above-mentioned port in the Arctic Sea, near Kola, where he was only captured after a desperate struggle, as he had several vessels, one of which was armed with eight cannons, the crews numbering seventy-two. As many of his men as could not prove that they were serving under compulsion were put to death then and there. Mendoses and two of his officers afterwards suffered the same fate at Copenhagen. Such was the rough and ready justice of those days.

In 1616, Munk was in the North Sea on the same errand, as lieutenant to Frants Brockenhuus, who had three ships under his command, but he returned early, as there was no need of their presence.

Meanwhile Munk had again turned his attention to private enterprise in the Arctic Seas, and particularly to the Arctic Whale Fishery, which was then just commencing to become a source of profit to various nations, but in which the inhabitants of Denmark and Norway had hitherto taken little or no part, although so favourably situated for it. A company, in which Munk was a partner, was formed at Copenhagen; but there was this difficulty: that the chase of the whales, and the proper treatment of their huge bodies for the extraction of oil and whalebone, was an art with which nobody in Denmark was properly familiar. In order to make a beginning, skilled hands had, therefore, to be secured from abroad. None at that time had a greater reputation for knowledge of everything belonging to the whale fishery than the seamen from the coasts of the Bay of Biscay. The Biscayans were the original whale-fishers of the world, and had carried on the Atlantic Whale Fishery for centuries with so great vigour that the species of whale which they hunted had become well-nigh extinct, and the fishery would have ceased if whales (particularly the Greenland Whale, closely resembling the Biscayan Whale) had not been discovered in great numbers in the Arctic Seas,[1] to which, consequently, the Biscayans transferred their operations. Munk, therefore, decided to procure men from these parts, as, indeed, was the custom in England in those days.

---

[1] For a long time it was thought that Greenland Whale was none other than that anciently hunted in the Bay of Biscay and the Atlantic, which, it was imagined, had retired from its pursuers to the Arctic Seas; and it is barely forty years ago that the stranding of a specimen, a female with its young, at Pampelona, afforded the great authority on whales, Professor Eschricht, an opportunity of proving that they are distinct species (*Balæna mysticetus* and *B. biscayensis*).

With this view he set out in November 1616, and proceeded to St. Jean de Luz, the head-quarters of the Biscayan whale-fishers. There his efforts to engage men were not successful; but in Bordeaux he was able to make arrangements with a certain Jan Lonighem, a Biscayan, who undertook to supply eighteen men skilled in the fishery. It appears that some person in authority (whose name is given as the Count of Gramante) threw difficulties in the way of the men leaving the country with Munk, in order to extort a large bribe from the latter. But Munk arranged with the men to go by themselves to Amsterdam, where he joined them. Several other companies for carrying on the whale-fishery were afterwards formed in Denmark, one of them under the King's immediate patronage, and others followed Munk's example in engaging Biscayans; but Munk has the credit of being the first to introduce this industry into Denmark, where it has since been very flourishing, though Munk himself lost money over it. He was interested in three whaling voyages, and it even seems as if he went out himself in 1617, for his biographer says that he was obliged to give up this business "because the King had lent him to go to India".

The fact was that Christian IV, ever alert, had resolved to avail himself of certain—at least apparently—favourable opportunities for opening up trade with India. An East India Company had been formed in Copenhagen in 1616, powerfully supported by the King himself; but it was not till 1618 that the first expedition was sent out, for which the Company obtained from the King leave to employ the most travelled and experienced officer in the Danish Navy, Jens Munk. In the biography of 1723, we are told that, on the 20th of February 1618, Munk received orders to get ready for this expedition three ships, called *Christian*, *Kjöbenhavn*, and *Öresund*. He was, however, left to make his own terms with the Company as regards his service; and, as he did not consider that the Company fulfilled the promises originally made to him, he asked and obtained the King's leave to decline. However, Munk showed his interest in the enterprise by subscribing a round sum of money towards it. The expedition, fitted out on a larger scale than appears to have been intended at first, sailed in November, 1618, under command of Ove Gjedde.

In the following year (1619), Jens Munk's old chief, Admiral Jörgen Daa, died, as it seems, in poor circumstances; and it is recorded that Munk charged himself with the expenses of his funeral, which, however, the family afterwards refunded. He was soon again in active work; and, instead of going to India round the Cape, Munk was, in 1619, sent out on an attempt to reach the far East by the Passage which at that time—particularly since the discovery of Hudson's Bay—was generally believed to exist round the North of America, but which still had to be discovered. The historian, Niels Slange, states in explicit terms that it was Munk himself who originally proposed this expedition;[1] and, if this be so, it is not difficult to understand how Munk may have been led to conceive such a plan, considering his restlessly active nature and the adventurous spirit of which he had given proof since his early youth. For years he had been familiar with the northern seas, where the passage would have to be sought, and he would very naturally be attracted by the idea of exploring the far western portion of them, where he had not yet been. The discoveries of English explorers were known over the whole of Europe, and would excite as lively an interest in Denmark as anywhere, particularly because the supposed passage was thought to be situated not far from Greenland, in which country a great deal of interest continued to be taken in Denmark. Munk himself was just the man to feel a desire to emulate those discoveries and to secure for his native country a share in the advantages that might result from the discovery of a passage. The very fact that he had not been able to come to terms with the Danish East India Company may very possibly have been an additional inducement to him; for it was commonly thought that the northern route would prove very much shorter than that round the Cape, and Munk may have flattered himself that he should be able, by discovering it, to put the churlish Directors of that Company to shame.

---

[1] *Op. cit*, p. 424.

At the same time, it should be borne in mind that Slange's work, though of great value, is by no means so reliable that we should not be justified in doubting, on reasonable grounds, an otherwise-unsupported statement of his, an instance of which we have already pointed out. As a matter of fact, there is nothing beyond Slange's statement to show that Munk himself had been mainly instrumental in setting this undertaking on foot. No direct evidence either way has been discovered; and, as regards the indirect evidence offered by his narrative, the reader must judge for himself whether it appears more like that of a man engaged in realising a pet scheme of his own than the report of a man who does his best to carry out the orders of his superiors. To us, the latter seems the more probable, though it may well be that Munk had had his interest drawn to the problem, and had expressed a desire to command the expedition when once it had been decided upon.

What has been said above of the disposition of the King of Denmark fully explains how he may have been led to resolve upon such an expedition, whether suggested by anybody else or not. Indeed, there is a fact on record which seems to prove that the matter had been thought of some years before. Amongst some documents referring to Munk, now preserved in the Danish State Archives,[1] there is a paper endorsed: *Mr. Haldz*

---

[1] *Indkomne breve til Cancelliet, 1621.*

Engelske Styrmand hans Relation om America ("The Statement of Master Hall, the English pilot, concerning America"). This purports to contain the opinion of an English pilot, called Hall, on the probability of a passage to India round or through the North of America. It is rather carelessly worded, but the main portion of it runs thus in English :—

"Unto 70 and 75. There he verges to the W. or the S.W., according to how open the sea is, because there, where land is marked on the map near Anian and that Strait, there is doubtless water. The reason is as follows: 1°. When he was in Greenland the last time, now lately, he found such a strong current, which flowed to the N.W., that it was not possible otherwise than that there must be an open sea near the Strait of Anian; nor is this so narrow as it is indicated in the marine charts, or on the globe; for, where there is land on the globe, there is open sea and water. 2°. The same he has experienced some years before, when he sailed to the East Indies. They had there an Indian pilot, who missed the Course, so that they were in great danger of their lives. Then they observed a similar strong current, which they followed, considering where that flowed to there must be open sea, and thus they reached a good harbour. 3°. Many books and authorities are of opinion that there is a passage through the Strait of Anian."

After a reference to Stephanus Gomez, the statement continues :—

"Besides, he would attempt to proceed towards the West in 61 and lxj degrees, because he thinks that there, too, there is a passage through by water. When one has passed through the Strait, one is close to Cattaio, China, and the Tartar ports, and near to East India. *N.B.*—This is only the fifth part of the length of the other route."

Some other quotations follow. There is neither signature nor date on the paper, which is evidently penned, not by Hall, but by some other person accustomed to write Latin (with which the Danish is interspersed) who had received this information from the English pilot—no doubt James Hall, who had been employed on the Danish expeditions to Greenland in 1605-6-7. The words "When he was in Greenland the last time, now lately" (*Der hand wor nu seniste gang vdj Grönland*), taken literally, imply that this statement was taken down not long after 1607, at the latest. In any case, the wording of it, and the absence of any allusion to the discovery of Hudson's Strait and Bay, hardly seem compatible with the supposition that it was written so late as 1619, many years after Hall's stay in Denmark and subsequent death. On the face of it, this paper would seem to show that when those expeditions to Greenland turned out so barren of results, in proportion to the expense incurred, there was in some official quarters a thought of attempting a search like that afterwards instituted by Hudson and those who followed in his track—a circumstance which would, of course, facilitate the adoption of such a plan in 1619.

Before proceeding further, we may note in passing that some writers[1] have stated that the object for which Munk was sent out in 1619 was the re-establishment of communication with the ancient Scandinavian colony in Greenland, an error which

---

[1] For instance, Major, in his valuable treatise *The Voyages of the Brothers Zeno* (Hakluyt Society, 1873), p. lxvii.

may be traced to J. H. Schlegel's abbreviated German translation of Niels Slange's above-mentioned work on the history of Christian IV. Slange states,[1] amongst the notable events of the year 1619, that, in that year, a Greenland Trading Company, strongly supported by the King, was established at Copenhagen, and sent out two ships. After giving some details concerning this company, he proceeds, in a new paragraph, to report that in that year Jens Munk was sent out with two ships, called respectively, *Enhiörningen* (*The Unicorn*) and *Lamprenen* (*The Lamprey*), in order to discover the North-West Passage. Schlegel appears to have misunderstood these statements as referring to one and the same event; and, very unfortunately, he condenses Slange's account in the following manner[2]:—"After this, a Greenland Company was formed in Copenhagen, which received great advantages from the King, and equipped two ships, *The Unicorn* and *The Lamprey*," after which he proceeds to describe Munk's voyage. This is, no doubt, the source from which the erroneous statement has crept into German and other works.

That Munk was selected to lead the expedition of 1619 was very natural, even if he had not himself either suggested the undertaking or solicited the command, because he was no doubt the fittest

---

[1] Slange, *op. cit.*, p. 424.
[2] *Geschichte Christian des Vierten . . . von Niels Slangen verfasst . . . Kürzer vorgetragen . . . von J. H. Schlegeln* (Copenhagen, 1757-1771), iii, p. 126.

commander that could be found amongst the Danish naval officers at the time. He was not only a brave man and an experienced practical seaman—many of his colleagues may have been his equal in these respects—but, by his voyages to Nova Zembla, he had gained some actual experience in Arctic navigation. Besides, though not possessing scientific training (as, indeed, he himself admits in his book), he was an unusually intelligent man, of rare perseverance, resource, versatility, and trustworthiness —in fact, just the man to deal conscientiously and successfully with such peculiar combinations of circumstances as might be expected to arise on a voyage of the kind in question.

About the terms on which Munk served on this expedition—whether any special pay or other encouragement was given him, or promised him in case of success—nothing is known. The only Royal favour recorded in regard to Munk at the time in question is the following:—He was then (it is not known since what year) a married man, his wife's name being Katherine Adriansdatter, and he had several children. By an order of April 8th, 1619,[1] Hans Steffenson, the manager of the Public School at Sorö, was ordered to take two of Jens Munk's sons on the foundation as soon as vacancies should occur.

The events of Munk's voyage of discovery in 1619-20 were narrated by himself in a book entitled

---

[1] *Sjæll. Tegn.*, vol. xxi.

Navigatio Septentrionalis (published at Copenhagen in Danish in 1624), which forms the chief subject of the present Book in this work; and there is, consequently, no occasion for us to dwell at length on those events in this place. Suffice it here to say that he left Copenhagen in May 1619, with two vessels, a small frigate, called *Enhiörningen*, and a sloop, called *Lamprenen*; that he wintered on the western coast of Hudson's Bay, in the mouth of a river for some time afterwards known as Munk's River, but now as the Churchill River, in order during the following summer to continue his explorations; but that, in the course of the winter and spring, the whole of the two crews succumbed to the scurvy, excepting Munk himself and two others, who, after having recovered, succeeded in re-crossing the Atlantic in the smaller of the two vessels, whilst the larger one had to be left behind. Munk landed on the coast of Norway on the 20th of September 1620, after a difficult and perilous voyage; but troubles did not leave him there. It appears that one of his sailors (probably one of the fresh crew which he at once obtained for his vessel) committed a murder whilst they were at Bergen, and fled from justice, on account of which Munk and his vessel were detained by the authorities, and released only in obedience to an express order of the King.[1] The vessel was laid up for the winter at Bergen, and Munk proceeded to Copenhagen, where he did

---

[1] *Norske Tegn.*, iv, fol. 187.

not arrive till Christmas Day, 1620, unfortunately, without having effected anything of what had been hoped for.

The failure of this expedition, which is stated to have cost (besides the many lives, the larger ship, and the ordinary stores) some 5,000 Rixdollars in cash, must, of course, have been very disappointing to the King, as well as to Munk himself; and so much the more so, as the misfortunes of the expedition seemed in the main to be due to preventable causes. There was no saying but that Munk, if he and his men had wintered in good health, might have succeeded in finding the supposed passage; whilst the sickness which carried off the crews almost to a man would naturally appear to be due (or, at least, to owe its terrible mortality) to insufficient preparations. As regards the necessity of specially warm clothing, Munk had gained experience on his expeditions to Nova Zembla; but he evidently had not any idea of the severity of the winter that would have to be encountered in Hudson's Bay. This was but natural, for, owing to the action of the Gulf stream, the temperature does not fall anything like so low in those parts of the Arctic Sea with which Munk was acquainted as it does under the same latitude in North America. He could not possibly have foreseen that, in a latitude below 59°—and he hoped to find the passage not very far North of that latitude—he would encounter a climate infinitely colder than in the North of Norway, in lat. 71°. He was prepared for a winter such as is experienced in the North of Norway, but not for a winter as it is at Churchill River, of the severity of which he had no conception. However, it would naturally appear, afterwards, that a good supply of fur clothing would have saved the expedition from the terrible effects of the cold. As regards the disease of scurvy, he was well aware that a diet mainly based on salt meat was disastrous; but, ignorant as he was of the character of the climate, he did evidently not anticipate so great a difficulty in procuring fresh meat as he actually experienced in the earlier part of 1620. It was reasonable to think that, if the expedition had been well supplied with smoked meat, such as is used extensively in the North of Europe, this source of danger might have been avoided. Finally, most people would suppose that better medical assistance than that which had been at Munk's command in 1619-20 might have averted the terrible mortality, which spared—and only just spared—three lives only out of sixty-four. Many minor defects in the equipment which had revealed themselves during the wintering at Churchill River might also easily have been remedied.

Considering that neither Christian IV, nor Munk, was of the temper that readily acquiesces in reverse, nothing would, under the circumstances, be more natural than the sending out, as soon as might be, of another expedition better equipped, in order to redress the failure. It is, therefore, not surprising that a statement to the effect that action in this direction really was contemplated is met with in the earliest account we have of what happened in this connection after Munk's return, viz., in La Peyrère's *Relation du Groenland* (Paris, 1647), a book to which we have had occasion to allude more than once in connection with the Expeditions to Greenland in 1605-6-7. La Peyrère explicitly says (p. 269) that Munk, after some years, became desirous of repeating the voyage in hope of better results; that he succeeded in enlisting the interest of several wealthy persons in the scheme; and that, in preparing for it, he availed himself of his sad experience, and strove to avoid the mistakes and defects of which he had become aware on the former voyage. Until lately, however, this statement has been considered doubtful at the best, because, in La Peyrère's account, it is closely interwoven with a fantastic story about Munk's death, which is alleged to have taken place just as the expedition was going to start. The absurdity of this story—to which we shall have to allude again—was demonstrated more than a century ago, and it was but natural that the discredit attaching to it should have been extended to the statement that a second expedition was at one time intended. Documents preserved in the Danish State Archives,[1] and to which M. Lauridsen was the first to call attention,[2] prove, however, that La Peyrère was rightly informed in so far that a

---

[1] *Indkomne Breve til Cancelliet, 1621.*
[2] *Jens Munks Navigatio Septentrionalis* (Copenhagen, 1883), pp. xlvi-li (see *post*, p. lvii).

second expedition really was intended; that considerable preparations were made for it; and that Munk, in superintending these, tried to improve in every respect upon the first equipment, according as experience had taught him. Only, the expedition was not a private undertaking, as stated by La Peyrère, but was fitted out by the King; and this took place immediately after Munk's return from his first voyage, not, as La Peyrère says, several years later. As La Peyrère also states, the expedition did not start; but the reason which he assigns—Munk's death at the last moment—is fictitious.

The principal of the documents referred to above is a sheet endorsed: *Jens Munk's Necessaria*. It reads thus in English:—

"Enumeration of all that I can think of now in haste, and that can be of particular use for this voyage.

1. Good medical men, particularly for scurvy.
2. Item: good victuals, and smoked meat in place of salted.
3. Item: good beer for the men, some wine and whisky.
4. For the people of [that is, who are to remain in] the country, flour, malt, some victuals, groats, and peas.
5. Item: all sorts of seeds and corn.
6. Item: sheep-skin clothing for the men, stockings, shoes and boots, fur shoes, blankets, overcoats.
7. Item: snow-shoes [*Skier*] wherewith to travel on the snow.
8. Item: some craftsmen—smith, shoemaker, tailor, bricklayer, cooper, carpenter.
9. Vessels for brewing, kettles, hand-querns, and some small millstones.
10. Pilot (*Styrmand*) not to be forgotten.
11. One who understands ores, and a person who can draw.
12. A large pinnace and three Norwegian jolly-boats.

"There is, however, much that is required for such a journey, but which one cannot think of in a hurry. I beg, therefore, that I may be informed, in particular, of the persons who are to supply all that is necessary for such a voyage, in order that I may not trouble Mr. Chancellor too much, and that everything may be ready in good time.

"Item: it is particularly necessary that the people who are to remain in the country should be mostly such as understand hunting and fishing, and know how to catch animals in the forest, in order that His Majesty may, in some measure, recover His expenses; for it appears that this would be the most profitable trade and occupation, and would not in any way be prejudicial to any expedition by land on the part of His Majesty. Finally, there must necessarily be a certain authority over them, for the better furtherance of justice and all order.

"For my own part, I am, with all due respect, ready to serve His Royal Majesty, my gracious Lord, with life and blood, wherever and whenever I am commanded, hoping that I, poor man, my wife and children may be provided for, so as to have what we can live upon. Likewise, I beg Mr. Chancellor to cause Peter Pai, or some physician, to be ordered to attend somewhat to me, that I may quite recover my health. God will recompense Your Worship."[1]

This memorandum bears neither date nor signature, but the contents leave no doubt as to its being a communication from Jens Munk stating, in obedience to the express orders of the King—which seem to have come rather suddenly on Munk—what he would require for a second voyage to the Arctic Regions. It is evident that Munk, taught by experience, had tried, as La Peyrère relates

---

[1] The Danish expression is a curious one, viz., *Strenghed*, iterally, "Your Severity"—a form of speech then in use in the North of Europe and in Germany.

to improve upon the outfit which had been provided for the first voyage. We also learn from unmistakeable expressions that Munk was intended, first of all, to return to the country where he had wintered, and to carry thither colonists, with a view of opening up a fur trade—or, at any rate, people who were to remain there some time.

That the original object of the first voyage—the discovery of a North-West Passage—was still to be pursued, appears from the second of the documents in question, which is inscribed, "A List of what will be required for the North-West Passage or Voyage". It is a memorandum setting forth what supplies had been ordered for the proposed expedition, with the names of the contractors—in one case, with the addition that Munk would give more detailed orders. The list is drawn up in accordance with Munk's requisitions. Special mention is made of remedies against scurvy, which were to be supplied by Peter Payngk (called Peter Pai in Munk's memorandum), the Court Apothecary—a man who enjoyed a great reputation for learning in chemistry, on account of which the science-loving Emperor Rudolf II at one time had him to reside with himself. Nor was the necessity forgotten of providing the expedition with "old and experienced surgeons, who possess a knowledge of medicine".

A third document in the same parcel is still more explicit as to the destination of the intended new expedition, and, moreover, gives a date. It is entitled: "Augmentation, according to H. M. the

King's gracious pleasure, of the Pay of the Crew which is to sail in this present Year, 1621, with Captain Jens Munk, to the North-West Passage." It appears from this paper that very considerable augmentations of pay were offered: for instance, besides clothes, the captain's pay was to be 200 Rixdollars a month—that is, as much as Munk's ordinary pay was *per annum*. The number in each of the different classes of men is not stated ; but, as there is mention of only one captain, one master-gunner, etc., probably only one large vessel, of about the same size as *Enhiörningen*, was to sail ; and, as "the sloop" is mentioned, *Lamprenen* was probably to sail again. There is nothing to show that any spare crew, with the necessary officers, were to be taken out in order to fetch home the abandoned ship.

Evidently the preparations for this new expedition were well in hand, and the question naturally suggests itself: Why did it not start? Mr. Lauridsen suggests,[1] on the strength of Munk's request for medical assistance, that his health may have suffered so much that he could not undertake the expedition at the time, and that this may have been the foundation of La Peyrère's statement that Munk took to his bed instead of starting on his voyage. Nor is this hypothesis, in itself, by any means improbable, although, of course, Munk may very well have been so much invalided as to require a doctor's care at the time when the new expedition was decided

---

[1] *Op. cit.*, p. lii.

upon, and yet have been quite restored by the time the expedition was to start. But there are several circumstances which would fully explain the postponement and final abandonment of the scheme, without that hypothesis. The order for the increase of the pay of the crew points to what may have been a serious difficulty. It was not a service on which men could very well be commanded to go against their wish, particularly after what had happened; and, even at very largely increased pay, it may have been difficult to get together crews such as Munk would care to take out. Still more would this hold good with regard to colonists, on whose exertions in obtaining fur the King would have to rely for some return for his outlay. The King is extremely likely to have given up the scheme altogether if he could not realise this part of it. A third point is not less important. Munk requested particularly that a *Styrmand* (that is, a mate) should not be forgotten; and this, of course, did not refer to an ordinary mate, who would be supplied as a matter of course. What Munk wanted was a man specially acquainted with the North-Western Seas. In 1619, he had had with him two English mates, who had been specially engaged to act as pilots. They were both dead, and Munk wanted the place of the principal of them filled by another thoroughly competent man. He had found his way home from the Churchill River by himself, and was, of course, perfectly able to sail out there again without assistance. But, beyond that, he was to search for a North-West Passage; and it is not difficult to understand that, for this purpose, he considered it indispensable to have at his side a man who, from his own personal experience, or from what he had learnt from others, knew as much about that problem and the chances of its solution as could be known beforehand. But such a man was very likely not to be found just when he was wanted.

Nor is it difficult to suggest considerations which may have caused the final abandonment of the scheme, when first it had been postponed for one or more of these reasons. The expedition to the East Indies by the Cape Route, on which Munk was to have served, proved very successful; and the King would scarcely have thought it worth while to spend more money on the uncertain venture of finding a North-West Passage if the second voyage for this purpose had been postponed until the trade had been opened by the ordinary route. Besides this, the complications arising out of the Thirty Years' War, which had commenced in 1618, could not but engross the King's attention. The probability of his being drawn into that conflict—as, indeed, he eventually was, with most disastrous results—must very soon have become apparent, and, in that case, there would be neither men nor money to spare for Arctic expeditions.

This last consideration also sufficiently explains why no notice appears to have been taken of an offer made in 1625 by a certain Carolus Joris, amongst other things, to fetch home the cannon which Jens Munk had left behind with his larger ship in Port Churchill.[1]

That it was not an easy matter to obtain men for such distant expeditions, seems to be proved by a fact connected with the first business on which Munk appears to have been employed after his return from Hudson's Bay. In the autumn of 1621, he was sent

---

[1] This Joris was probably none other than the well-known Dutch cartographer of that name, who already in 1615 had been to Davis Strait as mate (see S. Müller, *The Arctic North-West Passage*, Amsterdam, 1878, p. vii). We shall have to refer to him again as a cartographer in our Appendix A. His offer to the King of Denmark is contained in a report from an official in Iceland, preserved in the Danish State Archives (*Indkomne Breve til Cancelliet, 1625*), of which the following is a translation:—

Anno 1625, on the 7th of September, Master Jorris was at Bessestad, in Iceland, and states as follows:—That he was a pilot for Greenland to his Admiral, whose name is Adrien Diricksen Leffuerstein, who is now expected hither. Master Jorris, aforesaid, and he have agreed to go together to Greenland, and to meet for refreshment at Havnefjord in Iceland. The said Master Jorris reports thus of their voyage: that in Greenland they have obtained 170 barrels of silver ore, and think that it contains gold; they have also secured many horns of Unicorns, weighing together nearly 200 lb. Master Jorris, aforesaid, presents himself to the King's Majesty, if H.M. will accept his services to be employed on such voyages; likewise he offers to fetch back to H.M. the cannon which Jens Munk left behind him in America.—*Actum ut supra, Mr. Jorris Carolus, m. p.*

On a slip of paper, pasted on to the document, is written:—

"This is a true copy of the words which Master Jorris requested me to write down, which he has signed with his own hand, desiring that they might be submitted to H.R.M. In witness whereof, I have signed with my own hand, *Anno* 1625."

to Holland to engage men for the Danish East India
Company; and, in order to facilitate the execution
of this task, he was empowered by Royal Warrant
to promise any of the King's subjects who might
have fled the country on account of any unlawful
act, free pardon and safe return, if they agreed to
engage themselves for this service, unless they had
been guilty of murder or similar grave crimes.
How far he succeeded, we are not told ; but, in the
following year (1622), after having returned from
Norway, where he had levied sailors for the Fleet, he
was ordered to sea with a man-of-war, called *Neldebladet*, as convoy for the East Indiaman, *Water-
hunden*. He saw this vessel safe as far as the
Canary Islands ; and, on the return journey, he fell
in with a Danish squadron conveying the King to
Norway. His Majesty thereupon ordered Munk
to join the Fleet, and he did not return home till the
month of August.

The year 1623 brought Munk serious domestic
trouble, for which, perhaps, he was indebted to his
frequent absence from home. He was obliged to
divorce his wife, which entailed considerable legal
business. Very likely this unfortunate event was
the reason why the Manager of the School at Sorö
was now ordered at once to take in the two sons
of Munk, for whom places had been reserved in
1619; besides which, a third son was ordered to be
received as soon as a vacancy should occur.[1] Munk's

---

[1] *Sjæll. Tegn.*, xxii, f. 223.

family troubles did not, however, prevent his being actively employed by the King—in fact, there is on record an order from the King to the Municipal Authorities of Copenhagen, to hasten the legal proceedings connected with the divorce, because the King wanted Munk's services at sea.[1] He was thereupon sent with four ships to the coasts of northern Norway and Lapland, in order to put a stop to the encroachments of the Russians, who, in various ways, had interfered with Danish shipping and commerce. In this matter, he seems to have proceeded with perhaps too great vigour, so as to call forth complaints on the part of the Russians, particularly because at Kola he had levied a large sum as security for the claims of Danish merchants. His biographer of 1723 says that he cruised in those waters from May 1st to August 26th, and returned with good booty for the King, having done no harm to the Lapps (the inhabitants of the country, which had become subject to the Russians), but had treated them with all kindness. A short diary of Munk's, kept on this voyage, is still in existence.[2]

In 1624, Munk's account of his voyage to Hudson's Bay, entitled *Navigatio Septentrionalis*, was published, but he himself was continually on the move. In February of that year, he was despatched

---

[1] *Sjæll. Tegn*, xxii, f. 369.
[2] See the notice of the MS. of the *Navigatio Septentrionalis* in the Commentary.

to Pomerania and the neighbouring countries, to engage ship's-carpenters; and no sooner had he returned than he was sent out again to Mecklenburg, to carry a large sum of money to Duke Ulrich, the King's brother and Bishop of Sleswick and Schwerin, an errand which he successfully executed. Next, in the month of May, he was ordered with three ships to the North Sea, on the same service on which he had been so often employed—that of looking after pirates and unlicensed foreign vessels. On this occasion, he was instructed not to do the Russians any harm. There was at that time very great need of this kind of police-duty; and a second squadron was sent out to act in the same manner along the southern coasts of Norway, whilst Munk was engaged further north.

In February 1625, Munk received an addition of 100 Rixdollars to his pay, and was soon again in activity. In the same year, warlike operations commenced. Christian IV, besides being King of Denmark and Norway, was also a German Prince, in his capacity of Duke of Holstein, and was thus drawn into the Thirty Years' War on the side of the Protestant States. Although the actual fighting was carried on by land, divisions of the Danish fleet were employed in order to prevent the Imperialists from obtaining supplies by sea. Two such were sent out in the autumn of 1625; and Jens Munk was summoned in all haste to equip six ships which he was to command as Admiral, stationed on the Weser. In his letter to Munk,[1] the Chancellor requested him to come with all speed to Roeskilde, where he himself was—probably because the plague had been raging and was still prevalent in Copenhagen. With regard to this, he writes:— "Concerning the sickness, you need, next God's help, have no fear. The vessels shall be manned mostly with fresh and healthy crews." This letter was dated August 10th; and, before the end of September, Munk took up his station. His own ship was *Neldebladet*, which he had commanded before; and, amongst the others, were *Trost*, of Greenland memory, and *Lamprenen*, in which he had returned from Hudson's Bay. The latter, however, was lost with all hands, but under what circumstances is not known: thus both the ships Munk had taken out in 1619 were ultimately lost while under his command. In October, Munk returned to Copenhagen with most of the ships, whilst some of them wintered on the Weser, under command of Peter Kieldsen, the same who had been in Greenland under Lindenow in 1605.

In the spring of 1626, Munk resumed his command on the Weser. This is the last command of his mentioned in the biography of 1726—no doubt because Munk's journals, on which that biography is based, did not, as the author expressly states, extend further. It is known, however, from Slange's work and other sources that, in 1627, Munk

---

[1] *Sjæll. Tegn.*, xxvii, f. 91.

was again on the Weser, though at first only as second-in-command, Henrik Wind being Admiral; but, later in the year, Wind having been sent to the Elbe, Munk was Admiral himself.

In the following year (1628), Munk's career came to an end. We have already alluded to a somewhat romantic account of Munk's death, told by La Peyrère. It is to the effect that, when he had finished his preparations for a second voyage to Hudson's Bay and was on the point of departure, the King, in a conversation, upbraided him with the deaths among the crews on the first voyage, as if this had been due to Munk's mismanagement; and that, irritated by Munk's somewhat-spirited rejoinder, the King even went so far as to push him in the stomach with the point of his stick. This treatment Munk, it is stated, felt so keenly that he took to his bed in mortification and starved himself to death.[1] La Peyrère does not

---

[1] Le Capitaine Munck rendit compte de son voyage au Roy son maistre, qui le receut, comme l'on reçoit vne personne que l'on a creu perduë. Il sembloit que ce deust estre la fin des mal-heurs de ce Capitaine; mais son auenture est bigearre, et merite d'estre sceuë. Il demeura quelques années en Danemarc; où apres auoir long-temps resué sur les manquemēs qu'il auoit faits dans son voyage, par l'ignorance des lieux, & des choses, & sur la possibilité de trouuer le passage qu'il chercheoit pour le Levant; l'enuie le prit de refaire ce mesme voyage. Et ne le pouuant entreprendre seul, il engagea dans ce party, des Gentilshōmes de marque, & des Bourgeois qualifiez de Danemarc; qui formerent vne Compagnie notable, & equipperent deux Vaisseaux, pour ce long cours, sous la conduite de ce Capitaine. Il auoit pourueu à tous les inconueniens & à tous les disordres, qui luy estoient suruenus au premier voyage, & il estoit comme sur le point de

give his authority for this story; but there can be no doubt that he had been misled somehow, and that his account of Munk's death is simply one of his many mistakes, to the existence and probable causes of which we have alluded in another place.[1] Nevertheless, owing to the numerous reproductions of La Peyrère's book, this story was at one time very generally received, even in Denmark, where a translation of La Peyrère's book appeared in 1732,[2] and where his account of Munk's death was reproduced by one historian of note, Ludvig Holberg.[3] The latter certainly gives it only for what it is worth, but he ought to have known better than to repeat it, even as possibly true. Niels Slange, whose work appeared four years before Holberg's, mentions Munk's death in the following words:[4]—"The history

---

s'embarquer pour le second lorsque le Roy de Danemarc luy demanda le iour de son depart; et de discours à un autre luy reprocha que l'equipage qu'il luy auoit donné, avoit pery par sa mauuaise conduite, à quoy le Capitaine respondit vn peu brusquement; ce qui fascha le Roy, & l'obligea de le pousser du bout de son baston dans l'estomac. Le Capitaine outré de cét affront se retira chez luy, & se mit dedans son lict, ou il mourut dix iours apres, de deplaisir & de faim (*Relation du Groenland*, p. 268-271).

[1] See Book I (*Danish Expeditions to Greenland*), Introduction, p. xxii.

[2] See Bibliography, p. lx. In one of the Dutch reproductions (*Drie Voyagien Gedaen na Groenlandt*, p. 10), there is an illustration representing the interview between the King, who is seated, sceptre in hand, and Munk, who is standing before him in full armour.

[3] *Dannemarks Riges Historie* (1753), vol. ii, p. 668.

[4] Slange, *Kong Christian den Fjerdes Historie* (1749), p. 643.

of this year [1628] must now be concluded with [mention of] the decease of the brave and renowned navigator, Captain Jens Munk, which took place on the 3rd of June, a few days after having shown his bravery on the Fleet which was commanded by Pros Mund." J. H. Schlegel, in his abridgment of Slange's work, speaking of La Peyrère's book, says[1] :—" First of all, I must observe that what Peyrère states, on mere hearsay and without indication of date, concerning Munk's death (which is repeated by Holberg) is erroneous. For Munk died in the midst of the war against the Emperor, on the 3rd of June 1628, a few days after having shown his bravery in a naval engagement—consequently, under circumstances in which he cannot possibly have been thinking of a voyage to Greenland, or have died from vexation at the King's pretended ill-treatment of him. The address to the King, which forms the preface to his account of the voyage, shows that he was fully certain of the King's satisfaction." In speaking of Jens Munk's death, Schlegel says[2] :—" After having performed the voyage to Greenland, Jens Munk was employed every year in the service of the King. This fact confirms further what has already been observed in note 125 against the supposed occasion of his death. Holberg had scarcely any other authority

---

[1] *Geschichte König Christian des Vierten* (1771), iii, p. 126, note 125.

[2] *Op. cit.*, p. 231, note 246.

for this than Peyrère, who certainly, as an inquisitive traveller, learnt many things at Copenhagen, but may have misunderstood, or imperfectly remembered, much." It would be easy to accumulate evidence to corroborate this criticism—the fact that the preparations for a second voyage took place in 1621, immediately after Munk's return, is, of course, decisive; but it is not necessary, for no serious writer has given any credit to the story since Schlegel's time.

In 1628, a large Danish fleet operated in the Baltic under the King's own command; and that Munk at that time was considered one of the chief commanders in the Danish navy, may, perhaps, be inferred from the fact that a certain circular order to the captains has been entered on the Register of the Chancery, as having been addressed to Munk, in the King's own handwriting, with the addition that copies of the same were sent to all the others.[1]

There seems, however, to be some uncertainty as regards Munk's commands and movements in this, the last, year of his life. He is known to have been afloat, early in the year, on board *Den Flyvende Fisk* (*The Flying-Fish*); but it appears that, in the month of April, he came to Copenhagen on board *Hummeren*, though for what purpose is not known. At the time when his death occurred, the Fleet was off Stralsund, which was held

---

[1] *Sjæll. Reg.*, xviii, f. 294.

by the citizens and a Danish force against the Imperial army under Wallenstein; and the engagement in which Munk, according to Slange, had distinguished himself (but which Slange does not specify) may have been one which took place on one of the last days of May. Arnheim (or Arnim), the commander of the forces before Stralsund, having learned that it was intended to throw reinforcements into the fortress by sea, attempted to prevent it by means of a flotilla of boats, manned by soldiers, but the Danish Fleet frustrated this attempt after a smart engagement. If Munk was with the Fleet at the time, he was pretty sure to be employed on this occasion, which would have been a few days before his death, if Slange's date for that event is correct. But, although the author of the biography of 1723 gives the same date, the 3rd of June (Munk's birthday), stating that Munk's brother-in-law[1] had noted that he died on that day, it appears to be erroneous. It has been observed[2] that, according to the Treasury accounts, his salary was drawn by his wife down to St. John's Day [June 24th], "when he died"; and, according to the Parish Register of St. Nicholas, Copenhagen, he was buried in that church on

---

[1] That would be the brother of Munk's second wife, Margrethe Tagisdatter (daughter of Tage Eriksen, a Judge in Norway), who survived him. It appears not to be known when Munk married her, but he had no issue by her.

[2] *See* H. D. Lind, *Kong Christian den Fjerde*, etc. (Copenhagen, 1889), p. 196.

July 3rd, 1628. Perhaps the various statements may be reconciled by assuming that he fell ill shortly after distinguishing himself in the manner indicated, and that he died on June 23rd, which, by a clerical error, may have been corrupted into June 3rd, whereby both the biographer and Slange (who perhaps followed the latter) may have been misled. Supposing the body to have been brought back to Copenhagen, it might very well have been buried on July 3rd. There is no record of any monument to his memory in the church of St. Nicholas; and, if any ever existed, it would have disappeared in 1795, when a great fire destroyed the church, with the exception of the huge red-brick tower, which still forms a conspicuous feature in the centre of the city. Nor is any portrait of Munk known to exist.

Such were the principal events in the life of Jens Munk. They show him to have been a man of great ability in various directions, courageous and energetic, of great experience as a navigator, and enjoying, in an uncommon degree, the confidence of his sovereign and the esteem of his fellow citizens.

II.—*Bibliography of Early Accounts of Munk's Life and Voyage.*

Jens Munk's account of his voyage to Hudson's Bay in 1619-20—the only original one that we have—was published by himself, in 1624, at Copenhagen, under the title of *Navigatio Septentrionalis*.[1] It is illustrated by a map showing Greenland, Davis

---

[1] The full title is as follows :—*Navigatio, Septentrionalis. Det er: Relation Eller Bescriffuelse, om Seiglads oc Reyse, paa denne Nordvestiske Passagie, som nu kaldis Nova Dania: Igjennem Fretum Christian at Opsöge, Huilcken Reyse, Voris Allernaadigste Herre, Konning Christian den Fierde, vdi det Aar 1619. Naadigst Berammit, Oc til des Experientz afferdiget haffuer hans Majest: Skibs Captein, Iens Munck oc hans methaffuendis Folck, som offuer alt vare 64. Personer, met tuende hans Majest: Skibe, Enhiörningen oc Jagten Lamprenen: Samme Seiglads effter metgiffuen Naadigst Instruction, vdi Vnderdanigst gehörsomhed, saa meget muelig være kunde, er Tenteret, Men Capteinen effter höy Perickel vdstanden met Jagten, er icke vden selfftredie Igien til Norge hiemkommen, Met Bemelding om alle Circumstantier, Curs, Kaase oc Tilfald, det Farevand oc den Reysis Leilighed anrörendis, Aff forskreffne, Iens Munck Paa Hen oc Hiemfarten met flid Obserueret, Oc paa Höybemelte Kong: Majest: Naadigste Behaug vdi Tryck Publiceret. Syr: 43. Navigantes mare, enarrant ejus pericula. De som ferdis paa Haffuet, de sige aff den Farlighed, Oc wi som det höre, forundre oss, etc. Prentet i Kiöbenhaffn hoss Henrich Waldkirch*, ANNO M. DC. XXIIII. A rendering of this Title-page is prefixed to our translation of the text (see p. 1). The volume is a small quarto, 7½ inches by 6 inches, and unpaged; the collation being A to HIII, including title. The map is to face CIII (where a hand refers to it), the two woodcuts (marked with a star and a cross respectively) are to face, the first BIIII, and the second CIIII, in which places corresponding marks are inserted in the text.

Strait, Hudson's Strait, and Hudson's Bay; also by two woodcuts, on which various events are represented (according to the custom of the period) side by side, without divisions, although those events happened at quite different times.

This original edition seems now to be very rare. No public library in this country appears to possess a copy of it.

A second edition, consisting of a reprint of the original volume, with the addition of a biography of Munk, was published in 1723.[1] The text, which has been to some extent modernized in point of spelling, is marred by not a few misprints; and, though there is a copy of the map, the woodcuts have not been reproduced. Nevertheless, this edition is extremely valuable on account of the biography of

---

[1] The title-page of this edition, apart from slight modification and modernised spelling, is identical with that of the original edition, down to the words, *vdi Tryck Publiceret*, after which follow: *1624—Og nu anden gang efter manges Forlangede til Trykken befordret, og med forbemelte Capitains Liv og Levnets Beskrivelse, extraheret af hans egenhændige skrevne Journaller, formeeret.* KIÖBENHAVN, *Trykt udi Kongl. Majestets priviligerede Bogtrykkerie, 1723.* (*And now for the second time, at the request of many, published in print, and augmented with the Description of the said Captain's Life and Fortunes, extracted from his own autograph Diaries. Copenhagen: Printed in His Royal Majesty's privileged Printing-house, 1723.*) The text of Scripture is removed to the back of the title-page. The volume is a small pott octavo, measuring about 6½ inches by 4 inches, and the collation is as follows:—Title-page, pp. 1-2; the folding map; Preface, in form of address to the King, pp. 3-7; Munk's Narrative, pp. 8-72; Biography of Munk (in form of an Appendix), pp. 1-24.

Munk, which is stated to be extracted in the main from his own journals, a circumstance which seems to indicate that the anonymous editor was a member or friend of Munk's family. At the present time, Munk's papers have nearly all disappeared; and, but for this biography, we should have known next to nothing about his early life. Even with regard to the events of later years, when he had become a well-known personage in Denmark, the biography has preserved not a few interesting details which are not known from other sources. Of this edition, the British Museum possesses a copy (Press-mark, C. 32, *b*, 25).

A third edition, consisting of an accurate reprint of the edition of 1624, with an introduction and notes by Mr. P. Lauridsen, was published at Copenhagen in 1883.[1] The original map and the second woodcut are reproduced; a map of Hudson's Strait and Bay, according to our present knowledge, is added; and there is also a photo-lithographed facsimile of Munk's handwriting. This edition is chiefly valuable on account of some interesting additional information which Mr. Lauridsen has been enabled to produce from the Danish State-Archives.

Munk's autograph manuscript of the greater part of his book is still in existence; but it will be convenient to postpone our observations on it until we

---

[1] *Jens Munks Navigatio Septentrionalis. Med Indledning, Noter og Kort. Paa ny Udgiven af P. Lauridsen. Kjöbenhavn, 1883.* 8vo, lvi-58-[8] pp.

have placed before our readers the printed text, with which it will have to be compared. It will be found described and discussed in our Commentary.

The *Navigatio Septentrionalis* has never till now been translated into any other language, and its contents have become generally known only at second hand, through the same publication by means of which the contents of Lyschander's *Grönlandske Chronica* reached the world at large, viz., Isaac de La Peyrère's *Relation du Groenland*. We have already mentioned this book in connection with the Danish Expeditions to Greenland in 1605-7,[1] reserving a fuller notice for this place, as it is principally of importance with regard to Munk's voyage to Hudson's Bay, which La Peyrère included in his account of Greenland, because the latter name at that time was not unfrequently applied to all the lands north of Hudson's Strait.

As already stated, the author obtained the materials for his book during a stay in Denmark in 1644 and 1645, when he was one of the suite of the French Ambassador, M. de la Thuillerie. This circumstance procured him excellent introductions, and one of his principal informants was the learned Wormius, with whom he corresponded for several years. Nevertheless, the *Relation du Groenland* is disfigured by numerous inaccuracies, caused partly, no doubt, by the author's ignorance of the Danish language, but probably also in some measure by

---

[1] Book I (*Expeditions to Greenland*), p. xxii.

the evident fact that he wrote chiefly with the
intention of producing an entertaining book. Some
of his ill-founded statements have led to serious
mistakes concerning Munk and his voyage, which
have obtained very general acceptance on account
of the wide circulation of La Peyrère's book. It
will, therefore, be proper here to notice the different
editions, reprints, and translations of it, as far as we
are acquainted with them.

The original edition of the *Relation du Groenland*
was published in Paris in 1647.[1] The author's
name does not appear anywhere in it; but, as he
implies, in the very first lines, that he is the author of
the *Relation de l'Islande*, in which La Peyrère
names himself, the book is only anonymous in form.
It is illustrated by a map of the North Atlantic
and Hudson's Bay, mainly founded on that of Munk,
and by a folding plate, containing drawings of
Greenlanders, with their boats, etc., and of a skull
of the Narwhal, showing the true nature of its
"horn". These latter he obtained from Wormius,
who had destined them for his *Museum Wormianum*,
in which work (Leyden and Amsterdam, 1655) they
were afterwards inserted.

The *Relation du Groenland* was re-issued in 1663,[2]

---

[1] *Relation du Groenland. A Paris: Chez Avgvstin Covrbe, dans la petite Salle du Palais, à la Palme.* M.DC.LVII. *Auec Priuilege du Roy. 8°.* Eight preliminary leaves, including Title; Text, pp. 1-278; the Privilege [4 pp.]; a folding map to face p. 1, and a folding plate with figures, to face p. 144.

[2] Only the Title-page is reprint. In some copies, the imprint runs: *Chez Thomas Jolly, dans la petite Salle des Merciers, au*

and was reprinted in 1715, with reproductions of the map and other illustrations, in the first volume of J. F. Bernard's *Recueil de Voiages au Nord*,[1] of which there exists at least one later edition.

A Danish version of Bernard's *Recueil* was commenced in 1732,[2] but was not continued beyond the first volume, containing La Peyrère's treatises on Iceland and Greenland, and this is the only Danish translation of them. The maps and illustrations were not reproduced.

Palais, à la Palme, et aux Armes de Hollande. MDCLXIII. In others: *Chez Louis Billaine, au second pillier de la grand Salle du Palais, à la Palme, & au grand Cesar*, etc. That the two booksellers were partners is clear from the fact that the necessary permission for the issue of the book was granted to them jointly.

[1] *Recueil de Voiages au Nord, contenant divers memoires tres utiles au commerce et à la Navigation. A Amsterdam: Chez Jean Frédéric Bernard, sur le Rockin, près de la Bourse.* MDCCXV. 12°, vols. i-v. There is an enlarged edition in 10 vols., of which vol. i was published in 1731. La Peyrère's treatise occupies pp. 85-187 in the first edition, and has a separate title-page: *Relation du Groenland. Contenant l'Histoire des Voyages des Danois pour la decouverte de cette Terre. A Amsterdam: Chez Jean Frédéric Bernard, sur le Rockin, près de la Bourse.* MDCCXV. In the ed. of 1731 there is no separate title-page to La Peyrère's treatise, which occupies pp. 61-186.

[2] *Et samlet Udtog Paa de Reyser, Som Norden paa Ere foretagne, Udi hvilket indeholdes adskillige Beretninger, Som ere Til synderlig Nytte og Underretning baade for Handelen og Seyladsen. Udi det Franske Sprog först forfattet. Siden udi det Danske Sprog oversat, og med adskillige Historiske, Geographiske, og andre Anmærkninger saa og Registre formeret. Förste Part. Kiöbenhavn, trykt udi Hans Kongl. Majests privil. Bogtrykkerie, 1732.* 8°. La Peyrère's treatise on Greenland occupies pp. 117-299. The special Title-page is translated, but without imprint.

The earliest German translation appeared, in 1650, in the collection of Hulsius, of which it forms the twenty-sixth and last part.[1] It is somewhat abbreviated, all personal references, La Peyrère's notes on Spitzbergen, etc., being left out. On the other hand, a long notice of Hudson, borrowed from Hessel Gerritsz., is inserted as an introduction to the account of Munk's voyage, which has a special heading describing it as the chief item of the volume. The map is reproduced, some of the names being translated into German, the others into Latin. Some of the other illustrations are likewise reproduced, but the small drawings of a Narwhal's skull are replaced by others on a very large scale, occupying three plates. Besides the translation of La Peyrère's book, the volume contains a description of Spitzbergen, embodying some of La Peyrère's remarks, and a discourse on the Whale Fishery.

---

[1] *Die xxvi. Schiff-Fahrt, Beschreibung einer Höchst mühseligen vnd gantz gefährlichen Reyse, durch den See-verständigen Capitain, Herrn Johann Müncken, inn Jahren 1619, vnd 1620. verrichtet. Nach demer von Weyl and dem Durchleuchtigsten Fürsten und Herrn, Herrn Christiano IV. König in Dennemarck, Norwegen, etc., befelcht worden, mit zweyen Schiffen nach dem Freto oder der Enge Hudsons zu segeln, umb zu versuchen, ob nicht deren Gegend eine Enge, so Groenland von America abscheide, vnd also eine Durch-fahrt nach Ost-Indien zu finden: Sampt vorhergehender gar deutlichen Erläuterung dess Alten und Newen Grönlands, zu gegenwärtiger Schiff-Fahrts-Beschreibung insonderheit dienlich. Franckfurt am Mayn, Bey Christophoro Le Blon.* MDCL. 4°. Four preliminary leaves, including Title, and pp. 1-63, with a map and ten plates, of which four belong to the discourse on the Whale Fishery. The translation from La Peyrère ends on p. 45.

This German version was translated into Dutch, more or less abbreviated, and printed in Amsterdam under the title of *Drie Voyagien Gedaen na Groenlandt*, etc.[1] In this publication (of which the date is uncertain), the contents are re-arranged in a peculiar manner. It opens with the account of Munk's voyage, under the heading of *Journal van Ioan Monnick* (pp. 3-11, corresponding to pp. 36-45 in Hulsius); next follows the discourse on the Whale Fishery (pp. 11-15, corresponding to pp. 55-60 in Hulsius); after this comes *Voyagie na Groenlandt door Marten Forbisser* (pp. 15-18; in Hulsius,

---

[1] *Drie Voyagien Gedaen na Groenlandt, Om te ondersoecken of men door de Naeuwte Hudsons soude konnen Seylen ; om alsoo, een Doortaert na Oost-Indien te vinden. Alle ten versoecke van Christianus de IIII. Koningh van Denemarcken, etc. de eerste door Ioan Monnick, de tweede door Marten Forbisser, ende de derde door Gotske Lindenau. Als mede een Beschryvinghe, Hoe, en op wat wijse men de Walvisschen vanght. Item, een korte Beschryvingh van Groenlandt, met de manieren en hoedanicheden der Inwoonderen aldaer. t' Amsterdam, Gedruckt By Gillis Joosten Saeghman, in de Nieuwe-straet, Ordinaris Drucker van de Journalen der Zee-en Landt-Reyssen.* 4° Title and pp. 3-32. It is one of a series of similar accounts of voyages, all of which are printed with separate titles, signatures, and pagination, but without indication of the year of publication. They have been issued also collectively, with an engraved Title-page, under the title of *Verscheyde Journalen, van Zee en Landt Reysen, Mitsgaders de Beschrijvingh van de Landen en Volckeren, die gelegen syn onder den kouden Noordt-Pool. T'Amsterdam, Gedruckt by Gillis Joosten Saeghman.* The series is the sequel of a similar one, entitled, *Verscheyde Oost-Indische Voyagien: Met de Beschryvingen van Indien. t'Eerste Deel t'Amsterdam by Gillis Joosten Saeghman*. The first part of this series bears the date 1663, which appears to be the only date of publication given anywhere in the Collections.

pp. 24-26); next follows the account of the expeditions in 1605-6-7, under the title of *Journael van den Admirael Gotske Lindenau*, etc. (pp. 18-24; in Hulsius, pp. 26-35); finally, there is a *Beschryvingh van Groenlandt*, containing an account of the country and its ancient history, as well as of the voyages undertaken in search of it down to the close of the sixteenth century (pp. 25-32; abbreviated from Hulsius, pp. 6-21). The volume is handsomely illustrated, but neither the map nor the drawings of the original are reproduced.

A complete German version, by H. Sivers, was published at Hamburg in 1674, entitled, *Bericht von Gröhnland gezogen aus zwei Chroniken*, etc.,[1] in which the contents are left in their proper order, but divided into two books of fourteen and twelve chapters respectively, with appropriate headings. The first book treats of the ancient history of Greenland, corresponding to the first 117 pages of La Peyrère's work: the second comprises the remainder. The map and other illustrations are

---

[1] *Bericht von Gröhnland, gezogen aus zwei Chroniken: Einer alten Ihslandischen, und einer neuen Dänischen; übergesand in Frantzösischer Sprahche An Herren von der Mote den Wayer von einem unbenandten Meister, und gedruckt zu Parihs bey Augustin Kürbe ins Anno 1647. Jetzo aber Deutsch gegäben, und, um desto färtiger ihn zu gebrauchen, untershihdlich eingeteihlet Von Henrich Sivers. Hamburg, in Verlägung Johan Naumans und Jurgen Wolfs. Gedruckt im Jahr Christi.* 4°. Four preliminary leaves, including Title and pp. 1-70, with map and illustrations.

copied, the names on the former being turned into Latin.

Like the first German version of 1650, that of 1674 was also translated into Dutch and printed in 1678, augmented with historical and other notes to the various Chapters, and several independent pieces, referring to Nova Zembla and Spitzbergen. The title is *Nauwkeurige Beschrijvingh van Groenland*, etc.[1] The map and one of the original illustra-

---

[1] *Nauwkeurige Beschrijvingh van Groenland Aen Heer De la Mothe le Vayer; Verdeelt in twee Boecken, t'Eerste van't Oud (nu verloorne) Groenlandt, Gelegentheyd; Vindinghswijs; Besettingh met Inwooners; Beschrijvingh; Vrughtbaerheyd; Gewassen, Dieren, Zeewonderen, etc. 't Tweede van 't Nieuw (door 't soecken van 't Oud gevondene) Groenland, Beschrijvingh; eygenschap der Wilde, en veel andere seer aenmercklijke saken. Nevens 't kort begrijp der seldsaeme Reysen, gedaen om Oud-Groenland weer te vinden door M. Forbeisser uyt Engelland, in 't jaer 1577. Door Gotzke Lindenauw uyt Deenemarcken, in de Jaeren 1605. en 1606. Door Karsten Richards, in't Jaer 1601. Door 't Groenlandsch Geselshap te Koppenhagen, in't Jaer 1636. Met aenhangingh van't Dagh-verhael der wonderlijcke Bejegeningen des Deenschen Hoofdmans Johan Munck, in 't soecken van een wegh tusschen Groenland en America na Oost-Indien: Gelijck oock van den korten Inhoud en seldsaeme gevallen der Hollandsche en Zeeuwsche Scheeps-uytrustingh nae Nova Zembla, gedaen ten selven eynde: Der ontmoetingen van seven persoonen, noch seven, en noch andere seven gebleven op Spitzbergen, om aldaer t'overwinteren, e.s.v. Vertaeld, en met veelerley Historische Byvoeghselen doorgaens vergroot, door S. de V. t'Amsterdam. by Jan Claesz. ten Hoorn, Boeckverkooper tegen over t'Oude Heeren Logement. 1678. 4°.* Four preliminary leaves, including engraved Title and pp. 1-128, of which the translation of La Peyrère's book occupies 1-103 (in part); there is a copy of the map, and the original drawing of the Greenlanders is incorporated with the engraved Title-page, where they appear in the midst of a

tions are reproduced, the former with names mostly in Dutch, but a few in Latin. The headings of the chapters are, in some cases, slightly altered; and the tenth chapter of the second book of Siver's translation is divided into two, the description of Spitzbergen forming a separate chapter numbered eleven. The accounts of Munk's voyage to Hudson's Bay and of his intended second voyage and death follow, as in Siver's edition, where they are numbered as Chapters XI and XII; but, in the Dutch edition, they are not numbered at all.

In the following year (1679), the whole of this volume was translated into German, and printed at Nürnberg, with the title of *Ausführliche Beschreibung des theils bewohnt- theils unbewohnt-sogenannten Grönlands*, etc.,[1] which is the third

---

splendid forest; but the other figures are not reproduced. There is, however, a folding plate to illustrate the papers referring to Spitzbergen.

[1] *Ausführliche Beschreibung des theils bewohnt- theils unbewohnt-sogenannten Grönlands, in zwey Theile abgetheilt: Deren erster handelt von des Alt- (nunmhero verlohrnen), Grönlands Gelegenheit, Erfindung, Inwohnern, Fruchtbarkeit, Gewächsen Thieren und Meerwundern. Der andere: von dem Neuen (durch Suchung des alten, gefundenen) Grönland, Eigenschafft der Wilden, und viel anderen merckwürdigen Dingen mehr. Nebenst Einem Kurzem Begriff der seltsamen Reisen, so M. Forbeisser, Gotzke, Lindenau, Christian Richard und die Koppenhagen-Grönländische Gesellschafft, all Grönland wieder zu finden, in unterschiedlichen Jahren gethan. Mit Anfügung des Tagbuchs eines die Durchfahrt zwischen Grönland und America suchenden Dänischen Schiffes: wie auch des kurtzen Inhalts und seltsamen Zufälle der Holl- und Seeländischen Schiffsausrüstung nach Nova Zembla zu eben dem Ende vorgenommen: Samt Erzehlung*

German translation of the *Relation du Groenland*. On the map, however, the Dutch names are retained.

The first English translation of La Peyrère's *Relation* was published by Churchill in 1704,[1] under the title of *An Account of Greenland*. It is accompanied by a slightly-reduced copy of the map, and by copies of the other original illustrations, arranged together on one plate, so as to suit the shape of the volume. The names on the map are in English.

A very full abstract, which may be described as an abbreviated translation (not, however, including Munk's voyage), forms part of the Introduction to an English translation of Hans Egede's work on Greenland, of which the second edition appeared in 1818.[2]

A complete translation of La Peyrère's text was published, in 1850, by the Hakluyt Society,

---

der wunderbaren Zufälle, so dreymal Sieben Personen, welche den Winter über auf den Spitzbergen und der Mauritiusbay sich anfgehalten, begegnet, und wie elendiglich sie umkommen sind. Beschrieben, und mit verschiedenen Historoschen Anhängen durchgehends erklärt und erweitert durch S. von V. Nürnberg, in Verlegung Christof Riegels, 1679. Engraved Title, three preliminary leaves (including Title) and 131 pages; Map and one plate.

[1] *Collection of Voyages and Travels*, vol. ii (1704), pp. 447-478. There are several later editions of this work.

[2] *A Description of Greenland, by Hans Egede . . . A New Edition, with a Historical Introduction and a Life of the Author. . .* Second Edition, London, 1818, 8°.

accompanied by a copy of the map as it is in the original.¹

In conclusion, we may mention that the above-mentioned biography of Munk which appeared as an appendix to the second edition of the *Navigatio Septentrionalis*, in 1723, was reprinted in 1753 by C. P. Rothe²; and that, augmented with some details drawn from other sources, it also forms the substance of R. Nyerup's biography of Munk,³ as well as of all subsequent ones.⁴

---

¹ In *A Collection of Documents on Spitzbergen and Greenland*. Edited by *Adam White* (London, 1850, 8°), pp. 175-249. The Title-page of the re-issue of 1663 is reprinted, and the first paragraph of the text is detached from the body of the latter, and printed in the shape of a preface. The map is reproduced, but not the other illustrations.

² *Brave Danske Mænds .... Eftermæle*, by C. P. Rothe (Copenhagen, 1753, 8°), vol. ii, pp. 525-554.

³ *Archiv for Historie of Geographi*. Edited by J. C. Riise (Copenhagen, 1821), vol. ii, pp. 1-31.

⁴ All the above-mentioned editions, translations, and abstracts of La Peyrère's *Relation du Groenland* helped to spread throughout the world, and to perpetuate, the many erroneous statements concerning Munk's voyage which are found in the original work. In Denmark, of course, these errors never obtained much currency; but, even there, they were clearly, to some extent, received as true. Elsewhere, however, La Peyrère's account of Munk's expedition was almost implicitly accepted. So far as England is concerned, no detailed account of Munk's voyage has until now been published, except the translations of La Peyrère's work which appeared in Churchill's *Collection* (1704) and in the series of the Hakluyt Society (1850), which, of course, contain all the misstatements of La Peyrère's original work. There are, however, two other fairly-old and very well-known English works on Arctic Exploration in which a brief account of Munk's voyage appears; and

III.—*Notice of Voyages in Search of a North-West Passage preceding that of Munk.*

The remarkable series of voyages in search of a North-West Passage to Cathay, performed between the years 1576 and 1632, constitutes an exceedingly interesting and well defined chapter in the history of Arctic discovery. The series commenced with the

---

these may be most conveniently noticed here, though I admit that they do not really come under the head of this section. The first of these works is *A History of the Voyages and Discoveries made in the North, translated from the German* [Frankfurt-an-der-Oder, 1784, 8°] *of John Reinhold Forster* (London, dy. 4°, 1786), in which the account of Munk and his voyage occupies pages 470-471. Forster's account, though obviously condensed in the main from that of La Peyrère, is certainly not wholly so ; for, instead of inserting La Peyrère's fantastic accounts of Munk's death, Forster states that Munk was afterwards employed by King Christian IV in 1624, 1625, and 1627, and that he died on June 3rd, 1628—information which La Peyrère does not give, and which (if not derived direct from the 1723 edition of Munk's *Navigatio*) was perhaps drawn from Schlegel's or some other similar work. Moreover, Forster correctly identifies the harbour in which Munk wintered with Port Churchill, though many other English writers have identified it with Chesterfield Inlet. Probably Forster's account of Munk and his voyage, though very brief, is, as far as it goes, the most correct and reliable that has ever, until the present, appeared outside Denmark. The second of the two works to be noticed here is Sir John Barrow's *Chronological History of Voyages into the Arctic Regions* (London, dy. 8°, 1818), in which is an account (pp. 230-234) of Munk's voyage, which is obviously derived from that of La Peyrère (probably through the translation in Churchill's *Collection*), but is rendered still more unreliable through some further misstatements made by Barrow himself.—M. C.

first voyage of Sir Martin Frobisher in the first-named year, and closed with that of Captain Thomas James, who returned in the last-named year, after which the search for a passage completely ceased for more than a century. During this period of a little more than half-a-century, not less than seventeen North-West voyages were accomplished, all so far connected that they had the same object, each one of them being to a greater or lesser extent undertaken in order to follow up the results gained on those which had preceded it. The following is a complete list of the seventeen voyages, as the accounts of them have appeared in the volumes of the Hakluyt Society.

Voyages of the Early Series in Search of a North-West Passage.

No. of Voyage.	Year or Years.	Commander.	Narrative edited by	Year of Publication.	No. of Volume.
1.	1576	Sir Martin Frobisher	Admiral Collinson[1]	1867	38
2.	1577	,, ,,	,, ,,	1867	38
3.	1578	,, ,,	,, ,, [1]	1867	38
4.	1585	Capt. John Davis	Admiral A. H. Markham	1880	59
5.	1586	,, ,,	,, ,,	1880	59
6.	1587	,, ,,	,, ,,	1880	59
7.	1602	Capt. Geo. Weymouth	Thos. Rundall[1]	1849	5
8.	1606	Capt. John Knight	Clements R. Markham	1877	56
9.	1610-11	Capt. Henry Hudson	Prof. G. M. Asher	1860	27
10.	1612-13	Adm. Sir Thos. Button	Miller Christy[1]	1894	88
11.	1614	Capt. Gibbons	,, [1]	1894	88
12.	1615	Capt. Bylot and W. Baffin	Clements R. Markham	1881	63
13.	1616	,, ,,	,, ,,	1881	63
14.	1619-20	Capt. Jens Munk	Gosch and Christy	1890	97
15.	1625	Capt. Wm. Hawkridge	Miller Christy[1]	1894	88
16.	1631	Capt. Luke Foxe	Miller Christy	1894	88-89
17.	1631-32	Capt. Thos. James	,,	1894	88-89

The voyage of Captain Jens Munk, in 1619 (which, as will be observed, forms the last but three

---

[1] Only partially.

of the series), differs, in one respect, from all the others, in that it is the only one which was not despatched from England and commanded by an Englishman. Jens Munk was, as already stated, a Dane, and to Denmark belongs the whole honour of the enterprise. Munk's account of his voyage did not become known in England in time to be of use to those who followed him in the search ; but his own voyage was undertaken with some knowledge of what had been achieved by the earlier English explorers.

In order to enable our readers to form an accurate estimate of the relation of Munk's voyage to the other voyages of the series, it is necessary to turn back and to pass briefly in review those which preceded it. The earlier voyages which have a direct bearing upon Munk's expeditions are not numerous ; and the proceedings of those navigators who did not (as did Munk) seek a passage by way of Hudson's Strait may be noticed in a few words.

It is customary to ascribe to Captain Henry Hudson the credit of having been the first to discover, in 1610-11, the important waterways now known as Hudson's Strait and Hudson's Bay. Nor is this done without some reason ; for (as has been shown elsewhere[1]) Hudson was, practically speaking, the real discoverer of them. Still, the fact remains that the entrance of the Strait was probably known centuries before the date at which Hudson is

---

[1] *Voyages of Foxe and James* (Hakluyt Society, 1894), p. vi.

commonly supposed to have discovered it; while a portion, at least, of it had been explored and mapped, and the existence of the Bay had been indicated upon charts, at least half-a-century before that date.

Although there is no actual proof that the entrance to the very remarkable inlet which we now call Hudson's Strait was known to the Northmen in the eleventh and twelfth centuries, still there is no good reason to doubt that it was; for, as is well known, they had, from their colonies in south-western Greenland, sailed across what is now known as Davis Strait, and had discovered Labrador, Newfoundland, and Nova Scotia, in the last of which countries they had even attempted to establish settlements. It is hardly possible to doubt that, in so doing, they had ranged northwards along the coast of Labrador as far as the entrance to Hudson's Strait, more especially as we know that, on the opposite side of Davis Strait (that is, on the western coast of Greenland) they had ranged some ten degrees further to the north.

But the discovery of Hudson's Strait by the Northmen, though interesting, has little or no bearing upon the present question; for, although the fact may have been known to later explorers of that region, we have no evidence whatever that it was, and we may, therefore, regard the discoveries of the latter as new.

Writers of authority have stated explicitly that both Cabot in 1497 and Gaspar Corte-Real in 1501 ranged far enough to the northward along the coast of

Labrador to reach, and even to enter, Hudson's Strait; but, though this is by no means improbable, we are unable to find any definite record whatever in support of the statement.

After their time, many voyages were made by the Portuguese along the coasts of Newfoundland and Labrador, probably in the main for fishing purposes; but of the details of these voyages we know practically nothing, though we still have not a few of the charts which were made as a result of them; and it can hardly be doubted that a certain inlet shown on some of these charts—even on some of very early date—represents Hudson's Strait.

Coming down to a later period, we find that a large inlet on the coast of Labrador, in lat. 60°, is shown on the large *mappemonde* published by Gerard Mercator in 1569 under the name of *Golfam de Merosro*, and also in the famous atlas published by Abraham Ortelius in 1570 under the name *Baia dos Medaus* (*i.e.*, Bay of Sandbanks). This inlet has been identified by Dr. Asher[1] as Hudson's Bay and by Dr. Kohl[2] as Ungava Bay; but we believe neither of these writers is more than partially correct in his identification. That the inlet in question, as shown on these maps, and on many later ones to which it was transferred, was meant for Hudson's Bay or Hudson's Strait, or even for both, is probable; but we may observe that the

---

[1] *Henry Hudson*, p. clxxi.
[2] *Discovery of North America*, p. 384.

inlet has an earlier history which is too intricate and too remote for us to enter upon here, though we hope to discuss it in detail upon another occasion.

Hakluyt speaks[1] in a definite manner of what is, we believe (if the statement be true), the first recorded occasion on which Hudson's Strait was entered by any navigator; but unfortunately the record in question is vague and open to grave suspicion, notwithstanding the fact that Hakluyt says he makes the statement on the authority of an exceptionally reliable Portuguese gentleman. The statement is to the effect that, in the year 1574, "which [says Hakluyt] is not above eight years past", one Johannes Corte-Real, sailing in search of a North-West Passage, "founde, in fiftie eyghte degrees, a great entrance, exceeding deep and broad", into which he sailed twenty leagues southward, after which he was obliged to return. There can be no doubt that (if such a voyage really was made, and such a strait really discovered) that strait was Hudson's Strait, though the entrance to it lies in lat. 60°, not in lat. 58°; but one cannot avoid a suspicion that there has been some mistake as to the date, and that the voyage thus alluded to was really that of Gaspar Corte-Real in 1501. It seems not improbable that Hakluyt may have misunderstood his informant to say "eight" years when he really said "*eighty*", which would take one

---

[1] *Divers Voyages Touching the Discovery of America*, etc. (1582), [prelim., p. 4]. (See also the Hakluyt Society's reprint, edited by John Winter Jones in 1850, p. 7.)

back exactly to the time of Gaspar Corte-Real's voyage.

Although, therefore, there can be no doubt that Hudson's Strait had been discovered, and in part explored, long before, the earliest reliable record we have of its having been entered is that contained in the narrative of Frobisher's third voyage northwestward in 1578. It was entered by him on that occasion in mistake for the inlet a little further north which still bears his name, and he called it his "Mistaken Strait" in consequence. Frobisher himself believed that he had discovered a North-West Passage, and asserted, after his return home, that, had he not been concerned about the safety of the rest of his fleet, which had become separated from him, he both could and would have sailed through it into the Pacific. Circumstances, however, prevented any continuation of the search by Frobisher; and when (seven years later, in 1585) the search was recommenced under Davis, Frobisher's "Mistaken Strait" was completely neglected, because (for reasons fully explained elsewhere) it was supposed to be entered from the east coast of Greenland, instead of from the east coast of America.

Davis, nevertheless, in the course of his three voyages (1585-86-87) passed the entrance to Hudson's Strait, and observed the strong current setting out of it, which he spoke of as "the Furious Overfall"; but he had, of course, no idea that it was identical with the "Mistaken Strait" of Frobisher. On that occasion also, circumstances prevented its further exploration; for, when Davis returned to England, he found his country threatened by the Spanish "Armada", and every seaman and every ship was needed in its defence.

As regards Hudson's Bay, although we have no evidence that any navigator had, up to this time, penetrated Hudson's Strait far enough to reach the inland sea we now associate with Hudson's name, there had already appeared on some earlier charts (as stated above) a piece of water which occupies roughly the position of Hudson's Bay, and which we can only identify with that so-called "Bay"; and, as no white man is known to have reached it overland at so early a date, it may have been thus represented on the charts in question in consequence of information received from the Indians, just as Cartier, in his narrative of his second voyage in 1535, says[1] that he had heard a report as to the existence of the Great Lakes long before any white man had actually reached them—indeed, the charts above alluded to give some reason for believing that these reports as to the existence of the Great Lakes and Hudson's Bay were at first confused and jumbled up together.

For the resumption of the search after its discontinuance by Davis in 1587, we are indebted to the enterprise of the East India Company, which was incorporated by Queen Elizabeth on December 31st, 1600. On the 24th of July 1601, a letter

---

[1] Hakluyt's *Voyages*, vol. iii. (1600), p. 225.

written by one George Weymouth, a navigator, "touching an attempte to be made for the Discovery of a North-west Passage to the Est Indies", was submitted to a General Court of the Company. On the 7th of August, the proposals contained in the letter were adopted, the cost of the contemplated expedition being estimated at £3,000. A record of all the proceedings in connection with the preparations for this voyage is to be found in the first Minute Book of the Company, which has recently been published;[1] but, of the voyage itself, we have no account, except the meagre narrative of it given by Purchas,[2] who wrongly ascribes the enterprise to the Muscovy and Turkey Companies. Weymouth sailed on May 2nd 1602, and returned to England on August 5th following, this speedy return having been largely due to a mutiny among his crew. In his narrative of the voyage, which is vague and unsatisfactory, we meet with little or nothing of note, except a record of the fact that on the 26th of July he entered an inlet, which he describes as having been forty leagues in breadth, and into which he says he sailed "one hundred leagues west and by south". There can be very little doubt that the inlet was that now known as Hudson's Strait, although Weymouth seems to have entered it rather by accident than with the intention of following up the discoveries of Frobisher and Davis in that

[1] See *The Dawn of British Trade to the East Indies. . . .*, by Henry Stevens (London, 1886, 8vo).
[2] *Purchas his Pilgrimes*, Part III, pp. 809-814.

direction. Probably, indeed (for reasons already explained), Weymouth did not recognize it as the inlet Frobisher had spoken of as "The Mistaken Strait"; but he must have known Davis's description of the "Furious Overfall", in Hakluyt's work.

Weymouth's fruitless voyage seems to have damped the ardour of the East India Company; and, although another voyage under Weymouth was projected to start in the following year (no doubt to continue the exploration of the inlet Weymouth had reported), quarrels arose, and the enterprise was abandoned. After that, the East India Company never again set forth solely on its own account a voyage in search of a North-West Passage, though it several times afterwards co-operated with others of the great chartered trading companies of the day in despatching such voyages. Thus, in 1606, it combined with "The Company for the Discovery of New Trades" (more commonly called the Muscovy Company) in the dispatch of Knight's ill-fated and wholly-profitless expedition in search of a passage. Although we do not know precisely what were Knight's intentions, it is probable that they were to continue the investigation of the inlet entered by Weymouth in 1602; but his own death, and the severe injury sustained by his ship, frustrated whatever intentions he had.[1]

---

[1] For an account of Knight's voyage, see *Purchas his Pilgrimes*, vol. iii, pp. 827-831: also, *The Voyages of Sir James Lancaster ... and Captain John Knight*, edited by Mr. Clements R. Markham (Hakluyt Society, 1877), pp. 279-294.

Again some years were allowed to elapse without any attempt being made to follow up the discoveries of Frobisher, Davis, and Weymouth. Then, at last, came both the opportunity and the man. Henry Hudson (after three memorable, though unavailing, voyages in search of a North-*East* Passage to China, undertaken in the years 1607, 1608, and 1609 respectively) turned his attention north-westwards; and, in the spring of 1610, he sailed in Weymouth's old vessel, the *Discovery*, with the expressed intention of further exploring the promising inlet.[1] The Muscovy Company, the East India Company, and twenty-three private individuals (all of whom were eminent statesmen or leading merchants) bore the expense of setting forth the expedition.

Hudson's voyage in search of a North-West Passage (for our knowledge of which we are mainly indebted to Purchas[2]) is well known, chiefly on account of the importance of the discoveries made upon it, and of the tragic death of its commander. Hudson entered the inlet, now known as Hudson's Strait, on or about the 8th of July 1610. On August 3rd, having explored the entire length of the Strait, he entered what is now known as Hudson's Bay, being (so far as we know) the first navigator who ever did so. Sailing southwards, down its eastern coast, Hudson laid up his ship for the winter in what is now

---

[1] See *Henry Hudson the Navigator*, edited by G. M. Asher, LL.D. (Hakluyt Society, 1860), p. ccix.
[2] *Purchas his Pilgrimes*, vol. iii, pp. 576-608.

known as Rupert's Bay. On or about the 15th of the following June (1611), the ship was again free, and the voyage was recommenced. In the meantime, however, provisions had run low, and the crew viewed with natural apprehension the captain's expressed intention to continue his exploration westward. A few days later, they mutinied, placing Hudson, his son, and six others, in the ship's shallop, and deserting them, as has been so often related. Hudson and his companions were never heard of again, and the mutineers returned home, sailing as nearly as possible over the route by which they had come.

Discredited men as they were, they were bearers of news which, it is clear, excited the keenest interest in England on their return thither in the autumn of 1611. They could relate that they had sailed westward for six hundred miles, in the direction in which it was desired to discover a passage, until they entered a large open sea. That this sea was not the Pacific Ocean (or, as it was then called, "the South Sea") which they sought to reach, they must have known. Doubtless, they recognised that it was more or less land-locked, although no land to the westward, north of Cape Henrietta Maria, in lat. 55°, had been actually sighted; but they must have believed that, having got thus far towards the Pacific, but little was required to enable them to proceed for the rest of the way thither. Indeed, all contemporary evidence goes to show that, at the time, it was fully believed by all the leading geographers that the much-desired and long-sought passage westward to China, Japan, and the Indies by way of the North of America had, at last, been *actually discovered*, and that nothing remained to be done but to equip another expedition to sail through and more fully explore it.

That other expedition was got ready with the least possible delay, and sailed under Captain (afterwards Admiral Sir) Thomas Button at the earliest possible moment in the following spring. The influential position of those under whose auspices it was equipped is evidence of the importance of the results which were expected from it. A great trading company was (after the manner of those days) incorporated by Royal License, under the name of "The Company of the Merchants of London, Discoverers of the North-West Passage", with the Prince of Wales as its head and "Supreme Protector"; with the great Sir Thomas Smyth—then also Governor of the East India Company—as its Governor; and with 25 Peers of the Realm, 37 Knights, Baronets, or Court Officials, 38 Esquires, and 188 Merchants as its members—together no less than 288 persons, all of whom were eminent in their own lines at the time, either as leading statesmen, philanthropists, members of Parliament, or merchants. Very wide powers and valuable privileges (including a monopoly for ever of the trade through the passage) were granted to this Company, which, after the failure of its first and greatest expedition under Button, made several other energetic attempts to discover a passage.[1]

The main object of Button's expedition was (as already said) to continue Hudson's explorations to the westward until the Pacific (or "South Sea") should be reached; and the instructions Button received for his guidance whilst upon his voyage (which were drawn up and signed by Henry, Prince of Wales) show the absolute confidence felt at the time that this object would be successfully accomplished. No official or authoritative account of Button's voyage was ever published, probably because, although Button did not discover the passage, his observations still left grounds for hope that it might be discovered, and the Company of Discoverers naturally desired, therefore, to keep to themselves the knowledge which had been gained. Button's journals remained in his possession, we know, almost, if not quite, up to the time of his death; but, although he promised the use of them to Purchas when the latter was compiling his *Pilgrimes*[2], they were never sent and are now lost. For all we know concerning Button's voyage, we are indebted to the industry and inquisitiveness of Luke Foxe, who gathered what information he could about it from Button's companions, and published it in 1635 in his *North-West Fox*.

---

[1] For a full account of its inception and constitution, together with a *verbatim* reprint of its Charter, see *The Voyages of Foxe and James* (Hakluyt Society, 1894), pp. xxxviii-xlii and 642-644.

[2] *Purchas his Pilgrimes*, part iii, p. 848.

Button sailed in April 1612. He himself commanded the *Resolution*, while her consort, the *Discovery* (Hudson's old ship), was commanded by a Captain Ingram. He had with him at least two of the leading survivors of Hudson's expedition, namely, Bylot and Prickett. After reaching the western end of Hudson's Strait, Button sailed in a south-westerly direction across the Bay, passing the southern end of the Southampton Islands (which do not appear to have been seen by Hudson), where he bestowed the strange name of "Cary's Swan's Nest" on the cape still so-called. Late in July, or early in August, he encountered the western shore of the bay in about lat. 60° 40′ N., at a point which he named " Hope's Check", because there his hope of an easy passage westwards to the Pacific received a check. Thus was the western shore of the bay reached for the first time. Coasting southward, Button discovered and named Port Nelson, which he entered on August 15th. Here he wintered amid dire hardship. He himself was ill all the winter, and sickness carried off many of his men, which ultimately caused him to abandon his larger vessel, the *Resolution*. In the spring, sailing in the *Discovery*, he returned northwards, along the western coast. In lat. 60°, he encountered a race of tide flowing sometimes from the east, but sometimes from the west, apparently indicating the existence of a passage to the west ; for which cause, the place was called Hubbart's Hope, from Josias Hubert, or Hubbart, one of the crew. These expectations, however, were doomed to disappointment. Tracing the western coast of the bay as far north as lat. 65°, he reached a point which he named "Ne Ultra", somewhere in what is now known as Roe's Welcome. From this, satisfied that no passage leading westward was to be found there, he turned back homewards, coasting the south-eastern shore of the Southampton Islands. At the western end of Hudson's Strait, he paused to investigate a tide or current which Hudson's survivors had reported to flow from the north-west, down the large opening now known as Foxe's Channel. Button satisfied himself that such a current existed, and comforted himself with the hope of a passage in that direction; but the season was too advanced for further investigation and he returned home, arriving in England about the end of September 1613.

Keen must have been the disappointment felt in England on Button's return thither. His prolonged absence, caused by his having wintered in Hudson's Bay, had led to the belief that he had passed through the supposed passage into the Pacific, and had thus raised still higher the hopes first engendered by the discoveries of Hudson. But Button's return dashed all these expectations roughly to the ground; and the fact that he was able still to report hope of the existence of a passage leading westward in a fresh locality, must have gone but a short way towards appeasing the disappointment felt at its non-discovery in the locality in which it had been so confidently expected.

Nevertheless, the ardour of the "Company of Merchants of London, Discoverers of the North-West Passage", was not exhausted. Another expedition was at once organised to investigate the tide or current which had been observed by both Hudson's and Button's expeditions. It was despatched in March 1614, under the command of a Captain Gibbon, a near relative of Button and a companion on his voyage. The undertaking, however, proved a miserable failure. Gibbon even failed to enter Hudson's Strait, and spent the summer impounded among the ice in one of the bays upon the coast of Labrador.

By Gibbon's failure, a year of valuable time had been lost, and the source of Button's reported tide had not been further investigated. It was needful, therefore, that yet another expedition should be despatched for the purpose; and, in the spring of the following year, the same tireless company (or, at any rate, certain members of it) again despatched Hudson's old ship, the *Discovery*, this time under the command of Captain Robert Bylot, who had previously sailed in the same quest under Hudson, Button, and Gibbon successively, and who had with him as mate one William Baffin, a young seaman of exceptional attainments and ability. Bylot and Baffin accomplished little in the way of fresh discovery, but they made a careful survey of Hudson's Strait; and, at its western end, they explored (practically for the first time) the entrance to the large sheet of water we now call Foxe's

Channel, down which came the tide or current which, it was hoped, flowed through a passage from the Pacific Ocean. It must be admitted, however, that Foxe's Channel was not explored by Bylot and Baffin with sufficient thoroughness. Becoming embayed in one of the small inlets on the western side, they too hastily concluded that they had reached the extremity of the Channel, and relinquished further search; whereas, had they proceeded further north, they might have discovered the entrance to Fury and Hecla Strait, which has since proved to be a veritable "North-West Passage" though of no practical value. Upon the reported tide, Bylot and Baffin made numerous observations, but it did not appear to them to afford any evidence as to the existence or otherwise of a passage.

After the return home, Baffin expressed a somewhat-too-premature and too-dictatorial opinion that no passage existed *viâ* Hudson's Strait, and that, if one existed anywhere else, it would be found by exploring the northern portion of Davis Strait. Accordingly, in the following year (1616), Bylot and Baffin sailed again, under the same auspices, and in the same ship, in order this time to search Davis Strait. Their voyage was, in some ways, remarkably successful, and led to the discovery of what has ever since been known as Baffin's Bay; but, as it has no direct connection with our subject, it need not be further noticed here. It is needful, however, to say that they were again disappointed in their hoped-for discovery of a passage; and that, after their return home, Baffin expressed an opinion (in terms even more positive than those employed the year before in reference to Hudson's Strait) that there certainly existed no passage by way of Davis Strait—an opinion which, as we now know, was equally erroneous.

Apparently, even after all these discouragements, the enterprise of the Company of the Merchants of London, Discoverers of the North-West Passage, had not come to an end; for there is some reason to believe that, within the next few years, yet another searching voyage was despatched by it, at least in part. The voyage in question was that of Captain William Hawkridge, which most recent writers have ascribed to the year 1619. It seems to be quite certain, however, that this date is wrong. The point has been briefly noticed in Mr. Christy's *Voyages of Foxe and James;* but it deserves fuller consideration here, because, if the usually-accepted date for Hawkridge's voyage (1619) can be maintained, that voyage would have taken place in the same year as Munk's, and they must have been in Hudson's Strait at the same time. We believe, however, that this was not the case.

Concerning the voyage of Captain Hawkridge, we have absolutely no information except that given by Luke Foxe in his *North-West Fox*, published in 1635. Foxe, moreover, gives no clue whatever as to the year in which the voyage took place, or as to the names of its promoters. Rundall, however, in 1849, relying upon a certain passage in the Court

Minute Books of the Old East India Company,
asserted that the voyage was made in the year
1619, and that it was promoted by Sir John
Wolstenholme and his friends.[1] But an examination
of the record upon which Rundall relied shows that
it contains nothing whatever in support of his
assumptions. The record states (*Court Minute
Books*, vol. iv, fo. 114) that, at a "Court of Committees" (which, in modern parlance, would be
called a Board Meeting of Directors) of the East
India Company, held on the "20th of January 1617",

"Sr John Wolstenholme ... acquaynted them ... wth an intended
tryall to be made once againe in discou^{r}inge the Norwest passage,
wherein Mr Bullocke tenders his service, to proceede himselfe, if
Sr John Wolstenholme will procure my Lord Thr̄er to ioyne
annother in the pattent wth him, for the good of his child yf hee
dye, & will vndertake to end a difference dependinge betwixt him
and a gentleman. Receyuinge encouradgement to this new
Adventure, by reason that they vnderstand [that], in the bottome of
Botton's baye, wch runneth in 450 leagues from the mouth, where
a greate tyde of floode runnes, and riseth sometimes 17 or 18
foote in height, wch is supposed cannott bee butt by some Current
from the sea in some other place, wch in probabilitie may proue
the desired passage, whereof Mr Brigges hath a very greate hope.
But, whereas some made question of the sufficyencie and arte of
Mr Bullocke to vndertake the said discovery, they were enformed
that Mr Brigges approues of his skill and houldes him a man of
very good knowledge. And, therefore, Sr John Wolstenholme
moc̄ond thatt, seeinge this Companie have formerlie contributed
to the said discou^{r}ye, they would nowe proceede this one time wth
such a some as they shall thinke fitt, himselfe havinge such an
affec̄c̄on to the ac̄c̄on as that he intendes a good round Adventure
in his owne pticuler, & will psuade as many freindes as he may,

---

[1] *Voyages towards the North-West, 1496-1631* (Hakluyt Society,
1849), p. 151.

whereby to raise meanes to furnishe forthe 2 pinnaces, wch will cost 2000^{li}. And, seeinge the matter is small for this Companie, and that these workes bringe forth some good (as the [Arctic] whale fishinge was founde by the lyke occasion), yf the yssue proue good, this Companie are lyke to be ptakers of that good ; butt, yf itt should succeede otherwise, yet the deede is charitable: They, therefore, by erecc̃on of handes, did graunte an Adventure of 200^{li} towardes the same, to be disburst out of the Accompts of Fines."

Now, in the first place, it will be observed that the foregoing record contains no reference whatever to the year 1619. The date given is "January 20th, 1617", which, of course, corresponds to January 20th, 1618, according to our reckoning, and has nothing to do with 1619.

In the second place, it is observable that the record contains no reference whatever to Hawkridge, but that it relates to an intended expedition of a certain Captain Bullock, of which nothing whatever is known. It may be that Bullock's expedition actually took place in the year 1618, and that Foxe has wrongly ascribed it to Hawkridge ; or it may be that it took place in some other year, and that Hawkridge was the other commander who was to be joined with Bullock in the patent, and who, perhaps, in some way, managed to obtain the chief credit for the expedition. These are mere suppositions ; but, as has been elsewhere pointed out, Foxe's information about Hawkridge's voyage is so unsatisfactory that one is compelled to resort to surmise.[1]

---

[1] See *The Voyages of Foxe and James*, p. 249, *note*.

One thing, at all events, is clear: that Captain William Hawkridge did not make a voyage in search of a North-West Passage in either of the years 1618 or 1619—unless, indeed, there were two sea-captains of that name, of which we have no evidence. For the "Court Minute Books" and the volumes of *Original Correspondence* of the East India Company afford ample evidence that Hawkridge was in command of vessels belonging to that company in the East Indies and elsewhere from at least the early part of 1618 to the close of 1619. Thus, in a letter from Thomas Staverton to President Ball, written from Sambopa, in Macassar, on May 18th, 1618 (*Original Correspondence*, no. 651), there is a reference to "Richard Shortt, one of Mr. Hawkridg his Mattes", who was supposed to have deserted to a Spanish vessel. In another letter to President Ball, written from the same place on September 19th, 1618, Staverton says (*Original Correspondence*, no. 695) that a certain "Portingal" from the Moluccas had

"brought newes of the Shipp, the which (by many circumstances) I presume to bee true. He sayd [that] Mr Hawkridg had bine att Tyddore, where ptly through his owne good Carryadge, hee and all his Comp^a receeaued kind Vsadg from the Gouerno^r.... I make noe doubtt butt Mr Hawkridg hath had an honest Care in doing for, and looking to, the pties goods, &c. who soe vnfortunately left the shipp, as Mr Geo. Jackson, Wm Swetland," &c.

We next hear of Hawkridge in a letter (*Original Correspondence*, no. 784) to the Company from Captain Martin Pring, one of the Company's captains, dated from on board the *James Royal*, near the Isle of Becie, in the Strait of Sunda, on March 23rd, 1619, in which Pring says that, on October 22nd, 1618, he had arrived in the Road of Bantam :—

"Here [he says] wee found y⁶ *Thomas*, Mʳ Hawkeredge, maister, who arriued here the daie before from yᵉ Isle of Tidore, having narrowly escaped yᵉ fflemings & gotten about 40 pecul of Cloues, through yᵉ friendship of yᵉ Gouʳnour. The cause of his goinge to the Moluccaes was yᵗ hee had lost yᵉ Company of yᵉ 4 Shippes which afterwards were taken by yᵉ Dutch neare yᵉ Isles of Banda."

We next meet (*Original Correspondence*, no. 718) with the Minutes of a Consultation, held in Jacatra Roads on December 20th, 1618, for the ordering of the intended fight the following morning between the English and Dutch fleets. This is signed by fourteen captains in the service of the East India Company, including Hawkridge (whose autograph is reproduced hereunder), Sir Thomas

—*will: Hawkeridge.*

Dale being "Generall". Finally, we find (*C. M. B.* iv, fo. 464) that, at a Court of Committees held on December 3rd, 1619,

"certayne lʳes ... [containing accounts of the bad weather & of the narrow escape from shipwreck of the *James*] written from Silley by Mʳ Quoitmore, Mʳ Bennet, Mʳ Hawkeridge, and Mʳ Totten, from abourd the little *James* and *Suplye*, in the road of Silley, bearing date the 22ᵗʰ of November last, were nowe red."

Now we may regard it as certain, from the

position of the narrative of Hawkridge's voyage in Foxe's work, that that voyage took place between Bylot and Baffin's second voyage in 1616 and Foxe's own voyage in 1631 ; and, if (as has been already shown) it did not take place in either 1618 or 1619, it must have been despatched either in 1617 or after 1619.

Bearing in mind the very extraordinary energy with which the Company of Discoverers of the North-West Passage had hitherto followed up the search, never allowing a year to elapse after the return of one unsuccessful expedition without despatching another with the same object in view, it would be natural to conclude that Hawkridge's voyage was another belonging to the same series and despatched by the same tireless company in the year following the return of Bylot and Baffin (1617); but, in that case, it seems probable that we should find some mention of it among the ancient records of the East India Company, which we do not—unless, indeed, it was in some way connected with the intended voyage under Captain Bullock, already mentioned.

There is, however, another permissible supposition : we know that, in the spring of 1625, Sir John Wolstenholme and some of his friends were actively entertaining the project of another Arctic expedition, and that for this purpose the King had granted the pinnace *Lion's Whelp*,[1] but we have no

---

[1] See *The Voyages of Foxe and James*, p. lxxvii; the *Coke Papers*

record of any voyage resulting. It may be, however, that the voyage was actually made, and that it was commanded by Hawkridge, who, we know, lived until at least six years later.[1] This supposition is, perhaps, to some extent, supported by the fact that Foxe, in his book (p. 166, Ed. 1635), prints Hawkridge's voyage *after* a discourse by Purchas and Briggs on the probability of the existence of a North-West Passage, which follows Bylot and Baffin's voyages, though it has no special connection with them, and which (one might reasonably con-

---

(*Reports Roy. Hist. MSS. Comm.*, no. xii, 1888), vol. i, p. 183; *State Papers, Dom., Jas. I*, vol. clxxxv, no. 82; *Do., Chas. I, Warrant Book*, 21, no. 7; *Docquets*, June 25, 1625; *S. P., Dom., Chas. I*, vol. i, nos. 37 and 95; also Rymer's *Fœdera*, vol. xviii (1726), p. 166.

[1] *Voyages of Foxe and James*, p. 1. In addition to the information given in this place concerning Hawkridge, we may point out that he had formerly been in the Newfoundland trade, of which we have evidence in a statement by Captain Richard Whitbourne, who says (*A Discourse and Discovery of New-found-land*, London, 4°, 1620, p. [73]), that, in the year 1610, one morning early, as he was standing by the water's side, in the Harbour of St. John's, a strange and beautiful creature with a head and face resembling a woman, shoulders square and white like those of a man, and a fluked tail, swam towards him and approached so close to him that he retreated from the water's edge; "but the same came shortly after vnto a boate, wherein one *William Hawkridge*, then my servant, was, that hath bin since a Captaine in a ship to the *East Indies*, and is lately there imployed againe by Sir *Thomas Smith* in the like voyage; and the same creature did put both his handes vpon the side of the boate, and did striue to come in to him and others then in the said boate, whereat they were afraide, and one of them Strooke it a full blow on the head, whereby it fell off from them. . . . This (I suppose) was a maremaide." Captain Whitbourne was an Exmouth man.

clude) Foxe must have thought most fitting as a conclusion to his account of the voyages preceding his own.

It may be, therefore, that Hawkridge's expedition took place in 1625, not long previous to Foxe's; that Foxe only succeeded in obtaining information about it at the last moment; and that he then added it at the end of his account of North-West voyages previous to his own, after what he had intended as the conclusion of that portion of his book. That Foxe's narrative of Hawkridge's voyage was printed hurriedly, or under some other difficulty, seems certain, to judge from the confusion it displays.[1] If this supposition as to the date of Hawkridge's voyage should, hereafter, prove to be correct, it would also account for the otherwise inexplicable fact that no mention of Hawkridge's voyage occurs in *Purchas his Pilgrimes*, published in 1625. The industry of Purchas was so great that it is not easy to believe that, had Hawkridge's voyage taken place before 1625, he would not have heard of and mentioned it. The fact, too, that Whitbourne, writing (as quoted above) in 1620, makes no reference to any voyage made by Hawkridge in search of a North-West Passage, while he mentions his East Indian voyages, is against 1617 and in favour of 1625, as the date of Hawkridge's North-West voyage.

---

[1] See *The Voyages of Foxe and James*, p. 257, *note*.

We still remain, therefore, almost entirely in the dark as to the year in which Hawkridge's mysterious voyage took place, and as to whether it took place before or after Munk's voyage in 1619. It would, of course, be interesting if the point could be settled decisively; but, fortunately, it is by no means necessary for our present purpose that the doubt should be cleared up; for, even if Hawkridge's voyage did take place before Munk's, there is not the slightest evidence that Munk knew of the fact, or that it had any influence on his proceedings.

Leaving, therefore, the date of Hawkridge's voyage as uncertain, and of comparatively little consequence in this connexion, we may fitly conclude this survey of the voyages which preceded Munk's by stating how the problem of finding a North-West passage through Hudson's Strait and Bay stood in 1619, when Munk started on his expedition to attempt a solution of it. It will be found that the coasts of both the Strait and the Bay had been so far examined that there only remained four points which either really were as yet unexplored or insufficiently explored, or in which the existence of a passage was still thought probable, in spite of the negative results of previous expeditions.

Firstly, there was the waterway, now known as Foxe Channel, running northward from the western end of Hudson's Strait. This is still very imperfectly known; but, in 1619, it was totally unknown, except through the very cursory examination of its southern end made by Bylot and Baffin in 1615 (see p. lxxxv).

Secondly, there was the northern extremity of the channel now known as Sir Thomas Roe's Welcome. In 1619, this region had only been visited by Sir Thomas Button, who had more or less explored it in 1613, but who had turned back (without, apparently, sufficient cause) on reaching a point which, for a long time after, was known as "Button's Ne Ultra" (see p. lxxxiii). Button's examination had not been so detailed as altogether to preclude the hope of a westward extension of the channel.

Thirdly, it was thought by many that a passage would be found on the west coast of Hudson's Bay, at a spot known, since Button's expedition, as Hubbart's Hope (see p. lxxxii). Although Button's expedition failed to find any passage, Hubart did not, as it appears, abandon his expectation; and his views were adopted by many persons in England, notably by Professor Briggs. The latter seems to have thought that the passage would be found in the neighbourhood of what we now call Churchill Bay,[1] and with this view the latter was explored by Foxe and James. The question of Hubart's Hope will be discussed later on. Suffice it here to say that to this point an expedition might very properly be directed in 1619.

---

[1] See *Purchas his Pilgrimes* (1625), part iii, p. 848, and map.

Fourthly, there was the still-totally-unexplored southern coast-line of Hudson's Bay, between Hudson's westernmost point at Cape Henrietta Maria (see p. lxxix) and Button's easternmost at Port Nelson (see p. lxxxii).

The exploration of one or more of these four points might, therefore, as matters stood in 1619, very well form the object of further researches; and, when we come to consider Jens Munk's account of the expedition which started in that year under his command, it will be seen that it was probably directed towards the third of these points. In so far, it forms a direct continuation of the preceding voyages, although, of course, in other respects, it occupies a place quite outside the series of English expeditions.

Looking back on this series of voyages, it may seem to us, with our geographical knowledge, a somewhat unreasonable idea that a communication might exist between the western shore of Hudson's Bay and the Pacific, right through the mainland of the Continent of America. But it must be remembered that, at the time in question, the interior of North America was totally unknown, and there were no means of guessing whether it was all a solid continent or not.

As a matter of fact, nearly a century and a half elapsed after the date of Munk's voyage before the world was fully and finally convinced of the non-existence of a passage leading westwards or north-westwards from Hudson's Bay to the Pacific Ocean.

IV.—*Preliminary Observations on Jens Munk's Expedition to Hudson's Bay.*

In our sketch of Munk's life, we have already sufficiently explained the circumstances and considerations which may with probability be looked upon as having induced the King of Denmark to send out an expedition in 1619 for the purpose of attempting the discovery of a North-West Passage. It remains to consider the actual preparations made for the attainment of that object.

The first and most important subject to be discussed in this connexion would naturally be the instructions which, as we are told, were given to Munk, in his capacity as commander of the Expedition, according to the usual custom in such cases. But we meet here with the difficulty that, although Munk several times alludes to his instructions, he does not reproduce them; nor is any copy or abstract of them known to exist. We are, therefore, unable to supply the reader of Munk's account of his voyage with the guidance which a knowledge of his instructions would afford. It is, of course, generally speaking, quite feasible, from an account of this kind, to form more or less safe inferences as to what was intended to be done, and as to the manner in which it was to be done; but, as any discussion of these points would presuppose a very detailed knowledge of the text, we could not enter upon it in this place without largely anticipating what properly has to be said later on; and, after all, if, having deduced the contents of the instructions from the narrative, we were to pretend, by their means, to guide the reader to a right understanding of that narrative, we should simply be reasoning in a circle. Our observations on this subject must, therefore, be postponed, and will suitably find a place in connexion with what we have to say on the results of the voyage.

Before, however, leaving this subject for the present, we may observe that there is nothing at all surprising in the absence of any record of Munk's instructions; nor does there appear to be the smallest occasion for surmising, on that account, as has been done,[1] that the document has been purposely destroyed. It may be questioned whether any of the numerous similar documents of the same period are still preserved in Denmark; and it is certain that we should have known very little of their contents but for the office-copies entered in the registers of the Danish Chancery, to which we have already often referred. Such copies were, however, by no means always taken,[2] and Munk's instructions for this voyage are far from being the only ones of the kind which have not been so entered. No sufficient reason can be adduced for thinking this omission intentional. Even supposing (which is most improbable) that the document in question

---

[1] See Mr. Lauridsen's edition of the *Navigatio Septentrionalis*, p. xix.

[2] There is, for instance, no record of Cunningham's instructions in 1605, or of those of Godske Lindenow in 1606.

contained information which it was desired to keep secret, there would have been no occasion for not entering it in the books of the Chancery, where it would have been perfectly safe. For aught we know, therefore, the absence of any office-copy of Munk's instructions is purely accidental.

Without the text of Munk's instructions, we cannot tell with any certainty what he was directed to do, except in so far as it is disclosed by his narrative; but, in forming an opinion, we shall be much assisted by taking into consideration what information he, or those from whom he had his instructions, may be supposed to have been in possession of with regard to the main object of his voyage, and as to the ways and means of accomplishing it. In this respect, it may be observed, in the first instance, that, if (as the historian Niels Slange says) Munk really was himself the principal mover in the matter, he may reasonably be supposed to have thoroughly informed himself about it; in which case, we may fairly assume that the instructions given him mainly embodied his own propositions, as approved by the King. But, even if Slange's statement is not correct—and we have expressed our doubts concerning it (see p. xxviii)— we may rest equally well assured that every available source of information was drawn upon. In spite of his spirit and activity, Christian IV was neither rash nor imprudent, and was not likely to enter upon such an undertaking without obtaining all the information available concerning it.

The sources of information which, as a matter of fact, were open to the King and his advisers were of two kinds—partly literary (*viz.*, published books and maps), and partly personal (*viz.*, individuals possessing an actual acquaintance with Arctic navigation in general and with the problem of the North-West Passage in particular). As regards the former, only those would be of practical value which had been published since Hudson's last voyage in 1610, because the object of the new expedition was to follow up Hudson's discoveries. Of such publications, there were only two containing original matter, *viz.*, Hudson's map (as published by Hessel Gerritsz. in 1612) and Purchas' *Pilgrimage*, of which the third edition, published in 1617, contained not only additional information on Hudson's voyage, but an important though short notice on Button's voyage in 1612-13, together with some account of Bylot and Baffin's voyage in 1615.

That Hessel Gerritsz.'s map was known at Copenhagen can scarcely be doubted. Denmark was neither an unlettered nor an isolated country, even in those days. The writings of the Bartholins, the Wormius, and others, prove that the *savants* of Copenhagen were in too close communication with the rest of the world for a book attracting so much attention to remain unknown to them, particularly if written in Latin. Scholars are well aware how quickly, at that time, Latin books spread throughout Western Europe, on account of their being understood equally well everywhere—an advantage which was lost when scientific authors commenced to publish their works in the vulgar tongues. Moreover, the intercourse between Denmark and Holland was lively, and the Dutch language was understood by many in Denmark. Hessel Gerritsz. published the map in question in the summer of 1612, with an explanation in Dutch printed on the back; but a Latin translation quickly followed, and new editions of both soon appeared. Two German editions were published in 1613; and, in the same year, an abridged English translation found room in Purchas' *Pilgrimage*.[1] In some form, the map was doubtless known in Denmark; and that Munk was more particularly acquainted with the Dutch explanation of it may, perhaps, be inferred from the fact that, in referring to Lumley's Inlet, he spells the word Lumley's sometimes "Lomlis", as it is on Hessel Gerritsz.'s map, sometimes "Lomblis", corresponding to the spelling Lumbley in the Dutch explanation. There can be no doubt that Munk made use of this map in writing his published account of the voyage; but it is not certain that he had a copy with him on the voyage.

As regards Purchas' *Pilgrimage*, the case is different, in so far that, being an English book, it may not have been known in Denmark. But this makes little difference for our present purpose, because whatever information might be derived from that work became, in all probability, available to

---

[1] First Edition (1613), p. 624.

Munk and whoever had to draw up his instructions, through the medium of the personal sources of information which were open to them, and to which we must next turn our attention.

Thanks to the expeditions which had been sent out to Greenland and to Nova Zembla not many years before, men who possessed a certain measure of experience in Arctic navigation were not altogether wanting in Denmark at the time; but, as far as is known, none were to be found there who had been to the northern part of the Continent of America, or who had had any opportunity of acquiring particular knowledge of those parts of the sea which Munk's Expedition was intended to examine. The previous explorers of Hudson's Strait and Bay had all been English; and it was from England alone that men could be obtained whose assistance as pilots would be of any value. Such men were, accordingly, obtained; and, just as James Hall and John Knight had been engaged for the expedition to Greenland in 1605, so the services of two other Englishmen, William Gordon and John Watson, were secured for the voyage to Hudson's Bay in 1619. As will be stated more fully hereafter, there is some uncertainty as to the extent of the actual experience of these two men, and particularly as to whether either of them had been previously to Hudson's Bay. As regards Gordon, at any rate, it is known that he was acquainted with Baffin and, very likely, with other navigators who had been to Hudson's Bay; and he may therefore fairly be assumed to have been in possession of whatever knowledge about the Strait and Bay, and about the probability of a passage existing thereabouts, that was then known in England in circles interested in Arctic matters. Taking this into consideration, we shall probably not err if we state, as our belief, that so much at least as had been published by Purchas was at the disposal, directly or indirectly, of Munk and of those who planned his Expedition; and there would be nothing unreasonable in surmising that still further information had come to their knowledge through Gordon and Watson.

Purchas' notice of Button's voyage is of particular interest in this connexion. It is as follows:[1]

"This newes so incouraged the Aduenturers that, by the gracious assistance of . . . Prince Henry, the Aduenturers . . . pursued the action in a more Royall fashion, with greater shipping vnder the command of a worthy seaman, seruant to Prince Henry, Captaine Thomas Button, whose Discovery of a great Continent called by him New Wales, and other accidents of his Voyage, I haue not seene: only I haue seene a Chart of those discouered places, and I heare that hee passed Hudson's Strait and, leauing Hudson's Bay to the south,[2] sayled aboue 200 leagues South-West ward, ouer a Sea aboue 80 fathom deep, without sight of Land, which at length he found to be another great Bay. And, after much miserie of sicknesse in his wintering, notwithstanding hee was forced to quit the great ship, he beat and searched the whole Bay with very great industrie, euen backe againe almost to Digges Iland, neare which hee found the coming in of the great and strong tyde from the North West, which feeds both those huge Bayes."

---

[1] *Purchas his Pilgrimage*, 3rd Edition (1617), p. 926.

[2] It will be remembered that originally this name applied only to the south-eastern portion of the bay, as distinct from the western part, for some time known as Button's Bay.

If nothing more than this, and the negative result of Bylot's voyage in 1615, had been known in Denmark in 1619, one might naturally wonder that any expedition should have been then sent out at all to Hudson's Bay. It is, therefore, probable that it was further known at Copenhagen that, in spite of these explorers having failed to discover a passage westwards out of the Bay, the idea of such a passage existing was still entertained by many in England. We have stated above that, in 1619, there remained unexplored, or not sufficiently explored, four different points in the circumference of Hudson's Bay where a passage might still be sought for, and that, more particularly, it was by many considered not unlikely that an opening westwards would be found near a point on the west coast of the Bay called Hubbart's Hope. There is nothing unreasonable in supposing that this had come to the ears of the King of Denmark and his advisers, and that they thought the chance good enough to justify the sending out of an expedition.

As regards sources of information, we may finally observe that intelligence may probably have been obtained through the same channel (whatever that was) through which the services of Gordon and Watson were obtained.

Jens Munk's expedition consisted of two vessels, both belonging to the Danish Navy, probably selected by Munk himself, and equipped (as the custom of that time was) under his own superintendence, *viz.*, a small frigate called *Enhiörningen* (*The Unicorn*) and a sloop called *Lamprenen* (*The Lamprey*).

The name of the frigate was probably not derived from the Unicorn of the Ancients, but from the Narwhal, which is also called *Enhiörning* in Danish, and is mentioned by English writers of that period under the name of the "Sea-Unicorn". The fabled Unicorn of the Ancients was supposed to be a quadruped possessed of enormous strength and vital power, which was concentrated in its great frontal "horn". To the horn, therefore, marvellous virtue was ascribed, and it was eagerly sought for; but, as the animal did not exist, the real horn was, of course, not obtainable. Various substances, however, were sold for it, and amongst them fragments of the beautiful twisted tusks of the Narwhal. The Narwhal had been of course, known from early times to the mariners of the extreme North, but elsewhere it was unknown, and very few persons had any idea of the true origin of the so-called "Unicorn's horn". It was only at the time of which we speak that the animal became known to the world at large, through the narratives of whalers and other Arctic navigators, though it was some time before it was understood that the "horn" was really a tooth, and that it was not placed in the middle of the forehead, where it was often depicted—for instance, on Hall's maps of the coast of Greenland. It was thought a notable event, worthy of being chronicled by Niels Slange in his *History of Christian IV*, that, in the year 1605, a specimen of this animal, 30 ft. long (of which the tusk represented six), was captured off Iceland, the skull, with the tusk, being valued at between 30,000 and 40,000 Danish Rixdollars (about £6,000).[1] It was very likely this event which caused the frigate *Enhiörningen* to be so named; for she is not mentioned in the Danish records before 1610, when she was in the Baltic, in the fleet commanded by Mogeus Ulfeld. She was, therefore, probably built not long after the capture in question. In any case, the name, being that of a marine monster, was by no means unsuitable for a man-of-war.

Enhiörningen was probably a good ship, as she is mentioned several times as being in commission; but nothing is known with certainty about her armament. Of the cannon belonging to her, which were found long afterwards at her wintering-place in Hudson's Bay, one is described as being of about the size of a 3-pounder; another, an 8-pounder, appears to have been of brass; and Munk mentions two falconets of iron. As her crew only numbered 48, she cannot have carried more than six or eight pieces; and her armament, therefore, probably consisted of six brass 8-pounders and two iron falconets.

The name of *Lamprenen* (*the Lamprey*) seems odd; but similar names were not uncommon at the time in the northern navies, such as *Makrelen* (*the Mackerel*), *Hummeren* (*the Lobster*), *Den Blaa Orm*

---

[1] *Op. cit.*, p. 220.

(*the Blue Snake*), and others. Vessels of her class were chiefly used for transport and victualling—in short, as tenders. The earlier history and subsequent fate of this sloop have already been related in our account of the life of Jens Munk (see pp. xxi and xlviii).

The crews numbered at the outset 48 and 16, respectively, inclusive of officers. One of the sailors committed suicide, and another died, soon after leaving Copenhagen; in whose stead, three others were shipped in Norway, making a total of 65 when the expedition left Europe, of whom only three returned. Of the commander himself, we have already given a full account. His lieutenant was Mauritz Stygge, belonging to a now-extinct noble family, which, however, never was of any particular note. Being a nobleman, he is described by Munk as an "honourable and well-born man." It appears that there was in the Danish Navy a Captain Enevold Stygge, who in 1616 had commanded *Enhiörningen* in the North Sea. Very possibly he was this young man's father.

The chaplain was Hr. Rasmus Jensen, of whom nothing further is known. He is styled "*Hr.*", a description now applied to everybody in Denmark, like "Mr." in England; but at that time it was used only for noblemen and clergymen.

There were two surgeons with the Expedition, one on either vessel. The one on board *Enhiörningen* is described as M. Casper Caspersen, and has with great probability been identified[1] with a certain Casper Rottenburg—most likely of German extraction—who, on April 25th, 1619, shortly before the departure of the Expedition, was appointed an army and navy surgeon. He is described in the Danish as *Bardsker*, a corruption of the German word *Bartscheerer*—that is, literally, beard-cutter or barber, which at that time was a proper designation for surgeons. Even such a celebrated man as Ambrose Paré styled himself only *tonsor perpetuus* to Charles IX of France. Nowadays, all surgeons in Denmark must have a University education; but, in Munk's time, and for a long time after, they were, almost without exception, men who had learnt to perform surgical operations, but were otherwise almost destitute of medical knowledge. Physicians were always University men; but no physician or properly-educated medical man would condescend to perform ordinary surgical operations himself. On board ship, particularly in time of war, surgeons were of course indispensable, and were provided, but no physicians; and the consequence was that, although the naval surgeons sometimes— at a later period always—were taught the elements of the medical art in an empirical manner, the medical assistance available on board ship was mostly very inefficient. Surgeons were classed with ordinary handicraftsmen, like tailors and shoemakers, and,

---

[1] *Jens Munks Navigatio Septentrionalis*, ed. P. Lauridsen (Copenhagen, 1887), note 35.

like those, were described as *Mester* when qualified to carry on business on their own account. This is the meaning of the "*M.*" preceding the name of Casper Caspersen, who appears, however, to have been a particularly ignorant specimen of his class. The surgeon on *Lamprenen*, David Volske by name, had no such prefix, and was, therefore, no doubt, an even inferior person.

From an entry in the registers of the Danish Chancery,[1] it appears that Jens Hendrichsen, whom Munk describes as "skipper", was the master of *Lamprenen;* but nothing further is known of him. The same remark applies to Jan Olluffsen, the skipper or navigating officer of *Enhiörningen*.

Munk had four mates or *Styrmænds*, two of them —William Gourdon (or Gordon, as the name is spelt by modern writers), and John Watson— being Englishmen, whilst the two others—Hans Brock and Jan Pettersen—were Danes or Norwegians. How these four mates were distributed on the vessels is nowhere expressly stated; but, as both the Danes are designated as second mates, whilst Munk describes Gordon as his chief mate, the latter was no doubt chief mate on board *Enhiörningen*, and acted as pilot to the Expedition. Hans Brock was probably second mate of the same ship, and Watson chief mate of *Lamprenen*, with Jan Petterson as second.

As regards the antecedents of Gordon, there is,

---

[1] *Sjæll. Reg.*, xvi, p. 429.

perhaps, room for some little uncertainty. A William Gourdon or Gordon is mentioned in several accounts of Arctic voyages in the early part of the seventeenth century; but there is no direct proof, either that these statements refer to one and the same person, or that any of them refer to the man who sailed with Munk as chief mate in 1619. In *Purchas his Pilgrimes*, we find an account[1] of a voyage to Cherie Island in 1603, which is stated to be written by William Gorden, who acted as factor and overseer. Next, we have an account in the same work[2] of a voyage made to the Petchora in 1611 for the Muscovy Company, which account is stated to be "Written by William Gourdon of Hull, appointed chiefe Pilot for Discouerie to Ob, etc." Purchas prints two other accounts of the same voyage by James Logan and William Parsglove, in which this William Gourdon is also mentioned.[3] It appears that he returned to London the same year, while they remained on the Petchora till the next summer. Both in Baffin's[4] and in Gatonbe's[5] account of James Hall's voyage to Greenland in 1612, a William Gourdon or Gordon of Hull is mentioned, who, according to the latter, served as master's mate on board the *Patience*. Again, a William Gourdon is mentioned

---

[1] *Op. cit.*, vol. iii, p. 566.   [2] *Op. cit.*, vol. iii, p. 530.

[3] *Op. cit.*, vol. iii, pp. 541-546 and 547-550.

[4] *Op. cit.*, iii, p. 833. See also Book 1 (*Expeditions to Greenland*), p. 126.

[5] Churchill, *Collection of Voyages*, vol. vi (1732), pp. 252 and 253. See also Book 1, pp. 105 and 107.

in Baffin's account of a voyage for the Muscovy Company to Spitzbergen in 1613,[1] but only in one place, and in such a manner that it does not appear whether Gourdon was of the same party as Baffin, or in what capacity he found himself in that place. Finally, we have an account in *Purchas his Pilgrimes*,[2] entitled " Later Observations of William Gourdon ... at Pustozera in the yeares 1614 and 1615", from which it appears that the author was in the service of the Muscovy Company, and, after performing a long and arduous journey by sledge in the winter, returned home in 1615, reaching Dort, in Holland, in the month of September of that year.

As already stated, there is no direct evidence to show that all these data refer to the same man; but it is undoubtedly the natural inference, and there is no evidence to the contrary. It is true that the William Gorden who went to Cherie Island in 1603, did so as factor and overseer; and the person of that name who was at Pustocera in 1614-15 in the service of the Muscovy Company seems to have acted in a similar capacity. But nobody will doubt that the latter was the same man who went to the Petchora in 1611 in the service of that same company, and he, we are told, was the chief pilot of the expedition. Nor would there be anything remarkable in the same man acting both as trader and as practical seaman—occupations which in those times

---

[1] *Purchas his Pilgrimes*, vol. iii, p. 720.
[2] *Op. cit.*, iii, p. 553.

were often combined. The above-mentioned James Logan was evidently a sailor as well as a trader. Moreover, it may be observed that the Gourdon who, with some others, performed the above-mentioned journey by land in the winter 1614-15, not only regularly records, sailor-fashion, the direction of the wind, the distances travelled, and the directions taken, but also carried nautical instruments with him, and several times notes the latitude of the places and the variation of the compass, according to his own observations. The question remains: Was this pilot and factor identical with Munk's chief mate? In this respect, we may observe, first, that he is the only William Gordon known at that time in any way qualified for that post; and, secondly, that, in the warrant by which Munk's mate was appointed, the name is spelt (no doubt according to his own statement) Gourdon, just as it is always spelt by Baffin, and mostly by Purchas.

The point just discussed is of interest not only with regard to the personal history of Munk's chief mate, but also (and particularly) with regard to the question whether he can be supposed to have had any previous knowledge of Hudson's Bay. If he had been with Hall in Greenland in 1612, he cannot have taken part in Button's expedition to the Bay in that year; and, if he had been to the Petchora in 1615, he cannot have accompanied Bylot and Baffin to Hudson's Bay in that same year, though he might have been with them on their famous expedition to Baffin's Bay in 1616. There is, however, no evidence at all of any William Gordon having been with them in any capacity. It may, moreover, be observed that, as he served in 1612 as master's mate, and was very disappointed at not being made master after the death of Hall,[1] and as he evidently held a superior position on the Petchora in 1614-15, we may be sure that he would not have sailed in 1615 in an obscure capacity. Taking all this together, it appears to follow that Gordon, when he sailed with Munk in 1619, cannot have had any knowledge at all of the western part of Hudson's Bay, and that most likely he had never even been in Hudson's Strait.

How Gordon came into the Danish service is not known. We have, however, in speaking of Hall's and Knight's engagements, already alluded to the fact that Christian IV of Denmark was brother-in-law to James I of England; and, as there were frequent communications between the two Courts by means of embassies and messengers, the King of Denmark cannot have lacked means for obtaining pilots. As the Muscovy Company enjoyed certain privileges from him, that Company may have been applied to; and if Gordon was, or for some time had been, in their service they may have recommended him.

To judge from the silence of English literature during the seventeenth century with regard to

---

[1] See Book I, *Expeditions to Greenland*, pp. 107 and 126.

Munk's voyage, it can scarcely have been widely known amongst the general public.[1] That, however, some persons were aware, both that an expedition had been sent and that an Englishman served as pilot, is evident from the following passage in a letter from John Chamberlain (the professional writer of news-letters) to Sir Dudley Carleton at the Hague:[2] "There is speach here that the King of Denmarke hath discouered the North-West Passage by the meane of an English pilote." The letter is dated London, April 29th, 1620, when Munk had not yet returned; and the rumour had probably originated in this very circumstance, it being concluded that, as Munk had not returned, he had probably succeeded in getting through to the Pacific. Similar inferences were drawn when Button did not return in 1612, and afterwards when James did not return in 1631. The rumour may, of course, have come to England from the Continent, but may also have come through the same quarter from which Gordon had been recommended to Christian IV.

Whoever had acted as intermediary in the matter, Gordon had doubtless been well recommended to

---

[1] It is particularly worth noticing that, in Luke Foxe's work, *North-West Fox*, there is no evidence that, up to the time of its publication in 1635, Foxe, in spite of his extensive and, on the whole, successful inquiry after the journals, charts, etc., of his predecessors, had even so much as heard of Munk's voyage, which took place twelve years before his own. Nor does the indefatigable Purchas refer in any way to Munk's voyage, though it took place five years before the publication of his great work.

[2] *State Papers, Dom., Jas. I.*, vol. cxiii, No. 92 (Cal. p. 140).

Christian IV., and had been engaged by him on account of his supposed experience and knowledge of the Arctic Regions in general, if not of the particular waters to which the Expedition was to sail. When Gordon arrived at Copenhagen is not known; but, in the diary of Christian IV. for 1619, there is a memorandum of the King having advanced "Willem Gordon" 200 Dollars on March 11th.[1] Under date of March 29th, 1619, Gordon was appointed mate *(Styrmand)* in the Danish Navy, to serve whenever and wherever he might be commanded to go, with a salary of 50 Danish Rixdollars monthly; "and [says the Royal Warrant[2]], if the said Villem Gourdon succeeds, by the help and guidance of God, in finding the Passage, which We most graciously will command him to search for, We have graciously granted him that he shall receive a recompense of two thousand Rixdollars."

Concerning John Watson's antecedents, nothing whatever is known. It may be taken for granted that he would not have been engaged if the Danish authorities had not had reason to believe that his services would be of particular use; and, in another place, we shall adduce reasons for thinking that he had been with Button in 1612. If so, he would really know much more of Hudson's Bay than Gordon. That the principal position was, neverthe-

---

[1] *Kong Christian den Fjerdes Dagboger* (Copenhagen, 1825), p. 52.   [2] *Sjæll. Reg.*, xvi, fol. 42.

less, given to the latter, may, perhaps, be explained by the supposition that Watson had previously only filled subordinate positions, while Gordon was, we have reason to think, a man of considerable experience and had filled responsible positions. Very likely, too, Watson was inferior to Gordon in education.

Hans Brock was most probably the same who had served under Munk on his voyage to Nova Zembla in 1610 (see p. xvii); but of Jan Pettersen nothing further is known.

A nephew of Jens Munk, Erik by name, accompanied the Expedition, but in what capacity is not stated. He was a son of Jens Munk's elder brother Niels, whom we have mentioned several times, and who had died in 1617. Probably the young man was destined for the navy, and was permitted to accompany his uncle as a volunteer.

The remaining members of the crews do not call for any particular observations. Complete lists of the crews are rarely, if ever, met with in accounts of voyages, because, generally speaking, they would be devoid of interest. Yet cases do sometimes occur where it would have been of interest if we had had means to ascertain whether a particular man had taken part in an expedition, even only as a common sailor. We have, in fact, just mentioned such a case with regard to John Watson. In this case, there would be no difficulty in extracting from Munk's narrative an almost complete list of the sailors, because Munk mentions the names of nearly all in noticing their deaths; but, as none of them (except, perhaps, the two Englishmen) had been in those parts before, and as they all perished excepting the two who returned with Munk, but whose names are not mentioned, it would be of no practical use.

It will be observed that the men are mostly designated by their Christian names, with the addition sometimes of their occupation (carpenter, cooper, &c.), but generally, also, of their father's name, with the termination "*sen*," and, in many cases, of the place from which they hailed. Family names were, at that time, rare in Denmark, except amongst the higher classes. Two persons of the same name, and whose fathers also had the same name, were distinguished by adding the name of the homestead, village, town, or (in the case of persons hailing from afar) province to which they belonged. By paying attention to this, it will be seen that there is no foundation at all for Barrow's statement[1] that "the vessels, it would seem, were mostly manned by English sailors, who no doubt had been employed on some of the former expeditions for Arctic discoveries or on the whale fishery." In reality, Munk's sailors came from all parts of the Danish dominions. At least nine were from Norway, whilst others came from Halland, from Bornholm, from Copenhagen, from the island of Als, in Sleswick, and from elsewhere.

Such was the composition of the Expedition

---

[1] *A Chronological History of Voyages into the Arctic Regions* (London, 1818), p. 230.

which set out from Copenhagen for America on the 9th of May, 1619. We shall now let Munk himself give his account of the voyage, to which we have appended a few notes which seemed necessary. The main part of the explanatory matter, however (being much too bulky to be conveniently conveyed in the form of foot-notes), will be found in the Commentary following immediately after Munk's text. This Commentary is so arranged that it may be read independently of the text; but readers who may wish to consult the Commentary together with the text will have no difficulty in doing so, by means of the references to the pages of the text placed in the margin of the Commentary.

In a separate concluding chapter, we propose to discuss the geographical results of the voyage.

NOTE.—It should have been mentioned on p. lxvi that, besides the translation of La Peyrère's original treatise, which is noticed there, the Churchill *Collection* of voyages also contains an English translation of the first German version of the *Relation du Groenlande*, which the editors seem to have mistaken for an original work. It is found in the first volume of the *Collection* (1704, p. 544-569), and is entitled *An account of a most dangerous voyage performed by the famous Capt. John Monck in the years 1619 and 1620 . . . . Translated from the High Dutch original, printed at Frankfort upon the Maine, 1650.* The map and the illustrations are reproduced. There are consequently two versions of La Peyrère's treatise in the Churchill *Collection*, with maps and illustrations, both first published in 1704. They are both found in all the editions.

NAVIGATIO SEPTENTRIONALIS:

THAT IS, A

RELATION

OR DESCRIPTION OF A VOYAGE

In Search of the North-West *Passage*, now called
Nova Dania, through *Fretum Christian;*

WHICH VOYAGE

OUR MOST GRACIOUS MAJESTY KING
CHRISTIAN THE FOURTH WAS GRACIOUSLY PLEASED
TO COMMAND IN THE YEAR 1619;

And, in order to accomplish it, sent out his Majesty's Sea
Captain, Iens Munk, together with a Crew numbering in all
64 Persons, in two of His Majesty's ships, *Enhiörningen*
and the Sloop *Lamprenen;*

WHICH SAME

EXPEDITION WAS, SO FAR AS WAS POSSIBLE,

Carried out with most implicit obedience to the *Instructions*
Graciously given; but the Commander, after incurring great Peril,
returned back to Norway with the Sloop and only two others;

COMPRISING AN ACCOUNT OF ALL THE CIRCUM-
stances, Courses, Directions, and Occurrences, concerning that
Sea and the Particulars of that Voyage;

BY THE SAID

IENS MUNCK

Diligently observed on the Journey there and back, and
published by His said Royal Majesty's Most
Gracious Command.

ECCLUS. 43.

Navigantes mare, enarrant ejus pericula.

They that sail on the sea tell of the Dangers thereof; and, when we hear it
with our ears, we marvel thereat, etc.

Printed in Copenhagen by Henrich Waldkirch.
ANNO M. DC. XXIIII.

Most Mighty, Highborn Prince
and Lord, Sire,

CHRISTIAN THE FOURTH,

King of Denmark, Norway, the Vends, and the Goths, Duke of Sleswick, Holstein, Stormarn, and Dithmarschen, Count of Oldenburg and Delmenhorst, etc., My most gracious Lord and King:

Grace, Prosperity and Peace from God by Jesus Christ our Lord.

OST GRACIOUS LORD AND KING. Inasmuch as Your Royal Majesty, in the year of 1619, now past, after gracious consideration, commanded that I should sail forth with two of Your Majesty's ships, *Enhiörningen* and the sloop *Lamprenen*, in order to search for the North-West Passage, and, with regard thereto, graciously gave me instructions, which, by the help and assistance of God, I have followed, in most submissive obedience, as closely as human energy and power, with the utmost diligence, could on that sea and in that difficult navigation. And, although, after having returned from that voyage, I at once presented myself before Your Royal Majesty, in order most humbly to report on the events of the said journey, I had, nevertheless, the intention afterwards to put into writing a further description of the said journey, with all its circumstances, for publication, in order that Your Royal Majesty might be enabled graciously to hear a much clearer account thereof; and this I should long ago have humbly caused to be submitted to Your Majesty, but I have been occupied in consequence of other pressing commands of Your Majesty and in journeys, to which I am most humbly in duty bound towards Your Royal Majesty; so that I have not been able before now to publish this written account. I have now, therefore, revised and looked through my observations concerning the said voyage, the navigation, the sounds, known and unknown countries, harbours, straits, courses and directions, with all the circumstances, and whatever happened upon it, from the beginning to the last event, as far as this said passage could be searched for with the most careful possible examination and investigation, which I have truthfully written down day by day, according to the changes of the navigation and the incidents of the voyage; and I have thereupon described it all in this small treatise, in the most humble hope that Your Royal Majesty will graciously approve of it, and that every right-minded man who obtains knowledge of the circumstances of this endeavour will rightly consider and judge, that it has been done to the honour of Your Majesty's name and government, and that Your Majesty will graciously understand the good of the kingdom, and choose as far as possible that which now and ever can serve the welfare of the subjects. I, at the same time, most humbly pray that Your Royal Majesty will graciously accept both me and this small work of mine into Your favour and gracious protection, and always be to me a kind Lord and gracious King; and may God Almighty preserve Your Royal Majesty in lasting health and prosperous government.

Given at Copenhagen, the 1st of November, 1624.

Your Royal Majesty's
Humble and dutiful servant,
IENS MUNCK.

A
RELATION
Or Description of a Voyage and Expedition in search
of the North-West Passage, now called NOVA DANIA,
through FRETUM CHRISTIAN,

Wherein are Described all the Circumstances of that
Expedition, the Navigation, Straits, known and unknown
Countries, Harbours, Sounds, Courses and Directions,
which occurred upon that Voyage and all that happened
worth knowing, from the Beginning
to the End.

In the Name of the Holy Trinity,
AMEN.

NNO DOMINI, 1619: His Royal Majesty our most gracious Master's ship *Enhiörningen* and the sloop *Lamprenen* having, according to His said Majesty's gracious orders, been properly made ready, provided, and prepared with crew, equipment, provisions, ammunition and other necessaries for the voyage and expedition to search for the North-West Passage: I, Iens Munck, in the name of God, sailed with the said two ships, from Copenhagen into

the Sound, on the 9th of May; and there were then on the ship *Enhiörningen* forty-eight, and, on the sloop *Lamprenen*, sixteen persons.

I waited for wind in the Sound until the 16th of May, which was Whitsunday. I then sailed out of the Sound.

On the 18th of May, it happened, early in the morning, while we were sailing along, that one of my men, as he was walking on the deck, suddenly jumped overboard a distance of quite two fathoms and plunged his head under water, without, however, as it appeared, sinking so quickly as he desired. But, as it blew hard, no one could save him, which I should much have wished. He, therefore, went down and was lost.

On the 25th of May, when off Lister,[1] the sloop sprang a leak, so that I was obliged to run into Karmsund,[2] in order there to discover the leak in that vessel; and, on examination, I found that three bolt-holes had been left open by the carpenters, and afterwards filled with pitch; which defect I thereupon caused to be remedied without delay, in order to be able to continue the voyage. While I stayed there at Karmsund, one of my two coopers died; wherefore I caused three young men to be engaged at Skudenes,[3] in the place of those who had died, so as to maintain my full complement of men.

On the 30th of May, I sailed from Karmsund, further to continue my voyage, and shaped our course West-North-West for Heth Land,[4] which we accordingly passed on the 2nd of June.

On the 4th of June, in the morning, steering to the

---

[1] An island situated close to, and west of, the southern extremity of Norway.

[2] A sound between the Island of Karmö and the main-land, branching off from the north side of Bukken (or Stavanger) Fjord.

[3] The principal village on Karmö.

[4] Old Danish for Shetland.

West, we sailed round the East end of Ferröe, which is called Syderöe,[1] about four miles[2] to the West of it,[3] and then shaped our course West and West-by-North, until we came alongside Greenland.

On the 11th of June, I ascertained what quantity of provisions had been consumed, and gave definite orders as to how the stores should be served out for consumption—*viz.*, in this wise : the steward's book showing the provisions received by him was, according to the tenour of my instructions, always to be kept in the cabin ; and, whenever he opened a barrel of goods, he was to enter it in the book, and, in his weekly return, to state how long it had lasted, with indication of the day and hour when it had been finished, as well as of the weight or measure, according to the kind of goods, which all was to be in keeping with the orders and rules he would receive with regard to the board, befitting the circumstances of the time. In this way, I secured always an accurate account of what had been consumed and of what still remained in store of all kinds of Provisions and Drinks.

Item : we sailed on thus, in a westerly direction, until the 20th of June, when we found ourselves some miles to the North of the southern promontory of Greenland, in 61 degrees 25 minutes, though about 15 or 16 miles from land, where we encountered much ice, so that we were obliged to turn Eastwards again, towards the sea. Finally, we kept sailing to and fro, with gales and bad weather, until the 30th of June, when we sighted the southern Cape of Greenland, which the English call Cape Farwell, and which is situated in 60 degrees 30 minutes. Doubtless, whoever named that place thus, did not intend to return thither. The

---

[1] The southernmost island of the Færö group.

[2] Ancient Danish sea-miles, equal to 4·6807 English miles. About fifteen, therefore, go to a degree.

[3] For explanation of this obscure passage, see the Commentary.

southern promontory of Greenland is a high land, very rugged and uneven, with high jagged mountains; but it was not possible to obtain a true drawing or exact knowledge of those high mountains on account of the great quantity of ice which covers them and renders the said countries quite unrecognizable. We had then arrived at *Fretum Davis;* and, as regards the entrance to the said *Fretum Davis,* much ice was encountered there, and one must be particularly attentive here, carefully to avoid the ice. The reason is that, on the eastern side, Greenland trends mostly to the North-East-half-East, so that all the ice which comes from the East is turned into a South-Westerly direction; similarly, in *Fretum Davis,* Greenland trends mostly North-West-half-North, as also, upon the whole, does *Fretum Davis,* out of which unspeakably much ice comes forth, all of which meets off Cape Farewell, which projects as a triangle; for on both sides of the country there is floating an abundance of ice, which emerges from the numerous large fjords which exist in those countries.

Item: if one shapes one's course too much to the west, towards the American side, much ice is likewise encountered, and one may then easily be driven out of one's course, because the current with the ice sets principally to the South-West. Likewise, whoever intends to sail into *Fretum Davis* or *Regis* must keep to 60½ degrees from Cape Farewell; and, if it is possible to have Cape Farewell in sight, then he may choose his course as he thinks best into that said water, being particularly careful in calculating and noting exactly what variation there is, otherwise he will steer a wrong course: and this he must observe and pay great attention to, before he proceeds beyond 56 degrees with a westerly course.[1]

Now, to resume the account of my course and the con-

---

[1] For explanation of this passage, see the Commentary.

tinuation of my journey: When I had got free of the ice in 60 degrees and a half, the longitude of Cape Farewell, I steered my course West by North, according to a true course, two points allowed for the variation; on which track we, at times, encountered much ice; being, however, then in open sea, we were able in a measure to avoid it. A portion consisted of large masses, attaining to near 40 fathoms above the water, which, to those who have not seen them, may perhaps appear incredible, but which, nevertheless, is according to truth.

On the 8th of July, we sighted the land on the American side, but could not reach the shore for the quantity of ice. That same midday, we were in $62\frac{1}{2}$ Degrees latitude[1]; and we then sailed to and fro outside the ice and could not effect anything.

On the 9th of July, in the night, there was such a fog and great cold that icicles were hanging from the rigging one quarter long,[2] so that none of the men could stand the cold. On the same day, however, before three o'clock in the afternoon, the sun was shining in the same place so hotly that the men threw off their overcoats, and some of them their jackets as well. Then I stood in amongst the ice, into a great bay, which, in the opinion of the pilots, according to the latitude we were in, should have been the proper entrance to *Lomblis*, or *Hotson*, Strait, but which, after long investigation, we found not to be the right entrance. We found there much ice, which comes out of three large fjords; for which reason we have named the said places *Iisefiorde*, as they may properly be called.[3] It is situated in the latitude last mentioned, viz. $62\frac{1}{2}$

---

[1] The land seen was probably Lock's Land (see the Commentary).

[2] That is, a quarter of a Danish *alen* (= 2·059 feet, English measure) A "quarter" would, therefore, be a trifle over 6 inches.

[3] That is, "Ice Fjords", together forming, no doubt, Frobisher's Strait or Bay; by Davis called Lumley's Inlet.

degrees, and extends as far as *Munckenes* trending South-South-East-half-South and North-North-West-half-North. We shaped our course southerly along the coast, which we found to consist everywhere of broken land and high rocks, until we came to *Munckenes*, as it is now called, which forms the real North side of the entrance into *Hotson* or *Lomblis* Strait, which is now called *Fretum Christian*.[1]

On the 11th of July, we had beautiful clear weather with sunshine, in the middle of the day, though there was much ice ; and we then obtained the true latitude in which *Munckenes* is situated: *viz.* 61 degrees 20 minutes ; and that island which, in my Instructions, is stated—as a guide for finding the entrance—to be situated at the said entrance, in 62½ degrees, we found in 60 degrees 40 minutes.[2] In this respect, however, there may possibly be an error, because we could not come sufficiently near to the said island on account of the ice. This is here particularly to be noted : that whosoever happens hereafter to navigate the said *Fretum Christian*, or *Hotson*, should always shape his course so that he does not get below 61¼ degrees, in order that he may not be drawn from his course by the powerful current which sets the hardest towards the South, or by the strong ebb which comes from *Freto Christian* ; because, in that same *Freto*, the water rises and falls, with an ordinary tide, five fathoms or more, the water being, at the same time, very deep ; according to which anyone intending to sail that way may know how to guard himself. Concerning our entering into, and sailing through, the length of the said water, *Fretum Christian*, and what happened there, what course we steered, what ice we found, what occurred in the channel,

---

[1] Munkenes is, doubtless, the southern extremity of Resolution Island, probably Frobisher's Hatton's Headland. The question of Munk's names for Hudson's Strait is fully discussed in the Commentary. [2] This would be one of the Button Islands.

as well as in divers places on shore—all this took place *ut sequitur.*

On the 12th of July, I sent my lieutenant[1] with some of the crew on shore at *Munckenes*, in order to fetch water and to ascertain what was to be found there, because it seemed a likely place for finding harbours and for obtaining water. In the evening, they returned with water, and reported that there were harbours but no anchorage; nor could we lie there in safety from ice. We were, therefore, obliged to choose the better of two bad alternatives, because nowhere in the channel could we see open water. Half a mile from *Munckenes*, I caused the lead to be thrown, and reached the bottom at 150 fathoms. On the same day, I shot two or three birds with a gun; but, at the last discharge, the same gun burst into pieces, and took the brim clean off the front of my hat.

On the 13th of July, towards evening, we were in the greatest distress and danger, and did not know what counsel to follow, because we could not advance any further by tacking, the ice pressing us hard on all sides. Being, then, in such a perilous situation, all the officers considered it most advisable to take in all the sails and fasten the sloop *Lamprenen* to the ship *Enhiörningen;* which, accordingly, was done. We then commended all into the hand of God; and, trusting to God's merciful assistance, we drifted along and into the ice again. This incident of the attack of the ice and the distress of the ships in the ice are shown on the plate accompanying this treatise.[2]

While we thus drifted forwards and backwards in the ice, in great danger of our lives, the ice displaced a

---

[1] Mauritz Stygge (see the Introduction).

[2] This incident is represented farthest to the right on the first woodcut, facing page 14.

large knee in the ship, which was situated under the peg of the head of the ship, and fastened with six large iron bolts; wherefore I set all my carpenters to work to set that knee straight again. But it was too big for them, so that they could do nothing with it in that place. I therefore had the ship swung round and turned, so that the side to which the knee had come into a crooked position drifted against the ice, and then ordered the rudder to be worked so as to turn against the ice in order that the knee in a measure might right itself again, which also was effected as perfectly as if 20 carpenters had been engaged in refitting it. Afterwards, the carpenters adjusted the bolts which had become bent. .

On the 15th of July, in the morning at daybreak, we got clear of the ice again, and then sailed on through the Strait, along the northern coast, tacking, from time to time, under the high coast to leeward, which was the northern coast, as aforesaid. Later in the day, the wind became more favourable to us, and we then sailed North-West, with small sails, between the ice and the land. In several places along the coast, there seemed to be good harbours; but at that time they were all full of ice; and, as the ice drifted with great force around us on all sides, I did not dare to send my boat away in order to ascertain whether a convenient harbour might be found anywhere. Towards the evening, we came to some small islands, which stretched away from the mainland in a more westerly direction.[1] Here we again encountered much ice, and stayed outside these islands all night, and until the 17th of July, without being able to effect any thing to our advantage. At last, we thought good to run into a harbour which we then found.

---

[1] Probably some nameless islets which are shown on the charts between the Lower and the Middle Savage Islands.

On the 17th of July, I ordered the sloop to sail before us to find where we could anchor, and followed afterwards with the ship. We then found a good harbour, where we cast anchor in the name of God. On the following day, I sent men out with orders to search everywhere diligently whether any people were to be found on the land, or whether there were any certain indications of people having been there. Towards midday, they returned without having noticed any people. They had, however, found many places where people had been, though not recently.

On the 18th of July,[1] whilst lying hidden with the ship and the sloop behind an islet, we observed that there were people on the southern side of the harbour; wherefore, I at once had my boat manned, and went myself thither in it. When the natives who were there saw that I was coming on shore to them, they remained standing, having laid down behind some stones their arms and what other implements they had by them. When, now, I approached them, they returned whatever salutation I offered them in the same manner; but they were careful to keep between me and the place where their arms were laid. I also observed this place carefully, and, going there, took up their arms and implements in my hand and examined them; upon which, they at once made me understand that they would rather lose all their garments, and go naked than lose their arms and implements; and they pointed to their mouths, thereby signifying that it was by means of their arms and implements that they obtained their food. When I again laid down their arms and implements, they clapped their hands, looked up to heaven, and showed themselves very merry and joyful. Thereupon, I presented them with knives and all sorts of iron goods. Amongst other things,

---

[1] The apparent confusion in the dates here is discussed in the Commentary.

I gave one of them a looking glass, but he did not know what it was; wherefore, I took it from him and held it before his face, so that he could see himself. When he did so, he quickly took the looking glass from me and put it into his bosom. After this, they, in like manner, gave me presents of what they had: *viz.* different kinds of birds and seal-flesh. One of my men, who had very swarthy complexion, and black hair, they all embraced, no doubt thinking that he was one of their nation and countrymen. The appearance of this people, as well as of their arms and implements, is represented on the accompanying plate.[1] ✶

ON the same day, towards evening, I set sail again; and, on the 19th of July, I was again in front of the ice, and for some time kept beating to and fro. However, I had no hope of getting through the ice at that time, and therefore returned to the harbour where I had had intercourse with the natives, intending and hoping to become further acquainted with them. But it was altogether in vain; for, though I remained lying there until the 22nd of July, none of the natives came to me, although I had before presented them with various gifts; nor did they return to fetch their fishing gear as long as I continued lying there; from which it is to be concluded that they are, doubtless, subject to some authority which must have forbidden them to come to us again. The while I now remained in that harbour, hoping that the ice during that time would drift away, I ordered my crew to fetch water and wash their clothes. Some of them, I sent inland to shoot reindeer, which in that place were found in great numbers.

On the 22nd of July, towards evening, finding that none

---

[1] The interview with the natives is represented in the left-hand upper corner of the annexed woodcut.

of the natives would come to me, I made ready to sail from there, and caused His Royal Majesty's Arms and Name, *Christianus Quartus*, to be set up there; and I named the said harbour *Rin Sund*, because in that place we shot some reindeer.¹ Wherever we found the fishing nets of the natives lying, we deposited near them various kinds of our goods, such as knives and all sorts of iron tools, after which we set sail. The same harbour is a very good one, because one may lie there in safety from any wind whatever.

On the 23rd of July, in the morning early, when it became day, we found ourselves entirely surrounded by ice on all sides, so that we could not get away from it on either bow or in any direction. We, therefore, made *Lamprenen* fast to *Enhiörningen*, both ahead and astern, shot down the topmasts, as a violent gale was commencing, and then drifted whither the wind or the ice might carry us. We were at that time unable to see open water anywhere. In the night next following, the ice pressed on us so hard, and we were so firmly fixed in the ice, particularly to leeward, that we could not give way on either side, and the ice crushed four anchors to pieces on the bow of the sloop *Lamprenen*. At the same time, the ice forced itself underneath the keel of *Lamprenen*, so that one might pass one's hand along the keel from stem to stern, as the plate shows.²

The 24th of July, we remained so firmly fixed in the ice that the vessels could drift nowhere, either forwards or backwards, because the ice was lying firm between the

---

¹ Probably a sound between the main-land and some islets, near the shore, not far East of the place named Jackman's Sound, on the Admiralty Chart. The shooting of a reindeer is represented in the lower left-hand portion of the woodcut, facing page 14.

² There is no illustration of this incident on either of the wood-cuts.

shore and us; and the ice which came from the sea pressed us very hard, because a violent gale was blowing from the South-East, straight in-shore.

On the 25th of July, we were likewise hardly pressed by the ice; nor could we discover open water anywhere. On this occasion, I nearly lost in the ice two men who were ordered to fetch back a grapnel, which had been thrown on to a large mass of ice in order to enable us thereby, to some extent, to turn the ship, so that she might not get too much speed, as there was a very strong current. On the same day, the rudder-head[1] on the ship *Enhiörningen* was broken to pieces. *Item:* on the night next following, the ice and the current carried us in between the main land and some islets,[2] in such wise that ten pilots who had year by year navigated this water could not have steered the ship better through the said islets than the ice and the current carried and drifted her without injury.

On the 26th of July, we found ourselves entirely hemmed in by ice on all sides, so that we could nowhere manage to get an anchor in the ground, nor could we get any hawser on shore. The ship, however, remained in the same place all day, drifting neither outwards nor inwards, so that we were now in the greatest distress and danger. We did not know of any measures that we could take, but commended the whole matter into the hand of God, and prayed devoutly to Him for help and guidance. On the same day, we all gave something for the poor, each according to his means.

---

[1] This term is to be understood as used, not of the real rudder-head, but of the casing enclosing it, which used to be found in the officer's cabin in old-fashioned men-of-war, and which also was called the rudder-head. This is what is meant by the now obsolete term *Roerlade*, used by Munk.

[2] These islets (probably nameless rocks close to the shore) cannot be identified.

On the 27th of July, we drifted amongst some islets,[1] and, as much as we drifted in shore with one tide, we drifted back again with another. So much ice was at the same time floating round us that it was impossible anywhere to get on shore, even if one could have gained the whole world thereby.

On the 28th of July, we succeeded, by dint of much work and trouble, in entering a small bay between two islets, where we at once let go three anchors into the ground and carried two hawsers on shore. At the lowest ebb, we shortened our distance so much that we had scarcely water under the keel; but, when the flood returned, we were so much shaken and pressed by the ice that we had much more work close to land than we had had at sea amongst the ice. A large mass of ice, which was standing aground in 22 fathoms, split into two; and this ice caused such big waves and heavy rolling that the sloop *Lamprenen*, which was fastened to the side of *Enhiörningen*, had nearly rolled aground, if we had not quickly got her clear of *Enhiörningen*. An anchor also was dashed to pieces against the bow of *Enhiörningen* before the rope by which she was fastened could be cut.

On the 29th of July, we had plenty to do with the ice, which on all sides pressed against us, while we were lying in a little bay amongst some islets.

On the 30th of July, we were likewise in great distress caused by the ice, and had much troublesome work in order to keep the ice from the ships, as before mentioned.

On the 31st of July, we were carried inwards by the flood tide at its highest, over some rocks which, at the lowest ebb, were left dry, something like four fathoms

---

[1] We have no means of identifying the islets mentioned here and on the following day. Probably they were nameless rocks near the coast in the neighbourhood of Icy Cove.

above water[1]; and thus we came into a small bay, where we were somewhat more secure against the ice than before. The men were now so entirely worn out that they could not any longer have sustained the hard work entailed by pushing the great quantity of ice from the ship, and by the incessant veering and hauling.

August the 1st. When the crew had now rested somewhat, and we had obtained a little more quiet, a fourth part of the men went on shore together to try whether there was any game that we could shoot, in order to get fresh meat; but, though we saw some reindeer, they were so very shy that we could not get near them. If I had had two or three good dogs, they might have been of advantage to us; however, in time, we got some hares in that place. As for the men who meanwhile remained with the ships, they were not idle at any time, but were continually at work in stopping and keeping off the ice, in order that the ships might be preserved without damage.

On the 5th of August, the ice commenced to thin somewhat and to drift away; wherefore, I had the hold trimmed and more ballast put in. I ordered the beer to be put into fresh casks, and water to be fetched. Everything was made ready, and I gave new orders with regard to the navigation: as to in what places and latitudes we might find each other again if, on account of fog, we should become separated, although such meeting again would be a very uncertain matter.

On the 8th of August, so much snow fell that all the mountains were covered with it and appeared quite white; on the deck, the snow was more than a quarter deep.[2]

---

[1] A similar incident is reported by Abacuck Prickett as having happened to Hudson at some islands near the northern shore of the Strait, which, in consequence, he called the Isles of God's Mercy (see *Purchas his Pilgrimes*, vol. iii, p. 598).

[2] See page 9, note 2.

On the same day, I had a seaman named Anders Staffuanger buried. As regards this harbour: we have called it *Haresund*,[1] because we caught many hares there; and I have there set up His Royal Majesty's arms and name, with large cairns. This harbour is situated nearly 50 miles inside *Freto Christian*, in 62 degrees 20 minutes, on the northern shore, close to a large bay, of which the direction is mostly northerly, and in which there would no doubt be something to do, but not till the month of August. Near this, to the West, there is still another bay, which also has a northerly direction. On account, however, of the very great quantity of drifting ice, it was not possible to advance as much as half a quarter of a mile from the ships by water.[2] *Item:* in the same place occurs much Russian glass,[3] and there also seemed to be some ore; but, as I had nobody with me who had knowledge of such matters, much investigation concerning it was not undertaken. I had, however, some barrels filled with the stuff in question, which I took with me. Concerning the people of this country, we saw at that time none; but everywhere we could see certain signs and indications of people having been there before, who had had their tents there.

On the 9th of August, we set sail with a North-west wind in order to continue our journey, and we shaped our course West-South-West, which, at that time, was the nearest to the wind that we could go; because we were then clear of the ice, excepting a few pieces which were drifting about here and there. At the same time, a very stiff and violent gale commenced; and, the wind and the

---

[1] Probably Icy Cove, or some place near it. The question is fully discussed in the Commentary.

[2] The bays referred to were no doubt those we now call North Bay and White Strait (see the Commentary).

[3] Talc, also called "Muscovy Glass" in books of that time. This mineral was noticed by several of the earlier Arctic explorers.

current acting against each other, such a high and hollow sea resulted that neither I nor anybody else on board had ever witnessed the like of it. The reason of this is the strong flood and ebb which occur here; because, when the wind and the current are opposed to each other, it causes a hollow sea if there be a gale, as the water rises and falls in these localities over five fathoms with an ordinary tide, as before mentioned.[1]

On the 10th of August, early in the morning, we came to the western side of *Freto Christian*, upon which the pilots steered a southerly course, supposing that we had arrived in a large bay,[2] which, however, was found to be otherwise. As we were now sailing in a southerly direction along shore, we found the land to be very high and broken, girt with many islands; and, no doubt, good harbours were to be found in many places, if one had diligently sought for such, and if time had permitted to do so.[3] Sailing thus along shore towards the South, we came at last to a large promontory, which is now called *Alecke Ness* Cape,[4] and which lies in about 60 degrees; here also a large bay enters, stretching inwards due South-West, where we came to a low and flat land,[5] which the English pilot intimated was the place which

---

[1] The Admiralty Chart shows that the rise and fall is 30 feet at the Isles of God's Mercy.

[2] That is, Hudson's Bay, as explained in the Commentary.

[3] The portion of the coast here referred to was the southern shore of Hudson's Strait, from Cape Hope's Advance to the islands of Ekkertaujok and Akpatok, with the northern coast of these islands, which coast they mistook for the western shore of Hudson's Bay (see the Commentary).

[4] The English equivalent would be Auk's Ness. It was probably the eastern end of the Island of Akpatok. The identification of this and adjoining localities presents a somewhat difficult problem, which is fully discussed in the Commentary.

[5] Probably the southern coast of Ungava Bay.

Danish Arctic Expeditions, 1605-1620 (Hakluyt Society, 1897).

we searched for.[1] But those words and that opinion were soon revoked. Into this bay, some fine inlets appeared to open; but, on account of the shortness of our time, which did not allow us to remain there long, we steered our course out of the said *Synder bogt*,[2] in order to continue our voyage and navigation further. The same Bay is situated in 60 degrees, or rather more southerly.

August 14th. When we had come nearly five miles out of the *Synder bogt*, we came to a large island, of which the North-Western extremity was very high land; but, on the South Side, it was full of ice; and, inasmuch as there were many birds flying to and from the land, and, as it appeared white, being covered with snow, we called the same *Snee Oeland*.[3] The shape of this land is shown in the accompanying map.

ON the 20th of August, the wind became easterly, wherefore we shaped our course West-by-North, allowance being made for the variation; and we were then in 62 degrees 20 minutes. We were then in our right track[4]; but, as it was very foggy, we could not see land on either side, although the channel was not above 16 miles wide in that place, between the main-land on each side. *In summa*, we sailed thus West-North-West-half-North until we found ourselves in 63 degrees 20 minutes. However, in the meanwhile, we were at several places which are not now named here, but which will be found diligently pictured and described in the sea-chart which has been prepared to

---

[1] The meaning of these words will be considered in our discourse on Munk's Instructions at the end of our Commentary.

[2] That is, the Southern Bay. The bay in question was Ungava Bay.

[3] Probably Green Island. The passage does not seem very logical but it stands in the original as we have rendered it (see the Commentary).

[4] That is to say: back in Hudson's Strait, sailing westward.

show this ☞ according to their dimensions, quantity and quality, size and shape. *Item :* the high islands which are found here-about are likewise depicted on the sea-chart.[1] Here one must be careful not to approach too near to these countries which are called *Iissner*,[2] for the reason that both the strong current from *Freto Christian* and that from *Novo Mari*[3] meet each other in that place; wherefore there is always a great deal of rippling, by reason of the strong current which runs there; and, generally, there is at the same time much ice drifting in that current, which cannot get away in either direction, because what drifts away with one tide, comes back again with another. *Item :* after advancing about ten miles westwards in the said part of the sea, one sights two islands which are called *Söster*[4]; and right round these one may pick one's way by sounding. But, if anyone desires to enter into *Novum Mare* and to steer his course to *Novam Daniam*,[5] then he should leave these two islands aforesaid half a mile or a whole mile to port, although he may well run on either side. Proceeding westwards in the track, he will then come upon a large, flat and low island, called *Digses Eyland*,[6] round which one may

---

[1] The map here referred to cannot be any other than the one facing page 21, which is marked with a hand, as there is none other. For further elucidation of this passage, we refer to the Commentary.

[2] Doubtless a misprint for *Iisver*, as it is spelled on page 54. It means a place where much ice occurs. The name is found on the map in the place indicated in the text, but the islands are not distinctly marked. On the subject of the "high islands" and Iisver, see the Commentary. The country called Iisver is probably Charles Island.

[3] Hudson's Strait and Hudson's Bay.

[4] More correctly, *Söstrene* (the Sisters). The islands in question must be the Digges Islands, but are not distinctly marked on the map, where the name also is misplaced (see the Commentary).

[5] Munk's name for the country near the Churchill River, on the west coast of the Bay.

[6] Without doubt, Mansfield Island.

also sail by sounding. It is a great pity that this island is not situated in a southern latitude, because it is both a large and a flat land. One may run right round it sounding the while, and whoever intends to enter *Novum Mare* may likewise run on whichever side of it he prefers; but it is better to keep to the North of it, because one does not meet so much ice there as on the southern side. I sailed right round the said island. *Item:* from the northern point of that island, which is now called *Digses Eyland*, to *Jens Munckes Vindterhaffn*[1] in *Nova Dania*, the course is South-West-by-South and South-West, three days and three nights sailing; and, when one commences to strike the bottom at 30 fathoms and less one may steer a somewhat more southerly course, until one sights the southern land, which is a low wooded country. Some low rocks, which form a narrow promontory, will then appear, on which two beacons are erected.[2] Whoever desires to enter the harbour must leave the beacons to starboard and sail in, steering South-West. A little way inside the entrance, there is a sunken rock under the water, but on the eastern side, so that one can pass it without difficulty.[3] One may then cast anchor in 7 or 8 fathoms, and afterwards easily find out everything inside, because the ship *Enhiörningen* (for reasons which will be explained hereafter) is lying about a mile farther up the river, behind a promontory on the western side. See the plate, as well as the accompanying map, relating thereto.[4] ✠

---

[1] That is, Munk's Winter-Harbour, namely, Port Churchill.

[2] These beacons had been erected by Munk himself, for the guidance of others who might visit the place after him. No Europeans are known to have been on shore there before Munk.

[3] Called by some "St. Mary's Rock".

[4] The "plate" here referred to is the woodcut facing, and marked with a ✠, which gives a bird's-eye view of the harbour. The map is the same which has been referred to already. There is no special map of the harbour.

SEPTEMBER 7th. When I now had come into the harbour aforesaid, though with great difficulty, on account of wind and storm, snow, hail, and fog, I at once ordered my shallop, which was divided into six parts, to be put together; and, during the night following, we kept a watch on the land, and maintained a fire, in order that *Lamprenen*, which, during the great gale and storm, had strayed from us, might find us again. She joined us on the 9th of September, having been under the northern land, where an open passage was supposed to exist, but there was none.[1] The crew having suffered much from the before-mentioned gale, and in other hardship and trouble, and a part in consequence being down with illness, I caused, during these days, the sick people to be brought from the ship on shore; and we gathered still some cloud-berries, gooseberries, and other berries, which in Norway are called Tydebær and Kragbær.[2] I also had a good fire made on shore every day for the sick, whereby they were comforted, and in time nicely regained their health.

On the 10th and 11th of September, there was such a terrible snowstorm and gale that nothing could be done.

September 12th. In the morning early, a large white bear came down to the water near the ship, which stood and ate some Beluga flesh, off a fish so named which I had caught the day before.[3] I shot the bear, and the men all desired the flesh for food, which I also allowed. I ordered the cook just to boil it slightly, and then to

---

[1] This subject is discussed at length in the Commentary.

[2] Red Whortleberries (*Vaccinium vitis-idæa*) and Crowberries (*Empetrum nigrum*).

[3] The Beluga, or White Whale, is particularly abundant in the estuary of the Churchill River. The shooting of the Polar Bear is represented in the centre of the woodcut, facing page 28.

keep it in vinegar for a night, and I myself had two or three pieces of this bear-flesh roasted for the cabin. It was of good taste and did not disagree with us.

On the 13th of September, I sent out both my shallop and the ship's boat, under the command of my second mates, Hans Brock and Jan Pettersen, with orders to proceed 8 or 9 miles along the shore, one on the western, the other on the eastern side, and to examine what accommodation the land afforded, and whether there were any better harbours there than the one we were in.

On the 16th of September, Jan Petersen returned, who had been investigating the localities on the western side; and he reported that, where he had been, no harbours could be found; the land was low, flat, and wooded, and there was scarcely any safe harbour to protect a boat properly. On the same day, there was a terrible snow-storm from the North-East.

September 18th. As we experienced nothing but frost and snow, we deliberated together as to what measures to take. Then all the officers thought it best, and it was finally resolved, that, inasmuch as the winter was coming on us very hard and severe, increasing and getting worse day by day, we should have the ship brought in somewhere, as well as the unfavourable circumstances would allow, behind some promontory, where she might be safe from drift-ice. On the same day, the ring broke on the anchor by which we were moored.

On the 19th of September, we sailed up the river, with the ship and the sloop, as far as we could, and stayed one night at anchor. On that night, the new drift-ice cut into both sides of the ship and of the sloop, to the depth of about two fingers'-breadths, so that I was obliged to have the ship brought nearer to the western shore by 8 cables' lengths, across a flat. It was a distance of nearly 900 fathoms across the flat, where the ship was in great danger, because the ground was covered with stones, and the ship could not well rest on it, on account of her being sharp-built. As the drift-ice got the upper hand, the ship stuck on a stone and became quite leaky, so that all the carpenters had enough to do during the ebb in order to make her tight again before the return of the flood.[1]

September 25th. As we had now secured the ship close under the land and brought the sloop on shore by means of a high tide, I caused the ship's keel to be dug down into the ground, and branches of trees to be spread under the bilge, packed together with clay and sand, in order that the ship might rest evenly on the bilge on both sides, and thus suffer less damage.

On the same day, Hans Brock, the mate, returned, having been to the eastward to ascertain whether better harbours could be found. He also reported that there were no harbours suitable for winter quarters in the places where he had been, but only flat, bare, and swampy land. During his exploration, he had been in great danger of losing his life amongst the quantities of new ice which floated forwards and backwards; and he lost a grapnel which they had with them, the rope having snapped on account of the bad condition of the sea bottom.

September 27th. Whilst we now thought that the ship was well protected against drift-ice and bad weather, such a tremendous drift of ice came upon us with a low ebb that, if the ship had not been resting so firmly on the ground, we should have been carried away by the ice. We were obliged to let go all four hawsers by which the ship was moored, and part of them went to pieces. By this breaking up of the ice, the ship also became so leaky that, at flood-time, we pumped out quite 2,000 strokes of water; the ship was, on the same occasion, moved out

---

[1] See the map of the harbour in the Commentary.

of the dock which we originally had made for her, and in which she was placed.

On the 28th of September, at high tide, we had the ship replaced in position and moored by 6 hawsers; and, during the lowest ebb, the leaks were looked for and made good again. Thereupon, I had a fresh dock made as before, in which the ship again was placed; and, at the same time, I ordered the carpenters and others who could ply an axe, to make five bridge-piles; the other men hauled timber and stones for these piles, which I caused to be placed before the bow of the ship, in order to turn off the ice so that it should not hurt us.

October 1st. Everything being now well finished, and the ship and the sloop well protected against ice and tempest, I ordered the hold to be cleared out, the cannon to be placed in the hold, and a part of our goods to be brought on shore, in order that the deck might be clear and the men have more space to move about, and also that the ship should not suffer too much from the great weight resting on her deck.

On the 3rd of October, I ordered the crew of *Lamprenen* to come on board *Enhiörningen* for their meals, so that there should not be more than one galley; and I gave orders to the cook and the steward as regards the board, in accordance with the Instructions I had with me and the requirements of the time and place.

On the 4th of October, I distributed to the crew, clothes, shirts, shoes, and boots, and whatever else could be of use as a protection against the cold.

On the 5th of October, I caused two large fireplaces, round each of which 20 men might easily sit, to be arranged on the deck, one before the mast, the other behind the mast, as well as a fireplace on the steerage,[1]

---

[1] A portion of the deck astern.

round which likewise 20 persons could be accommodated, in addition to that in the cook's galley, where he did his cooking; that he required to have to himself.

On the 7th of October and next following days, the carpenters were ashore with the men to cut timber and haul stones for breakwaters, which were made in order to protect the ship against damage from the ice, which sometimes drifted very much there during the rising of the tide and until the ebb was halfway out.

That same day, the weather being fine, I myself journeyed up the river to see how far I could get with a boat; but, about a mile and a half up, there were so many stones in it, that I could not advance any further, and had to return. I had brought with me all sorts of small goods, intending, if I had met any natives, to present them with some in order to become acquainted with them, but I could neither find nor perceive any. On my return journey, I came to a promontory and found there a picture on a stone, drawn with charcoal, fashioned like the half of a devil, wherefore I called the same promontory *Dieffuel's Hug*.[1]

In many places where we came, we could quite well see where people had been and had their summer abodes. Even in the place where the ship is lying, there are certain signs and indications of people having been there. In the forest, there are, likewise, in many places, great heaps of chips, where they have cut wood or timber; and the chips look as if they had been cut off with curved iron tools. I am of the opinion that the said people have some kind of idolatry connected with fire; because, wherever one finds places where they have had their dwell-

---

[1] That is, "Devil's Cape". It is, perhaps, Musketo Point, situated at the point where the river suddenly expands into the Estuary, and about one Danish mile (or four-and-a-half English miles) above the place where the vessels were lying.

ings in the summer near the seaside, some square places, nearly eight feet either way, are generally to be found, which are bordered with stones, and, at one extremity, are covered with thin flat stones and moss, whilst, at the other extremity, two flat stones are found standing upright, edgewise, about a foot apart ; on which two stones, a flat stone is placed, fashioned as if intended for a small altar, on which two or three small pieces of charcoal are placed, no fire or coals being observable elsewhere near. From this, I can only conclude that this has been used for their idolatrous worship ; and, if that is so, it is to be wished that these poor blinded pagans might come to the profession of the true Christian Faith.[1] As regards their food and mode of living : it would seem that they use much in a half-cooked state, because, wherever we found that they had had their meals, the bones did not seem to have been very well roasted.

On the 10th of October, I commenced to give the men rations of wine ; but beer they were allowed to drink according to their want, as much as every man himself liked. At the same time, I made regulations for keeping a watch, the fetching of wood, and burning of charcoal, as well as with regard to whose duty it was to be, during the day, to melt snow into water; so that everybody knew what he was to do, and how he had to conduct himself.

October 15th. During the night, the new drift-ice has again lifted the ship out of the dock in which she was placed ; but I at once ordered fresh branches to be thrown under the vessel at the next low water and the spaces to be filled up with clay and sand as before. In the same night, the ice carried one of the piers right away ; in consequence of which, I was obliged at once to order another to be built

---

[1] These places were the graves of the natives, as observed and described by several of the early explorers.

in the place of it, for the protection of the ship. As soon as the ice had become quite firm, the ship suffered no further damage.

On the 22nd of October, the ice became firm for good, as it was a terribly hard frost. On the same night, we caught a black fox.

After this day, the crew commenced to go on shore in the day time in pursuit of game. A part went into the forest to set traps to catch animals, and some of these built a hut wherein to lie *for glug*, as it is called in Norway[1]; another part of the men betook themselves to the open country for shooting, because there was plenty of ptarmigan[2] and hares,[3] as well as all kinds of birds, as long as the snow was not too deep; so that, before Christmas, there was enough of pastime. At that time, all the men liked to go into the forest or the open country for shooting, because they never went on shore when the weather was fine but that they carried home something good, which was a sufficient inducement to them to move about.

On the 30th of October, the ice everywhere covered the river, which, down to that time, could not freeze completely on account of the strong ebb and flow which prevailed. During these days, the frost was rather mild, and every day there was fine clear sunshine; wherefore I went on shore on the 7th of November with 19 men, and penetrated nearly three miles into the country, in order to ascertain whether any inhabitants were to be found. As, however,

---

[1] *Glug* signifies a window or similar opening. To lie *for glug* means to lie in ambush behind a *glug*, in order to watch traps or to shoot animals attracted by a bait, or otherwise.

[2] The Willow Ptarmigan of Hudson's Bay is identical with the European species (*Lagopus albus*), which being common in the North of Europe was well known to Munk and his crew under the name of *Rype*. This, accordingly, is the appellation used in the original. The early English explorers misnamed this bird "White Partridge".

[3] Probably the Polar Hare (*Lepus glacialis*).

there was a sudden great fall of snow, which was too heavy for us to make our way through, we were obliged to return without effecting anything by the journey. But, if we had had snowshoes, such as are used in Norway, and men that knew how to run on them, it is not improbable that we might have got far enough to find people. Otherwise, it is impossible to get along in these countries in the winter.[1]

On the 10th of November, which was St. Martin's Eve, the men shot some ptarmigan, with which we had to content ourselves, instead of St. Martin's goose[2]; and I ordered a pint of Spanish wine for each bowl[3] to be given to the men, besides their daily allowance; wherewith the whole crew were well satisfied, even merry and joyful; and of the ship's beer there was given them as much as they liked. But, afterwards, when the frost got the upper hand, the beer froze to the bottom, so that I was afraid of letting the men drink of it before they had well melted and boiled it again; for which reason, I had every fresh barrel, as it was taken up for consumption, boiled afresh, because, in any case, it was better than snow water, which otherwise would have had to be melted for drinking or mixing with wine. However, in this matter, I let the men follow their own inclination, because the common people, after all, are so disposed that, whatever is most strongly forbidden them, they, notwithstanding, are most apt to do on the sly, without considering whether it be beneficial or hurtful to them.

On the 12th of November, we had fine sunshine; and in the evening the sun was observed to set South-West-by-West. It is likewise to be noted that, hereabouts, the

---

[1] Others have made the same observation; and, amongst Munk's requisites for a second expedition, *Skier* (snow-shoes) are mentioned

[2] Roast Goose on the Feast of St. Martin is as obligatory in Denmark as Turkey on Christmas Day in England.

[3] Probably equivalent to: for each mess.

moon causes a full sea when in the East-South-East and West-North-West.

On the 15th of November, two of my men first commenced to lie *for glug* (as it is called in Norway) in a small hut which they had built for the purpose in the forest; and, in the first night, they caught two black foxes and a cross fox, which were all beautiful.

November 14th. In the night, a large black dog came to the ship on the ice, when the man on the watch observed him, and, not knowing but that it was a black fox, at once shot him, and, with much exultation, dragged him into the cabin, thinking that he had got a great prize. But, when, in the morning, we examined it, we found it to be a large dog, which no doubt had been trained to catch game, because he had been tied round the nose with small cords, so that the hair was rubbed off there.[1] His right ear was cleft, and perhaps his owner was not very pleased to lose him. I should myself have been glad to have caught him alive, in which case I should have made a pedlar of him, and have let him go home to where he had come from with small goods.

November 21st. During these days, the weather was very beautiful—as fine as could be expected in Denmark at that time of the year; the sea outside us was also quite clear, and the water open as far as we could see over the sea. It is, however, to be noticed that the ice on the sea drifts mostly according to the strength of the wind. *Item:* during all these days, as long as the fine and mild weather lasted, the men were every day in the forest, although the snow was very deep. Some of them shot ptarmigan, which were of great assistance to us; whilst others visited and put in order their traps, in which they caught animals.

---

[1] The Eskimaux generally muzzle their dogs on account of their thievish habits.

On the same day, a sailor who had long been ill was buried.

November 23rd. When the sun was in the South-West, there was an appearance in the sky as if there had been three suns in the heavens.

On the 27th of November, there was a very sharp frost, by which all the glass bottles we had (which contained all kinds of precious waters) were broken to pieces; wherefore it is to be observed that whoever intends to navigate such cold seas should supply himself well with tin bottles, or others that are able to resist the frost.

On the 3rd of December, the weather being very mild, I went out into the middle of the estuary, with some of the men, in order to ascertain how thick the ice was in the middle of the channel; and we found that the ice was seven Seeland quarters thick[1]; and this thickness it retained until long after Christmas, whether the frost was more or less severe. But, in quiet standing water, the ice became much thicker than seven quarters. As regards much of the drift-ice which floats forwards and backwards in the sea, and exhibits very great thickness: this ice comes out of the many large rivers and bays, and owing to the great force of the wind and the current, by which it is shoved together, it attains such great thickness, and thus floats away. Amongst this ice, there occur large masses rising quite twenty fathoms above the water; and some such masses of ice, which I myself have had examined, stood firm on the sea-bottom in more than 40 fathoms, which, perhaps, may seem incredible, but, nevertheless, is so in truth. Concerning such deep and high masses of ice as I have found: it is my opinion that, where many high and steep mountains are found, there is also very deep water. All the snow which is driven on to the mountains, having

---

[1] That is, about 3 feet 7 inches thick see p. 9, n. 2.

great weight, slides down by degrees; and, as soon as the snow comes into the water, in such cold places, it is at once converted into ice. Being every day in such wise increased, it at last becomes so thick and high; because, generally, where such high lands and mountains are found, there also such large and thick masses of ice occur.[1]

On the 10th of December, in the evening, about halfpast eight o'clock, the moon appeared in an eclipse. When the moon became full, it was surrounded by a large circle, which was very clear, and a cross appeared therein, which divided the moon both across and lengthwise. This commenced when the moon was in the East-North-East, and lasted till she came round to the East; then the moon commenced to come into the eclipse. The distance of the moon from the circle furthest from the moon was, on either side, equally, $20\frac{1}{2}$ degrees above my easterly horizon. When first the eclipse commenced, the moon was $15\frac{1}{2}$ degrees above my eastern horizon; but, at the time when the eclipse came to an end, the moon was 47 degrees above my southern horizon, and in the South-East-by-South; at 10 o'clock, it came to an end.

For further information concerning this eclipse of the moon, I refer the benevolent reader to the *Ephemerides*, where he can see year, month, and day when the said eclipse commenced and ended; and he will then learn with certainty what difference there is in the longitude of the places. This is my short and simple description of the said eclipse which I have seen and observed in the said place, hoping that the benevolent reader who has knowledge of these matters will take all I have said in the best

---

[1] Munk's theory of the formation of Icebergs is noticed in the Commentary; where, also, it is pointed out that those Munk here alludes to were seen by him in Hudson's Strait, not in the vicinity of his wintering-place, where none occur.

meaning, even though I have not here described every circumstance exactly as I ought.[1]

On the 12th of December, one of my two surgeons, the one on *Lamprenen*, David Velske by name, died, and his corpse had to remain on the ship unburied for two days, because the frost was so very severe that nobody could get on shore to bury him before the 14th of December; and the cold was then so intense that many of the men got frostbites on the nose and the cheeks when they met the wind with uncovered face.

On the 20th of December, the weather was fine and mild, so that the whole crew was on shore. A part of them went shooting, so that we might have some fresh meat for the approaching Christmas Holy Days; another part occupied themselves with getting wood and burning charcoal. In the evening, the men who had been out shooting returned and brought a number of ptarmigan and a hare.

On the 22nd of December, we had a sharp frost. I had a Rostock[2] barrel filled with water; and, in the morning, when they loosened the hoops of the barrel, it was frozen quite to the bottom, and was all ice.

On the 24th of December, which was Christmas Eve, I gave the men wine and strong beer, which they had to boil afresh, for it was frozen to the bottom; so they had quite as much as they could stand, and were very jolly, but no one offended another with as much as a word.

The Holy Christmas Day we all celebrated and observed solemnly, as a Christian's duty is. We had a sermon and Mass; and, after the sermon, we gave the priest an offertory, according to ancient custom, each in proportion to his means. There was not much money among the

---

[1] With regard to Munk's evidently-confused description of the eclipse, we must refer the reader to the Commentary.
[2] The beer of Rostock was then much prized in Denmark.

men, but they gave what they had; some of them gave white fox-skins, so that the priest got enough wherewith to line a coat. However, sufficiently long life to wear it was not granted to him.

During all the Holy Days, the weather was rather mild; and, in order that the time might not hang on hand, the men practised all kinds of games; and whoever could imagine the most amusement was the most popular. The crew, most of whom were, at that time, in good health, consequently had all sorts of larks and pastimes; and thus we spent the Holy Days with the merriment that was got up.

Anno Domini 1620.

JANUARY 1st. On New Year's Day, there was a tremendously sharp frost, and I ordered a couple of pints of wine to every bowl to be given the people, over and above their daily allowance, in order that they might keep themselves in good spirits. We had quite clear sunshine on that day; and we always had the hardest frost with a North-West wind. During these days, we had the sharpest frost that we had yet experienced during the whole winter; and at the time we suffered more severely from that terrible frost than from anything else.

On the 8th of January, and all the preceding days, the fearfully hard frost continued, with a North-West wind and clear sunshine. On that day, one of my sailors died.

On the 9th of January, the men recommenced catching some foxes and sables.

On the 10th of January, the priest, Mr. Rasmus Jensen, and the surgeon, M. Casper Caspersen, took to their beds having for some time felt very unwell; and, after that time, violent sickness commenced amongst the men, which day by day prevailed more and more. The illness which then raged was very peculiar, and the sick were generally attacked by dysentery about three weeks before they died. On the same day, my head cook died.

January 18th. On all these days, the weather was as mild as it ever could be here in Denmark at that time of the year; and all the men who were still in health were in the forest, each about his business, but principally shooting, in order to get some ptarmigan for the sick.

On the 21st January, it was fine clear weather and sunshine; and, on that date, thirteen of us were down with sickness. Then, as I had often done before, I asked the surgeon, M. Casper Caspersen aforesaid, who was also lying mortally ill, whether he knew of any good remedy that might be found in his chest and which might serve for the recovery or comfort of the crew, as well as of himself, requesting him to inform me of it. To this he answered that he had already used as many remedies as he had with him to the best of his ability and as seemed to him advisable, and that, if God would not help, he could not employ any further remedy at all that would be useful for recovery.

On the 23rd of January, died one of my two mates, Hans Brock by name, who had been ill, in and out of bed, for nearly five months. On the same day, it was fine weather and beautiful sunshine; and the priest sat up in his berth and gave the people a sermon, which sermon was the last he delivered in this world.

On the 24th of January, in the forenoon, there appeared to be two natural suns on the heavens.

On the 25th of January, when I had the body of my mate, the before-mentioned Hans Brock, buried, I ordered two falconets[1] to be discharged, which was the last honour that I could show him at that time. But the trunnion

---

[1] The "falconet" or "falcon gun" was a sort of small cannon, now obsolete.

burst off both falconets, and the man who fired them very nearly lost both his legs, so very brittle had the iron become on account of the sharp and severe frost.

On the 27th January, died Jens Helsing, seaman. On the same day my lieutenant, the well-born Maurids Stygge, took to his bed for good, after having been ailing some time.

Item: on the same day, the men saw the tracks of five reindeer which had been chased by a wolf, of which the footprints could also be seen; wherefore, I sent a party of the men in order to trace the said deer and wolf, hoping to obtain some of them. But, on account of a great fall of snow which overtook the men, they could not trace the said animals further, and returned without catching any.

On the 28th of January, the cold was so severe that a tin pot with some water in it, which the boy had forgotten in the cabin, had burst in the night by the frost; so that I do not know in what kind of vessels any precious waters may be preserved on voyages to such cold seas, as tin cannot stand.

On the 2nd of February, the frost was very hard. The men who were on shore obtained two ptarmigan, which were very welcome for the use of the sick.

On the 5th of February, a seaman, named Laurids Bergen, died. On the same day, I again sent to the surgeon, the before-mentioned M. Casper Caspersen, with an urgent request that, for God's sake, he would do his utmost, if he knew of any remedy or good advice; or else that, inasmuch as he was himself very ill and weak, he would let me know what medicine or remedy I could use in any way for the benefit of the crew; to which he answered, as before, that, if God would not help, he could not render any advice or assistance at all.

On the 6th of February, I went with three men to the opening by which we had entered, to see how matters stood with the ice in the sea; but, at that time, we could not see any open water, and in the evening we returned to the ship.

February 10th. During these days, the weather was rather mild, but there was much sickness and weakness amongst the crew. Two of them died on this day, after having been on their sick-bed for a very long time.

On the 12th of February, we caught two ptarmigan, which were very welcome for the use of the sick.

On the 13th of February, I ordered for each person at each meal in the day one-third of a pint of wine, and in the morning a whole measure of whisky, beyond the ordinary allowance.

February 16th. During all these days, there was nothing but sickness and weakness; and every day the number of the sick was continually increased, so that, on this day, there were only seven persons in health that could fetch wood and water, and do whatever work there was to be done on board. On the same day, died a seaman who had been ill the whole voyage; and one may truly say he was as dirty in his habits as an untrained beast.

On the 17th of February, one of my men, Rasmus Kiöbenhauffn, died; and, of the crew, there had then already died twenty persons. On that day, we got a hare, which was very welcome.

On the 20th of February, in the evening, died the priest, Mr. Rasmus Jensen aforesaid, who had been ill and had kept his bed a long time.

February 25th. During all these days, nothing particular has happened, except that the lieutenant's servant, Claus by name, who had been ill, died. In this last night, the frost has broken the bottom of a kettle which was used for melting snow in the daytime, a little water having been forgotten in it the evening before.

On the 29th of February, the frost was so severe that nobody could get on shore to fetch water or wood; and that day the cook was obliged to take for fuel whatever he could find. Towards evening, however, I got a man on shore to fetch wood. On that same day, I was obliged to mind the cabin myself: otherwise we should have got nothing to eat all day, because my servant had then also fallen ill and taken to his bed altogether.

On the 1st of March, died Jens Borringholm and Hans Skudenes; and, the sickness having now prevailed so far that nearly all of the crew lay sick, we had great difficulty in getting the dead buried.

On the 4th of March, the weather was mild, and we caught five ptarmigan in the open country, which were very welcome to us. I ordered broth to be made of them, and had that distributed amongst the sick; but, of the meat, they could eat nothing, because of their mouths being badly affected inside with scurvy.

On the 8th of March, died Oluf Boye, who had been ill nearly nine weeks, and his body was at once buried.

On the 9th of March, died Anders, the cooper, who had lain sick since Christmas, and his body was at once buried.

On the 11th of March, the sun entered Aries; it was then the Spring Equinox, night and day being equally long. In those quarters, the sun rose in the East-South-East, and set in the West-North-West at 7 o'clock in the evening; but it was not really more than six o'clock on account of the variation.[1] On the same day, the weather was fine and mild, and I had all the snow thrown off the deck of the ship and had it nicely cleaned. At that time, I had but few to choose between that could do any work.

March 21st. During all these days, the weather was changeable. Sometimes it was fine and clear; at other times, sharp and severe, so that nothing particular can be

---

[1] Some observations on this passage will be found in the Commentary.

recorded on that score. But, as regards the crew, the most part of them were, alas, down with illness, and it was very miserable and melancholy either to hear or see them. On that same day, died the surgeon, M. Casper, before-mentioned, and Povel Pedersen, who had both been ill almost since Christmas. Now and afterwards, the sickness raged more violently every day, so that we who were still left suffered great trouble before we could get the dead buried.

March 24th. All these days the weather was fine and mild, without frost; and we hoped now that, after this day, the weather would become favourable. One of the men, who got on shore and climbed a high rock, saw open water outside the inlet, which filled us with confident expectations.

On 25th of March, died the skipper, Jan Ollufsen, who had been ill in bed for 19 weeks. That same day, the weather was fine, and I was ashore myself and collected Tydebær (as they are called in Norway) where the snow had melted off. They were as fresh in such places as if it had been in the autumn; but one had to be careful to gather them at once: because otherwise they withered speedily.

On the 26th of March, it was also fine weather. I was on shore and gathered a quantity of berries, which I distributed amongst the men. They were very welcome, and did not disagree with them.

On the 27th of March, I looked over the surgeon's chest and examined its contents in detail, because, having no longer any surgeon, I had now to do the best I could myself. But it was a great neglect and mistake that there was not some little list, supplied by the physicians, indicating what those various medicaments were good for, and how they were to be used. I am also certain, and would venture to stake my life on it, that there were many kinds of medicaments in that surgeon's chest which the surgeon I had did not know: much less did he know for what purpose, and in what way, they were to be employed; because all the names were written in Latin, of which he had not forgotten much in his lifetime; but, whenever he was going to examine any bottle or box, the priest had to read the description out for him.

March 29th. All these days, the weather was rather mild. On the same day, died Ismael Abrahamsen and Christen Gregersen, whose dead bodies also were buried on the same day, according to our opportunity and ability at that time.

On the 30th of March, there was a sharp frost. On that day, died Suend Arffuedsen, carpenter; and at this time commenced my greatest sorrow and misery, and I was then like a wild and lonely bird. I was now obliged myself to run about in the ship, to give drink to the sick, to boil drink for them, and get for them what I thought might be good for them, to which I was not accustomed, and of which I had but little knowledge.

On the 31st of March, died my second mate, Johan Petterson, who had been ill in bed a long time.

On the 1st of April, died my late nephew, Erich Munck, and his and Johan Petterson's dead bodies were placed together in one grave.

On the 3rd of April, it was a fearfully sharp frost, so that none of us could uncover himself for cold. Nor had I now anybody to command, for they were all lying under the hand of God, so that there was great misery and sorrow. On the same day, died Iffuer Alsing.

On the 4th of April, the weather was so cold and severe that it was entirely impossible for anyone to get on shore and dig a grave wherein to bury the dead bodies which were in the ship.

On the 5th of April, died Christoffer Opslöe and

Rasmus Clemendsen, my chief gunner and his mate. On the same day, towards evening, died my boatswain, Lauritz Hansen by name ; and the number of men in health was now so small that we were scarcely able to bury the bodies of the dead.

On the 8th of April, died Villom Gorden,[1] my chief mate, who had long been ill, in and out of bed. On the same day, towards evening, died Anders Sodens, and his dead body and that of the above-mentioned Villom Gardon were buried together in one grave, which we who then were alive could only manage with great difficulty, on account of the miserable weakness that was upon us, in consequence of which, not one of us was well or strong enough to go into the forest to fetch wood and fuel ; and we were obliged, during those days, to collect everything that was in the ship and would serve for fuel ; when that was consumed, we were obliged to take our shallop for fuel.

On April the 10th, died the honourable and well-born gentleman Mauritz Stygge, my lieutenant, who had long been ill in bed ; and I took some of my own linen, wherein to wrap his body as well as I could. It was with great difficulty that I got a coffin made for him.

On the 12th of April, we had fine sunshine and some rain, which had not fallen in that locality for seven months. On the same day, we carried the lieutenant's body on shore, and buried it properly, according to our ability at that time.

On the 13th of April, I took a bath in a wine-cask, which I had caused to be prepared for the purpose ; and I utilized for this purpose all the kinds of herbs which we found in the surgeon's chest and thought serviceable. After that, my men likewise had a bath, as many of them

---

[1] William Gordon, the English pilot.

as could move about and were not too weak; which bath (thanks be to God) did us much good, myself in particular.

On the 14th of April, there was a sharp frost. On that day, only four, besides myself, had strength enough to sit up in the berth and listen to the homily for Good Friday.

The 16th of April was Easter Day. Then died Anders Oroust and Jens, the cooper, who had been ill and in bed a long time; and, as the weather was fairly mild, I got their bodies buried. On the same day, I promoted my captain of the hold to be skipper, although he was ill, in order that he might assist me somewhat, as far as his strength allowed, because I was myself then quite miserable and abandoned by all the world, as everybody may imagine.

In the night following, died Hans Bendtsen.

On the 17th of April, died my servant, Olluff Andersen, who, during seven years, had served me faithfully and well.

On the 19th of April, died Peder Amundsen, who had been long ill and was quite wasted away.

On the 20th of April, we had fine sunshine, with an easterly wind. On this day, we got three ptarmigan, of which we were very glad.

On the 21st of April, the sunshine was beautiful; wherefore some of the sick crawled forth from their berths in order to warm themselves by the sun. But as they were so very weak, some of them swooned, so that it did not do them any good; and I had enough to do before I got them back again, each to his berth. On the same day, towards evening, we obtained two Birckhöns,[1] of which we stood in great need in order to get something fresh for our comfort; which was due to God's special providence,

---

[1] This name is probably meant for the Black Grouse (*Tetrao tetrix*); but, as that species does not occur in North America, the birds in question must have belonged to some similar species, probably the Canada Grouse (*Dendragopus canadensis*).

because the sick could not eat any of the salted meat, but only broth of such fresh meat as we obtained.

On the 22nd of April, in the afternoon, I had a bath prepared in which we all, as many as were strong enough to move, bathed, and it did us good.

On the 24th of April, died Olluff Sundmöer, who was mate to the captain of the hold.

On the 25th of April, the wild geese began to arrive; at which we were delighted, hoping that the summer would now soon come; but, in this expectation, we were disappointed, for the cold lasted on much longer.

On the 27th of April, there was a sharp frost at night and a southerly wind. We felt the cold weather of these days more acutely than any other, and it caused us much hurt and weakness. On the same day, died Halffword Brönnie, who had lain ill more than two months; and it was with great difficulty that I got his body buried.

On the 28th of April, died Morten Nielsen, butler, and Thoer Thönsberg; and it was with great trouble that we four persons who were still able to move about a little managed to bury their bodies.

May 3rd and 4th. During all these days, not a man left his berth save myself and the under-cook, who still could do a little. On the last of the days mentioned, died Anders Marstrand and Morten Marstrand, boatswain's mate, who had both long been ill.

On the 6th of May, Johan Watzen,[1] the English mate, who was the fourth mate I had, died. The bodies of the last-mentioned dead were left some days, because the cold was so sharp and severe that none of us three poor men who still had a little strength left, could get them buried.

On the 7th of May, the weather became milder, and we managed to bury the dead; but, on account of our

---

[1] John Watson, the second English pilot.

extreme weakness, it was so difficult for us that we could not carry the dead bodies to their burial in any other way than by dragging them on a little sledge which had been used in the winter for the transport of wood.[1]

May 10th. These foregoing days, we had very severe cold and frost, which greatly weakened and hindered us; but, on this day, the weather was fine and mild, and great numbers of geese arrived; we got one of them, which sufficed us for two meals. We were, at that time, eleven persons alive, counting the sick.

On the 11th of May, it was very cold, so that we all remained quietly in our berths that day; because, in our extreme weakness, we could not stand any cold, our limbs being paralyzed and, as it were, crushed by the cold.

On the 12th of May, died Jens Jörgensen, carpenter, and Suend Marstrand; and God knows what misery we suffered before we got their bodies buried. These were the last that were buried in the ground.

On the 16th of May, it was very cold indeed. Then died the skipper, Jens Hendrichsen; and his body had to remain unburied.

On the 19th of May, died Erich Hansen Li, who, throughout the voyage, had been very industrious and willing, and had neither offended anyone nor deserved any punishment. He had dug many graves for others, but now there was nobody that could dig his, and his body had to remain unburied.

On the 20th of May, the weather was fine and mild and the wind southerly. It was a great grief to us that, whilst God gave such an abundance of various kinds of birds, none of us was strong enough to go into the country and shoot some of them.

---

[1] The incident of the sledge being used for burials is represented in the centre of the second woodcut facing page 23.

On the 21st of May, we had beautiful clear sunshine; and I and three others, though with great difficulty, went on shore, where we made a fire, and anointed our joints with bear's grease. In the evening, I and one other went on board again.

On the 22nd of May, the sunshine was as fine and warm as anyone could wish from God; and, by Divine Providence, a goose, which, three or four days before, had had a leg shot off, came near to the ship. We caught and cooked it, and we had food for two days off it.

As regards the birds which occur in this country: specimens of various kinds had arrived during the last week: *viz.* all kinds of Geese, Swans, Ducks of all kinds, Terns, Southern Pewits, Swallows, Snipes (a very good and toothsome bird), Gulls of all kinds, Falcons, Ravens, Ptarmigans, Eagles.

May 28th. During these days, there was nothing particular to write about, except that we seven miserable persons, who were still lying there alive, looked mournfully at each other, hoping every day that the snow would thaw and the ice drift away.

As regards the symptoms and peculiarities of the illness which had fallen upon us: it was a rare and extraordinary one. Because all the limbs and joints were so miserably drawn together, with great pains in the loins, as if a thousand knives were thrust through them. The body at the same time was blue and brown, as when one gets a black eye, and the whole body was quite powerless. The mouth, also, was in a very bad and miserable condition, as all the teeth were loose, so that we could not eat any victuals.[1]

During these days, when we were lying in bed so altogether bad, there died Peder Nyborg, carpenter, Knud Lauritzsen Skudenes, and Jörgen, the cook's boy, all of

---

[1] The disease was undoubtedly scurvy.

whom remained on the steerage; for there was then nobody that could bury their bodies or throw them overboard.

On the 4th of June, which was Whit-Sunday, there remained alive only three besides myself, all lying down, unable to help one another. The stomach was ready enough and had appetite for food, but the teeth would not allow it; and not one of us had the requisite strength for going into the hold to fetch us a drink of wine. The cook's boy lay dead by my berth, and three men on the steerage; two men were on shore, and would gladly have been back on the ship, but it was impossible for them to get there, as they had not sufficient strength in their limbs to help themselves on board, so that both they and I were lying quite exhausted, as we had now for four entire days had nothing for the sustenance of the body. Accordingly, I did not now hope for anything but that God would put an end to this my misery and take me to Himself and His Kingdom; and, thinking that it would have been the last I wrote in this world, I penned a writing as follows:—

INASMUCH as I have now no more hope of life in this world, I request, for the sake of God, if any Christian men should happen to come here, that they will bury in the earth my poor body, together with the others which are found here, expecting their reward from God in Heaven: and, furthermore, that this my journal may be forwarded to my most gracious Lord and King (for every word that is found herein is altogether truthful) in order that my poor wife and children may obtain some benefit from my great distress and miserable death. Herewith, good-night to all the world; and my soul into the hand of God, etc.

JENS MUNCK.

JUNE the 8th. As I could not now any more stand the bad smell and stench from the dead bodies, which had remained in the ship for some time, I managed, as best I could, to get out of the berth (which no doubt was due to God's fatherly Providence, He being willing still to spare my life), considering that it would not matter where, or among what surroundings, I died—whether outside, amongst the others that were lying dead, or remaining in the berth. When, by the assistance of God, I had come out of the cabin, I spent that night on the deck, using the clothes of the dead. But, next day, when the two men who were on shore saw me and perceived that I was still alive—I, on my part, had thought that they were dead long ago—they came out on the ice to the ship, and assisted me in getting down from the ship to the land, together with the clothes which I threw to them ; for the ship was not farther from the shore than about twelve or fourteen fathoms. For some time, we had our dwelling on shore under a bush, as may be seen on the accompanying plate[1] ; and there we made a fire in the day time. Later on, we crawled about everywhere near, wherever we saw the least green growing out of the ground, which we dug up and sucked the main root thereof. This benefited us, and, as the warmth now commenced to increase nicely, we began to recover.

While we thus continued on shore, the sailmaker, who before had been extremely weak, died in the ship.

June 18th. When the ice drifted away from the ship, we got a net for catching flounders out of the sloop ; and, when the ebb had run out one quarter, we went out dryshod and set it. When the flood returned, God gave us six large trout, which I cooked myself, while the two others went on board *Lamprenen* to fetch wine, which we had not tasted for a long time, none of us having had an appetite for it.

As we now thus every day got fresh fish which was well cooked, it comforted us much, although we could not eat any of the fish, but only the broth, with which we drank

---

[1] See the centre of the woodcut facing p. 23, near the top.

wine, so that by degrees we recovered somewhat. At last, we got a gun on shore and shot birds, from which we obtained much refreshment; so that, day by day, we got stronger and fairly well in health.

June 26th. In the name of Jesus, and after prayer and supplication to God for good fortune and counsel, we now set to work to bring *Lamprenen* alongside *Enhiörningen*,[1] and worked as diligently as we could in getting sails ready for us. But herein we encountered a great difficulty and much anxiety, because *Lamprenen* stood high on the shore, having been carried up by the winter's flood. We were consequently obliged first to unload all that was in her, and then to look out for a high spring tide in order to haul her out. In this we succeeded, and brought her alongside *Enhiörningen*. When we got on board *Enhiörningen*, we were obliged first of all to throw overboard the dead bodies, which were then quite decomposed, as we could not move about or do anything there for bad smell and stench, and yet were under the necessity of taking out of *Enhiörningen* and placing on board *Lamprenen* victuals and other necessaries for our use in crossing the sea, as far as we three persons could manage.

On the 16th of July, which was Sunday, in the afternoon, we set sail from there in the name of God. At that time, it was as warm in that country as it might have been in Denmark, and the cloudberries were in bud. There was such a quantity of gnats that in calm weather they were unbearable. A quantity of rain also fell every day at this time of the year. Before setting out from there, I drilled two or three holes in *Enhiörningen*, in order that the water which might be in the ship might remain when the ebb was half out, so that the ship should always remain firm

---

[1] The former, it will be remembered, had been hauled on shore (see p. 26).

on the ground, whatever ice might come,[1] as is to be seen on this plate.[2] And I have called the same harbour after myself, JENS MUNCKES BAY. All that has happened here is found depicted in this plate.[3] ✠

On the 17th of July, towards evening, I met much ice, and I stood off and on in front of the ice; but, in the course of the night, the weather being calm and misty, we stuck firm in the ice. I then let go the boat of *Enhiörningen*, which I had taken in tow for the purpose of having it for use if I should come near to land anywhere.

On the 20th of July, we were altogether drifting with the ice, when a large white bear came close to the ship. When he saw us, he took to flight across the ice and through the water, followed by a large dog I had with me, which strayed from the vessel in consequence, and never returned, though a couple of days after we could still hear him howl. I guessed that we were then about 40 miles from land.[4]

On the 22nd of July, there was a severe gale, so that the ship drifted with great speed; and, each time it struck against the ice, it was as if it had struck against a rock; at that time, the ice broke my rudder; and, if I had not succeeded in throwing a grapnel on to a large mass of ice, by which I could turn the ship, so as to prevent

---

[1] At this point, Munk's original MS., preserved at Copenhagen, ends.

[2] The word in the original is *Kort*, which would ordinarily mean "a map"; but it is used by Munk as signifying a drawing. There is, however, no illustration on the woodcut of the harbour illustrating the measures taken for the safety of the ship.

[3] The reference is to the woodcut marked with a cross and facing page 23.

[4] Munk's miles being ancient Danish sea-miles (see p. 7, *n.* 2), there must be some mistake in this figure, but we have no means of correcting it.

her from drifting too fast, both the ship and we would have been lost that day.

On the 24th and the 25th of July, we continued drifting in the ice, made fast to an iceberg in order that the ship should not drift so fast and suffer too much damage.

On the 26th of July, we got clear of the ice. I then tried an easterly direction, between the ice and the southern land, and found sandy bottom in 38 fathoms, and then kept beating to and fro; but I did not succeed[1] in getting through that way.

On the 27th of July, in the afternoon, I again fell in with the boat of *Enhiörningen*, which I was obliged to let go ten days before, when first I was caught in the ice.

On the 28th of July, I kept tacking between the ice and the land, from 10 and 15 fathoms back to the ice again in 45, 46, and 48 fathoms; and then I came to the conclusion that it was vain to hope to get past the ice on the southern side.

On the 29th of July, I stood North-West again.

On the 30th of July, I became again fixed in the ice, the fog being so thick that it was difficult to exercise sufficient vigilance.

On the 1st of August, I got free of the ice again and sailed North-West; and, in the course of the day, the wind became so high that I took in the foresail and let her drift with one sail.

On August the 4th, I sailed on between the ice and the land to the West.

On the 5th of August, the ice came against me so strongly in the night that I was obliged to come into 12 fathoms before I could double that strip of ice; and

---

[1] The corresponding word in the original is *formodet* (supposed), which does not seem to give sense. We therefore suspect it to be a misprint for *formaaede*, and have translated accordingly.

it is to be noted that the ice drifts, following the direction of the shore, principally towards the South.

On the 6th of August, I came again into deep water in 45 fathoms, and then steered East-North-East, without observing any ice.

On the 8th of August, I sailed 40 miles in 24 hours, East-North-East.

On the 9th of August, I had sailed 38 miles, when the wind shifted to the East, with a sharp frost.

August 10th. A heavy gale from the East, compelling us to lie by, with cold, fog, and frost.

On 11th of August, the weather was changeable; the wind somewhat easterly. I stood to the North and, at daybreak, made the mainland on the North-Side, called the *Kolde Hug*, which is in 62½ degrees.[1] Here I found the bottom in 20 fathoms, about a quarter of a mile from the shore. From the southernmost point, the coast trends North-East, being flat land without forest; and I steered East-North-East, about five miles from the land. In 40 fathoms, the bottom is hard and stony.

On the 12th of August, I sailed East-North-East, with a light breeze.

On the 13th of August, in the morning early, I arrived off the North-East point of *Digses Eyland*,[2] where much ice was encountered near the land. Towards the South, this land is low and flat, and the Eastern point is in 63 degrees[3] For a night and a day, we stood off and on, on

---

[1] The statement at the beginning of this entry refers to the small hours of the night between the 10th and the 11th. Munk reckoned his days, for the purpose of his journal, from midnight to midnight. The point at which he arrived at daybreak (*Kolde Hug*) can only have been Cary's Swans Nest, on Coats Island, though the latitude is a little too high.

[2] That is, Mansfield Island (see p. 22, *n*.).

[3] For explanation of this statement, see the Commentary.

account of much ice meeting us, which we could not get through.

August 14th. In the morning, when I found myself so much beset with ice on all sides, and the land on both sides close to me, I took in the mainsail and, with the foresail, worked myself through the ice where it was thinnest. Towards noon, I came into clear water. I then observed to starboard some high islands, South-West from me, and then I steered East-South-East. The two islands were *Sösteren*, which are indicated on the map, and were to port when I sailed home. The others are called *Iisver*, situated under the mainland to starboard when I sailed home. And this is the entrance to *Fretum Christian* coming from *Novo Mari*.[1]

On the 15th of August, I found already much ice in that channel between the lands, though scattered, so that it was nothing but "luff on" and "hold firm the grapnel".[2] Much snow fell, and the wild geese commenced briskly to fly south again.

August 16th. I found myself under the northern coast of *Fretum Christian*, or Huttsom Strait, and then shaped my course East by South, which was South-East-by-East according to a true course.

On the 17th of August, the wind was North-Westerly, and I steered South-East, according to a true course, allowance being made for the variation. That night, we

---

[1] The questions here arising out of Munk's description of his course are fully discussed in the Commentary. Suffice it here to say that he passed from Hudson's Bay (*Novum Mare*) into Hudson's Strait (*Fretum Christian*) through the narrow channel between the Digges Islands (the *Söster*) and the main-land.

[2] The meaning of this passage, which we have translated literally, is that those orders had to be repeated continually, whenever they overtook a large ice-floe. The proceeding is described in the Commentary.

had much fog and cold; but, in the daytime, fine sunshine and nice weather.

August 18th. Until noon, fog and westerly wind; and towards evening, we sighted *Munckenes*.[1] From this cape, the coast trends, on this northern side, northerly towards *Fretum Davis*, and inwards towards *Fretum Christian*, North-West-half-North.

On the 19th of August, we had a strong westerly wind and thick weather. We sailed in those 24 hours 40 miles; and, in places, large icebergs were drifting.

On the 20th of August, there was a nice moderate breeze, and we sailed then 30 miles.

August 21st. All night rain, with a North-East wind; in the daytime, a stiff breeze; and we sailed in those 24 hours 20 miles.

August 22nd. In these 24 hours, we sailed, with the mainsail and a stiff breeze, 36 miles.

On the 23rd of August, we sailed 27 miles; and our latitude was 58 degrees and 44 minutes. On the same day, towards evening, the wind fell off, fortunately enough, because I was obliged to take up and woold my pump, which did not work properly.

August 24th. A gale from the East. During these 24 hours, we sailed South-South-East, about 20 miles; and at noon we steered northwards.

On the 25th, 26th, and 27th of August, it was altogether calm.

On the 29th of August, we got a good North-West wind again, and our course was East-by-North; but the wind shifted to North with a gale, so that we had to take in all our sails, and the pump did not forget us.

On the 31st of August, we set sail again, but only

---

[1] Probably Hatton's Headland (see p. 10, *n.*).

the small mainsail; and we had nothing but tempest and bad weather.

September 1st. Before a wind which could move men.[1]

September 2nd and 3rd. Again storm and tempest from the South-East. Towards evening, we were obliged to take in the sails altogether and to lie-to, working the pump.

On the 4th of September, we had tremendous rain and wind, amounting to a gale, and we could not at all leave the pump. Towards the evening, the wind commenced to be more favourable; and, as we were quite exhausted with pumping, we drifted the whole night without sails, in order to get some rest, as far as the pump would allow of it.

September the 5th. At noon, I observed in 58 degrees 59 min. The wind was westerly, with rain and rather a rough sea.

September 6th. All night, the wind was light; in the morning, the wind commenced to fall off.

On the 7th of September, I observed in 59 degrees 15 minutes. There was a nice moderate breeze. We triced up the tack; but, early in the day, the wind fell off again.

September 8th. I observed in 60 degrees 19 minutes. The wind was again a little to the West, but light.

On the 9th, 10th, and 11th of September, we had all kinds of wind and foggy weather; but, in the evening, towards night, a gale sprang up, and our foresail was torn from the bolt-rope, so that we three men had plenty to do to get it in, and then the ship was half full of water.

---

[1] We give this as the most probable literal rendering of the words in the original: *Den 1 Septemb. For en Vind huad men Kunde berøre*, and we take the sense of this obscure passage to be that they sailed on before a wind strong enough to blow a man off his legs. At the same time, it must be admitted that *berøre* in Danish does not (at least, nowadays) mean to move, but only to touch. The corresponding word in Low German, however, is used in that sense, and there are a few other touches of Low German in the text.

September 12th. In the course of the night, the wind shifted to the West and blew hard; our topsail-sheet was blown to pieces, the topmast-stay broken asunder, and the great parrel too; so that it was very anxious work for us three.

On the 13th of September, I conjectured ourselves to be in the longitude of Hethland[1]; and we then descried a ship, to which at last we approached so near that we could speak to the people on board; and I requested them to assist me; but, though I got alongside him twice, he could not help me, because the wind was too high.

On the 14th of September, we made the Orkney Islands.

On the 15th of September, we passed the Orkney Islands, and the wind shifted entirely to the South-East.

On the 16th of September, we sailed 20 miles, steering East by North, towards Norway, as near to the wind as possible.

On the 17th of September, we continued to sail East by North.

On the 18th of September, I changed the course to a more southerly one in the 20th glass.[2]

September 19th. Compelled to lie-to all day during a gale.

On the 20th of September, we saw Norway.

On the 21st of September, we came to harbour South of Allen[3] in a flying gale, not knowing the locality. When I had come inside the rocky islands into a large fjord,[4] I could find no anchorage, and was obliged all

---

[1] Shetland (see p. 6, *n.*).

[2] The old sand-glasses ran for half-an-hour. Twenty glasses would, therefore, mean 10 o'clock.

[3] A small island, generally called Alden, on the west coast of Norway.

[4] Probably the outer part of Dalsfjord, which is just north of Sognefjord.

day to beat to and fro inside the rocks, because I had only half an anchor. Towards evening, when I saw that nobody came out, I steered into a bay, where I dropped that half of an anchor, and thus remained, without being moored, as I had no boat wherewith to carry a hawser on shore. Late in the evening, a peasant came there by accident; and I was obliged to threaten him with a gun to make him come and assist me in getting a hawser on shore. In the morning, I at once proceeded in the same boat to His Majesty's bailiff in Sundfiord,[1] and requested him to procure fresh victuals and men that could run the ship into Bergen.

As I now had seen the ship safe, and had returned into a Christian country, we poor men could not hold our tears for great joy, and thanked God that He had graciously granted us this happiness.

On the 25th of September, I came myself to Bergen, and went at once to physicians to obtain advice and remedies. I also ordered at once drink and medicine to be prepared and forwarded to my two men by the hands of a skipper whom I sent to the ship to take care of it in my place.

On the 27th of September, I wrote home to Denmark, to the High Authorities, to report that I had arrived there.

---

[1] Properly spelt Söndfjord, which is the name of the district in which Dalsfjord is situated.

THANKSGIVING.

ALMIGHTY AND ETERNAL GOD, Gracious Father, and Heavenly Lord, Who has commanded us to call upon Thee in all necessity and adversity, and also dost promise that Thou wilt graciously hear our prayer and save us, so that we may thank Thee for Thy loving-kindness and Thy wonderful acts, which Thou doest towards the children of men: I have now, on this long and perilous journey, been in danger and necessity, in which I have nevertheless experienced Thy gracious help and assistance, in that Thou hast saved me from the icebergs, in dreadful storms, and from the foaming sea. Thou wast my highest pilot, counselor, guide, and compass. Thou hast led and accompanied me, both going and coming. Thou hast led me out of anxiety, disease, and sickness, so that by Thy help I have regained my health, and have returned to my native country, which I entirely believe to be Thy doing. Nor has it been accomplished by my own understanding or providence, wherefore I humbly and heartily give thanks to Thee, O Thou my gracious Father. And I pray that Thou wilt give me the grace of Thy Holy Spirit, that I may henceforth be found thankful to Thee in word and deed, to Thy honour and glory, and for the confirmation of my faith with a good conscience. To Thee, O Holy Trinity, be Praise and Thanksgiving for ever, for these and all Thy benefits.

To Thee alone belongs all Power and Glory
for ever and ever.
AMEN.

Isaiah, Chap. xliv.

Fear not, for I have redeemed thee. When thou passest through the waters, I will be with thee, that the rivers shall not drown thee.[1]

---

[1] The passage is Isaiah xliii, 1, 2. The translation is in accordance with that of Luther, slightly differing from the English version.

COMMENTARY
ON
JENS MUNK'S
NAVIGATIO SEPTENTRIONALIS.

I.—Observations on the Text.

On Munk's Manuscript.

We have already mentioned (p. lvii) that Munk's original manuscript of the greater part of the *Navigatio Septentrionalis* is still in existence. Previous editors of Munk's book have paid little or no attention to this manuscript; but it is in reality of great interest and of considerable importance for the proper understanding of the printed text. As we shall, therefore, have to refer to it frequently in the course of this Commentary, we may suitably preface the latter with a description of it.

The manuscript of the *Navigatio Septentrionalis* belongs to the University Library at Copenhagen (*MS. Additamenta, No. 184*). It is written in a small quarto book of 50 leaves, measuring 7¾ in. by 7 in., and bound in a limp parchment cover. On the front of the cover are these words: *Captien Jens Munks Beschrifning om den Reise 1619* (Captain Jens Munk's Description of the Voyage in 1619). Near the top of the cover are written a few lines, which are difficult to decipher on account of the ink not having adhered to the smooth surface; but what is legible reads thus in English: "The 14th .... Mr. Rasmus has said .... the world has been standing less than six thousand

years, and . . . . Master Gordon says that the world has been standing more than six thousand years, and . . . ." On the inside of the cover, the two first verses of the 91st Psalm are written in Danish. Near the top of the first page is the following heading: *En liden Memorial Paa Nogelle Synderlige stöker att Komess i Hu som Navigationen vedt Kommer* (A little memorandum of some particular matters to be remembered concerning the navigation). A line has, however, been drawn through this heading, and another title written underneath, as follows: *Beskriffuelse Om Jenss Munckes Reyse som hand Anno 1619 begyndte Den 9 Mai Paa den Norduest Passasie, Kiena att Vpsöge, och huad Sig Paa Same Reyse haffr tildraget* (An account of the voyage of Jens Munk, which he commenced in the year 1619, on the 9th of May, to the North-West Passage, in order to find a way to China, and of what happened on the same voyage). Below this is a prayer in Danish, apparently a daily Thanksgiving, to which are appended these words in Portuguese: *Alquen na gloria quer Emtrar sempre deue de comesar Vida Noua Vida* (To whom the Glory. From the commencement of life, one ought always to strive to enter upon the New Life). On the back of this leaf, nothing is written except an addition of money in Danish currency. On the front of the second leaf, there is only a quaint prayer of Munk's own composition.[1] The reverse of the leaf is blank. Near the top of the third leaf are these words: *Reysen begyndes* (The voyage is commenced); after which follow the first lines of the text, which read thus in English:

"On the 9th of May, sailed from Copenhagen, as that day was a Sunday.

"16th. Sailed out of the Sound.

"18th. In the morning early, as one of my crew was walking," etc.

---

[1] The following is a translation: "O, Thou Lamb of God that bearest the sins of the world, have mercy upon us, and grant us graciously a fair wind, and speed us well thither, where we wish to be, so that His Royal Majesty's expedition and voyage may be well performed; that I may deserve thanks, and have the good will of my master and the grace of God, friendship and a good conscience; that I may not do my neighbour any hurt, further than what I am graciously commanded. Be with me, O God, in all my ways, and be always my companion and true guide, for the sake of Thy holy name. Amen."

The text continues from fol. 3 to the front page of fol. 49, at the foot of which it stops abruptly after Munk's statement about the measures taken for the safety of *Enhiörningen* before leaving the place where they had wintered. In the middle of the front page of fol. 6 is a blank space. The front page of fol. 9, the back of fol. 11, the back of fol. 13, and the front of fol. 14, are all blank, having been intended (as the context shows) for the insertion of illustrations. On the front page of fol. 28 is a rough outline, intended to illustrate the appearance of three suns, on the 23rd of November (see p. 33). Finally, on the front page of fol. 30, is a drawing in illustration of the eclipse of the moon which occurred on the 10th of December, 1619 (see p. 34). On the back of fol. 43 commence Munk's notes written during a cruise in the North Sea in 1623 (see p. xlvi), which are continued to the obverse of fol. 49. On the remaining three pages are some accounts, perhaps not written by Munk. The MS. is in good condition, and bears no trace of having been in the printer's hands.

From this description, several inferences may be drawn. The words on the cover, referring to the conflicting opinions of the chaplain and Gordon about the age of the world, seem to prove that Munk actually had the volume with him in Hudson's Bay, as he would scarcely have put them down thus, years after the death of these men. The original heading near the top of the first page shows clearly that the volume was at first intended for notes on the navigation, probably of the same kind as those referring to the cruise in 1623, which occupy the last leaves of it. The insertion of the prayers also seems to indicate that the volume was intended for daily use. It was evidently when Munk changed his mind and utilised the volume for a more elaborate account of the voyage, that he substituted a new and more appropriate title for the original one. The facts that the manuscript of the *Navigatio Septentrionalis* contained in this book only narrates the outward voyage and the wintering, and that the remainder of the volume is mostly occupied by notes on Munk's cruise in the North Sea in 1623, lead to the inference that Munk was engaged in the composition of his book in the winter and early spring of 1622-23, but was interrupted by the duties devolving upon him in connection with the fitting-out of the ships. It seems that he took the volume before us with him on board, intending to continue the work while at sea; but that, instead of doing so, he made use of the remaining leaves in the manner stated. That he did not afterwards continue his account of the voyage of 1619 in the same volume is fully explained by the want of space.

Several blunders prove that the *Navigatio Septentrionalis* was not printed from the MS. before us, but from a copy which must have contained also the continuation of Munk's account; but neither this nor Munk's original log-book are now known to exist.

The fact that, in many places, events are alluded to which happened long after those to which the context refers, proves that the text of the *Navigatio Septentrionalis* is not merely an amplified copy of what Munk may have written down on the voyage, day by day; but the manner in which Munk has worked up his material is not everywhere the same. In some parts, he relates the events in detail, as they happened, under their respective dates, sometimes more fully, sometimes so briefly that his statements appear as mere transcripts from his log-book, in which, now and then, not even the present tense of the verbs has been altered to the past. Other portions, on the contrary, are very much condensed, notably his account of the voyage from the Færö Islands to the Continent of America, between the 4th of June and the 8th of July, during which time only two dates are mentioned in connection with the navigation: *viz.*, June 20th and 30th; and that of the voyage from Haresund into Ungava Bay, up Hudson's Strait and across Hudson's Bay to Churchill Harbour, which occupied the period from August 10th to September 7th, during which likewise only two dates are mentioned: *viz.*, the 14th and the 20th of August. In these portions, Munk only gives a summary of events, introducing isolated extracts from his notes by means of the word *Item*.

As regards the relation of the printed text to the MS. (as far as it reaches), we may observe in general that the former differs from the latter, not only in its more correct spelling and grammatical construction, but also in being more or less amplified in most places. We have no means of deciding with certainty whether this is due to Munk himself or to some literary "improver", and in the latter case to what extent; but it can scarcely be doubted that such a person was employed to write up some

Ref. to Page of Text.

parts. The contrast between the grandiloquent verbosity of the Title-page and the Dedication (which are not found in the manuscript) and the simplicity of diction prevailing in the narrative itself, is too glaring to allow us to ascribe those portions to Munk himself. A comparison between the printed account of the departure from Denmark and Munk's simple statement in the manuscript, as quoted above, reveals the same contrast; but the rest of the book (except a few passages) agrees so much better with the manuscript, though somewhat amplified from it, that it would seem as if Munk very soon decided to dispense with this process of ornamentation.

On the Outward Voyage.

Page 5   Munk brought his ships out of the harbour of Copenhagen on the 9th of May. He adds in the MS., "as that day was a Sunday," referring, no doubt, to a superstitious belief, still prevalent in many places, that Sunday is a lucky day for the commencement of any enterprise, just as Friday is still more generally considered unlucky. As the Sound is a narrow thoroughfare, sailing ships are often detained there by unfavourable winds; and this happened in Munk's case, so that a whole
Page 6 week elapsed before he finally weighed anchor and left Elsinore on Sunday the 16th. The correctness of this date is confirmed by the following entry in Christian the Fourth's diary for this year under that date: *Seilede Enhiörningen og Lamprenen paa den Seilads norden om. Den Almægtigste give det til Lykke*[1] (*Enhiörningen* and *Lamprenen* sailed on the voyage round by the North. May the Almighty make it prosper).

In spite, however, of a Sunday having been chosen both for the first and for the final start, it would not be surprising if many on board looked forward with misgivings, because they had not proceeded very far before one of the crew committed suicide— an event which many would look upon as a bad omen.

Their course necessarily lay northwards as far as the Scaw, and after that westerly as far as Lindesnæs, the southernmost promontory of Norway, in lat. 58°. From this point, their nearest

---

[1] R. Nyerup, *Kong Christian den Fjerdes Dagbøger* (Copenhagen, 1825), pp. 56-57. The passage is quoted, in German, by J. H. Schlegel, in his translation of N. Slange's *History of Christian IV*, iii, p. 126.

route would be through the channel between the Orkney and the Shetland Islands, which is in lat. 59° 30′; they would therefore naturally for some distance follow the Norwegian coast, which gradually trends round towards the north from Lindesnæs; and this was fortunate, as another event of bad omen happened just then, the sloop springing a leak when they were off Lister, an island just west of that cape. It was necessary to seek harbour in order to have this seen to; and, following the coast as he did, Munk was able to find one, without going much out of his way, by sailing into Bukken (or Stavanger) Fjord. Near the entrance of this bay, on the north side, is an island called Karmö, separated from the mainland by a strait called Karmsund; and to this place Munk repaired. In the printed text of 1624, the name is given as *Karsund;* but there is no such place in the neighbourhood, and, as the manuscript has quite plainly Karmsund in all three places where it occurs, *Karsund* is merely an error of the copyist, which we have corrected in our translation. Another sailor having died while they were here, Munk engaged three additional hands at Skudenes, which is the principal place on Karmö.

Ref. to Page of Text.

Page 6 *(continued)*

After leaving Karmsund, they did not take the nearest route, south of the Shetland Islands, but passed to the north of the latter in 61°—for what reason does not appear. On the 2nd of June, they passed the northernmost point of Shetland (in old Danish, Hethland), and two days after they passed the Færö group. With regard to this latter point, however, Munk's expressions are anything but clear. His words are "steering to the West, we sailed round the East end of Ferröe, which is called Syderröe, about four miles to the West of it." In the first place, it would clearly be impossible to sail round the east end of any island four miles to the west of it. In the second place, none of these islands is called Færö, though the name is used in the plural (in Danish, *Færöerne*) of the whole group, each island having a separate name, as Strömö, Sandö, Syderö, etc.[1] Finally, Syderö does not form the eastern extremity of the group, but

Page 7

---

[1] The only *Færö* in the singular is a small island west of the Orkneys, in English called Fair Isle (see *Expeditions to Greenland*, p. 57, note 4). By analogy, the Færö Islands ought in English to be called the Fair Isles.

is (as the name implies) the southernmost island of them all. In the MS. the passage originally read "round the southern end", which is correct and intelligible; but the word *Synner* ("southern") has been altered to *Öster* ("eastern"). The probable explanation of this puzzling passage seems to be that Munk, after having rounded the northern extremity of Shetland, steered west, so as to pass clear of the Færö group, leaving it to starboard, but that he missed or was driven from his course in the night, and, in the morning of the 4th of June, came up with Syderö to the east of the island, instead of to the south of it. If so, he would be compelled to change his course, and to sail round the southern extremity of the island, in order to get a clear start westwards for Greenland. Supposing, further, that, after having done so, they followed the western coast of the island for some distance northwards, before resuming their proper course for America, and that they were four miles to the west of the islands when they finally left them, this may have been what Munk meant by his statement that they sailed round Syderö, four miles to the west of it. The substitution of "the east end" for "the south end" is difficult to account for; but it may, perhaps, have been caused by Munk remembering that when they first saw Syderö on that morning they had it to the west of themselves.

The miles mentioned here and elsewhere in Munk's account are ancient Danish sea-miles, of which about 15 go to a degree. They are, consequently, equal to four English sea-miles or about $4\frac{1}{2}$ ordinary English miles.

The passage from Syderö to Greenland occupied 16 days. During this time, nothing remarkable seems to have happened, as Munk passes it over in silence, as far as the navigation is concerned. Meanwhile he directed his attention to a very important matter—the proper economy as regards food. It is not stated for what length of time the vessels were provisioned; but, as it was foreseen that the expedition might have to winter, it may be assumed that they had ample supplies on board. The proper victualling of the ships under his command seems to have been a point on which Munk was always particular; for, in his annotations concerning his expedition to the northern coasts of Norway in 1623, he has recorded that he was not satisfied with the supply he had received, but that his demand for more had not been successful. Possibly, also, he may have had in mind Hudson's mistake in this respect. At any rate, he made such arrangements as would enable him at any time to ascertain what he might still count upon, and to calculate how long it would last.

Ref. to Page of Text.

Page 7 (continued)

On June 20th, Greenland was sighted, but at a considerable distance. Munk estimates that they were some 15 or 16 Danish miles (about 70 English miles) from land; and, as the mountains in the southern part of Greenland exceed 2,000 ft. in height, this is not impossible, though it would require very clear weather indeed to see them so far off. We are not told in any way whether Munk intentionally approached the east coast of Greenland a little north of Cape Farewell, and then dropped down to the Cape, or whether the same thing happened then which seems to have happened on approaching Syderö—*viz.*, that he had steered too northerly. The former would be in keeping with the advice which he gives a little further on—namely, that in crossing Davis Strait for Hudson's Strait it is preferable to start from Cape Farewell, which, on account of the strong southerly current, would be more easily attained by making for a point on the east coast north of the Cape than by steering directly for it. However this may be, Munk's account of his first approach to Greenland does not appear self-consistent; for he says that, when they found themselves "some" miles north of Cape Farewell, they were in lat. 61° 25'; but, even if we take Munk's own estimate of the latitude of the Cape, as given in the printed text, *viz.*, 60° 30', they would, in 61° 25', be nearly 14 Danish miles north of the Cape—a distance which Munk could scarcely have meant by the word "some". If we turn to the manuscript for elucidation of the point, we find that the approach to Greenland is described in the same words, but the latitude in which they saw the land is given as 60° 25'. At first sight, this seems to offer an easy explanation, as 61° 25' might be a mere copyist's error for 60° 25'. The sequel of the printed text, however, shows that such a surmise would be inadmissible; for, a little further down, we find the latitude of Cape Farewell given as 60° 30', which is clearly inconsistent with their having found themselves in lat. 60° 25', some miles north of the Cape. It is evident that the figure 60, which appears in the manuscript where the approach to Greenland is described, has intentionally been altered in the printed text to 61, and that it is owing to an oversight that the expression, "some" miles north of Cape Farewell, which is incon-

5 2

Ref. to Page of Text Page 7 (continued) sistent with that change, has been left unaltered. If we look further in the manuscript, we find that, after the statement that they sighted Greenland in lat. 60° 25', some miles north of Cape Farewell, no other latitude is mentioned in connection with the Cape; in the next place, where it is spoken of, and where the printed text inserts lat. 60° 30', the manuscript does not mention any latitude at all; finally, where Cape Farewell is referred to in connection with the crossing of Davis Strait, and where the printed text again inserts lat. 60° 30', the MS. merely says "the latitude aforesaid", which must mean 60° 25', the only figure that has been mentioned. All these statements in the MS. are in harmony with one another, and imply a latitude for Cape Farewell not very far from the true one. We have no means of guessing why Munk's original statement was altered; but, as it is so much more self-consistent and in keeping with actual facts than that of the printed text, we are inclined to look upon the former as the more correct one.

It may be observed, in passing, that Munk cannot have been induced to alter the indication of the latitude of Cape Farewell by consulting the map of Hessel Gerritsz.; for on the latter that promontory is placed in lat. 59°. This is as much too southerly as the figure given in Munk's printed text (60° 30') is too northerly, the correct latitude being 59° 45', as confirmed by the latest explorer of the Cape, Lieut. Holm, who was able to observe on the spot itself.[1]

If it was really in lat. 61° 25' that Munk and his party first saw Greenland, the point observed can, of course, not have been Cape Farewell, but would probably have been the high promontory on the east coast in lat. 61° 21', called Kunerinak in the Greenland language, and on the Danish maps Cap Tordenskjold.[2]

Bad weather and the great quantity of ice which, as is usually the case, they met in the neighbourhood of Cape Farewell drove them out to sea again; and it was not till the 30th of June, after a ten days' struggle with storms and gales, that they (whether for the first or second time is not clear) sighted Cape

---

[1] *Medd. om Grönland*, vol. vi (1883), p. 165.

[2] See Map of the East Coast of Greenland from Cape Farewell to lat. 63° 45', by Lieutenants G. Holm and V. Garde, in *Medd. om Grönland*, vol. ix (1889), plate XVI.

Farewell. This they seem to have recognised without hesitation, which is easily understood when it is remembered that Gordon had been with Hall when the latter made the Cape in 1612.[1] Munk's description of Cape Farewell agrees perfectly with those of other writers. The mountains close behind the Cape are more than 2,000 ft. high, and very rugged and wild in appearance. He expresses regret that he could not obtain a drawing of the Cape, meaning, as his words imply, one of the kind made by navigators in order to enable others to recognise the localities where they had been; but the explanation he gives seems scarcely sufficient, because the snow and ice which, he says, obscure the real features of the country, alter, of course, very little during the short summer. From the fact that Munk mentioned a draughtsman amongst his requisites for a second voyage, it might, perhaps, be concluded that the real reason why he could not obtain a good sketch of Cape Farewell was the want of a competent person to do it; but the same person who drew the bird's-eye view of the wintering-place could surely have made a good sketch of Cape Farewell. A sketch of it, exhibiting markedly the features indicated by Munk, is prefixed to the above-quoted paper by Lieut. Holm. So impressed was Munk by the forbidding aspect of the place, that he suggested that whoever called it Cape Farewell doubtless did not mean to come there again; but, as a matter of fact, that was not exactly the case, if Gatonbe was rightly informed, that Davis so named the Cape because he could not come near the land by six or seven leagues for ice.[2]

In passing we may observe that, although in Denmark the name *Cap Farvel* is now always applied to the Cape Farewell of English navigators (the Statenhuk of the Dutch, the Umanarsuak of the Greenlanders), it was not always so. Until not very long ago *Cap Farvel* in Danish meant the southern extremity of the island of Sermersok, in about lat. 60° 10'. It is, nevertheless, an error when the "Clerk of the *California*", after stating[3] that the Dutch gave the name of Cap Vaarwell to a promontory west of

---

[1] See Book I, *Expeditions to Greenland*, p. 89.
[2] See Book I, *Expeditions to Greenland*, pp. 89-90.
[3] *An Account of a Voyage for the Discovery of a North-West Passage by Hudson's Streight*...., by the Clerk of the "*California*" (London, 1748, 8vo), p. 11.

Ref. to Page of Text.
(Page 8 continued)

Cape Farewell, in about lat. 61°, continues, "the same Cape which Munk so named in the year 1619, when he took his departure from thence to America". In the first place, the Danish usage alluded to is of much later date than Munk; and, in the second place, Munk speaks expressly of the promontory as the one "which the English call Cape Farewell".

From Cape Farewell, Munk crossed Davis Strait in search of the great inlet, which, at that time, was still supposed by many to lead to the hoped-for North-West Passage; but, before narrating his experiences in seeking this, he offers some remarks on the navigation in those parts. At first sight, these observations do not seem to convey any very clear meaning. His words are as follows:—

"*Item*, if one shapes one's course too much to the west, towards the American side, much ice is likewise encountered, and one may then easily be driven out of one's course, because the current with the ice sets principally to the south-west. Likewise, whoever intends to sail into *Fretum Davis* or *Regis* must keep to 60½ degrees from Cape Farewell; and, if it is possible to have Cape Farewell in sight, then he may choose his course as he thinks best into that said water", etc.

On the face of it, this reads like advice offered to navigators intending to sail into and explore Davis Strait, and appears to be mainly to the effect that they should keep the middle of the channel; but, if it is thus understood, it seems a curious and impracticable instruction that they should keep to 60½, whether this be taken as meaning latitude or longitude; nor does there appear to be any reason why one should be better able to choose a right course having Cape Farewell in sight. But the fact is that, although Munk does not expressly say so, he had in mind, when he wrote this, only the particular task which had been incumbent upon him *viz.*, to cross Davis Strait, in order to find the entrance to Hudson's Strait. He wrote with a view of guiding others who, after him, should sail to the country which he had visited; and, when it is remembered that his account was written after his return home, when he had learnt that the proper entrance to Hudson's Strait was not (as he had been instructed from home) in about lat. 62°, but just north of lat. 60 30', his direction is quite intelligible. By the map, the course from Cape Farewell to Hudson's Strait would be very little to the north of west; but anyone steering so would, as he says, be carried too far south by the current. *Ref. to Page of Text.*

It will have been noticed that, in mentioning Davis Strait, Munk suggests an alternative name *Fretum Regis* (on Munk's map misspelt *Reij*). This was, of course, meant as a compliment to King Christian IV, but was scarcely intended seriously. The older name was too well established to be changed, and *Fretum Regis*, which occurs only once in the text, seems merely thrown in, as it were, in passing. *Page 8 (continued)*

At this point of his narrative, Munk draws particular attention to the necessity for careful observation of the variation of the needle, a matter which at that time had been taken up, particularly in England. We have seen (see p. xv) that he had observed it in his exploration of Kolguew Island in 1609. In saying that navigators ought to make special observations on this subject, and to note down the results, he makes use of the expression "*punctere*", which seems to mean that the amount of the variation should be marked by dots on the compass dial. This should be commenced, according to his advice, before coming beyond 56°; and, as this figure, of course, must refer to longitude, the question arises: From which meridian is this reckoned? As we shall be able to prove that, in working up his text, Munk made use of Origanus' *Ephemerides*,[1] in which the longitudes are reckoned from Frankfort-on-the-Oder, the 56 would probably have to be counted from that meridian; but as Munk had no means of determining longitudes at all while on his voyage, the figure must have been arrived at merely by dead reckoning. Munk does not say why he mentions longitude 56 as the point where navigators ought to turn their attention specially to this kind of observation before coming further west; but it may be grounded in the fact that some time before reaching that longitude Munk had crossed the line dividing the area of easterly declination, in which both Denmark and England were then situated, from

---

[1] *Ephemerides novae* . . . . . *a Davide Origano* . . . . . *accommodatae horizonti Francofurtano cujus longitudo est 36 part o min latitudo 52 part 20 min* . . . . . *Francofurti ad Oderam. Anno 1599* . . . . *4°*; or, more likely, the extended edition in three vols., with separate titles, viz., *Annorum priorum [posteriorum] 30* . . . . . and *Novae motuum coelestium Ephemerides* . . . . . *Francofurti ad Viadrum* . . . . . *1609*.

Ref. to Page of Text.

Page 8 (continued) the area of westerly declination, wherein he now found the variation increasing to a figure far beyond what he had ever observed before.[1] In the subsequent part of his narrative, Munk often states expressly whether the directions indicated are corrected by allowance for the variation or not —"by a true compass," as he calls it; but he does not always do so. At the same time, we have not noticed any instance where there is any necessity for thinking that he has omitted the correction in question. In a few places only, does he state the amount of the variation—curiously enough, always the same, viz., two points—and his statements agree fairly well with what is known from other sources. Munk's statement of the variation at Port Churchill is of interest as being the earliest known reference to the declination on the west coast of Hudson's Bay, and as indicating a considerable westerly displacement of the magnetic pole. Unfortunately, however, as will be shown hereafter (p. 122), it is not free from obscurity.

Page 9 After this digression, Munk resumes the account of his voyage; but the printed text has in this place been rendered meaningless by wrong punctuation. Translated as it stands, the printed text would read thus: "and this he must observe and pay careful attention to before he comes beyond 56 degrees with a westerly course, to come back to my course and further to advance the voyage. When I had now got clear of the ice", etc. But in the MS. there is a full stop after "westerly course", after which half a page is left blank, as if for the insertion of some intended remarks, which after all have been omitted. The new paragraph then commences thus: "Now to return to my course and to continue [the account of] my voyage. When I had now got clear", etc. The person who copied Munk's MS. for the press has run the two paragraphs together and misplaced the stop, whereby the whole passage has become quite unintelligible. Probably with the intention of mending the confusion thus created, he has omitted the word "now" and altered "my voyage" to "the voyage". We have corrected this corrupted passage in our translation.

In resuming the thread of his narrative, Munk says that he got clear of the ice "in 60½, the longitude of Cape Farewell": a somewhat surprising statement, because nowhere else does he

---

[1] See the first map in Prof. Christopher Hansteen's *Untersuchungen über den Magnetismus der Erde* (Christiania, 4, 1819).

indicate the longitude of any locality, and there does not seem to be any special reason for doing so here. The figure being, moreover, the same as that indicating the latitude of Cape Farewell, one is tempted to suspect another blunder of the copyist; but the MS. also has "longitude". The figure, too, is left in blank in the MS., showing that Munk had not got it in his notes, but had to obtain it from some other source, which would not have been the case if "longitude" had been a slip of the pen on Munk's own part for "latitude", for he gives the latter just before, presumably in accordance with his own observation. It cannot, therefore, be doubted that longitude is really meant. As in the case just mentioned, the figure is probably reckoned from Frankfort-on-the-Oder; nor is it far wrong on that supposition. In reality, Cape Farewell is 43° 53′ west of Greenwich, whilst Frankfort-on-the-Oder is 14° 34′ east of Greenwich, making the difference between Cape Farewell and Frankfort 58° 27′. That Munk indicates the point from which he started across Davis Strait by mentioning the longitude of Cape Farewell is easily explained by supposing that the ice, from which he had just got clear, had carried him back so as to leave him, as nearly as might be, south of the Cape.

Munk does not mention the date on which he started from the neighbourhood of Cape Farewell; but it was only on the 8th of July that they sighted the western shore of the Strait—having most likely been delayed by the ice descending Davis Strait. Munk describes it as "the American side", evidently not reckoning Greenland a part of America. Their land-fall is stated to have been in about 62½°, which would be off the northern part of Lock's Land (Hall's Island of Frobisher), which bounds the mouth of Frobisher's Bay to the north; and this accords with Munk's subsequent statements. Ice and fog at first prevented near approach to the land; but, when the latter cleared, Munk appears to have descried an opening in the ice-belt, through which he steered into a large bay. This, he says, the mates (meaning, doubtless, Gordon and Watson) supposed to be the entrance to Hudson's Strait, because of the latitude in which it was situated. From the sequel, it appears that Munk had been instructed to search for the Strait in about the latitude of 62½°; and the circumstance that in this place he refers, not to his instructions, but to the opinion of the pilots, may perhaps

Ref. to Page of Text.

Page 9 *(continued)*

Ref. to Page of Text.

Page 9 (continued) indicate that he did not agree with them. That Hudson's Strait really could be entered from where they were, through Gabriel Strait, they evidently did not suspect; in fact, when Munk says that the ice which he encountered in such great quantity came out of three large fjords, it seems as if Gabriel Strait must have been one of them—blocked, no doubt, by ice and appearing landlocked.[1] The second must have been the main channel of Frobisher's Bay; but the third cannot be accounted for except by supposing that the shallow bay on the north side appeared from Munk's point of view as the opening of a great inlet.

Munk says that, after long investigation, they came to the conclusion that this bay was not the right entrance to Hudson's Strait; but he does not say why they came to that conclusion. A little further down, however (see p. 10), he mentions that his instructions directed him to look for a certain island situated in 62° 30′, which should mark the entrance of Hudson's Strait; and it was very likely because they did not find or recognise any such island at the mouth of Frobisher's Bay that they decided to seek further south. That this Bay had been discovered long before by Frobisher and called by his name, they did not suspect, because, at that time, it was generally believed that the localities explored and named by Frobisher were situated on the east coast of Greenland; and that they did not recognise the bay as the Lumley's Inlet of Davis is easily accounted for—even supposing that they had a detailed knowledge of Davis's voyages—by the fact that the name of Lumley's Inlet had at that time, by mistake, become synonymous with that of Hudson's Strait, as we shall more fully explain hereafter. Under the circumstances, it is very natural that Munk should have bestowed a new name on the locality, and called it *Iisefjorde* (the Ice-Bays).

Page 10 Munk next followed the coast southwards until he reached a promontory clearly marking the entrance of a great inlet, with regard to which they satisfied themselves that it really was Hudson's Strait, though so much farther south than they had

---

[1] It may be noted that A. W. Graah applies the name *Iisefjorde* to Gabriel Strait. See the map in his *Undersögelses-Reise til Östkysten af Grönland* (Copenhagen, 1832), of which an English translation appeared in 1837.

been led to expect. Munk places this promontory in lat. *Ref. to Page of Text.* 61° 20', which, together with the terms in which he speaks of it, both in this place and particularly in narrating the return voyage (see p. 55), leaves no doubt that it was the southernmost headland on Resolution Island (as recognised already by A. W. Graah,[1] followed by Admiral Ravn[2]), most likely, though not certainly, the "Hatton's Headland" of Frobisher. For the reason already stated, it would not occur either to Munk or to the English pilots to identify the promontory in question with any place mentioned by Frobisher; and Munk was therefore perfectly justified in calling it after himself, *Munckenes* (Munk's Cape). Indeed, if it were not for the probability of this cape being identical with "Hatton's Headland", it ought now to be called *Munckenes*. The name of "Cape Best", which is applied to it on some modern maps, also occurs on Frobisher's map,[3] but belongs evidently to some headland east of Hatton's Headland—possibly Cape Warwick. As, however, the author of Frobisher's map evidently did not intend to give an accurate outline of Resolution Island, but only to mark the position of it, no safe conclusion can be drawn from the map as to the meaning of the names in question. Cape Best is not mentioned in Best's text, but Hatton's Headland is spoken of, and that in terms which would apply with a good deal of probability to the southernmost extremity of the island.

Ref. to Page of Text. Page 10 (continued)

Much less (if, indeed, anything) can be said in justification or excuse for the bestowal of a new name on Hudson's Strait, viz., *Fretum Christian*. Whilst Munck only, as it were, interpolates the alternative name of *Fretum Regis* once in mentioning Davis Strait, he makes use of *Fretum Christian* in most places where he refers to Hudson's Strait, and generally without mentioning either of the two other names, Hudson's Strait and Lumley's Inlet. As, moreover, he introduces the name *Fretum Christian* with the same phrase which he makes use of in introducing the name

---

[1] *Op. cit.*, map.
[2] In an article entitled *Udsigt over de Reiser, som ere foretagne for at finde Nordvest Passagen* ("Review of the Voyages undertaken to find the North-West Passage"), in *Dansk Maanedskrift, 1860* (Copenhagen, 8°), p. 89.
[3] In Best's *True Discourse*, etc. (London, 1578, 4to).

Ref. to Page of Text.

Page 10 (continued)

Munckenes (*viz.*, "as it is now called") it is clear that he seriously meant to propose this new name for the Strait. Superfluous names are most objectionable in geography, and there is nothing specially to be said in favour of this one. At the same time, it must be remembered that Munk was not a professional geographer but a plain sailor, who may have thought that a name bestowed in honour of his King would at once command acceptance, at least at the side of the older less pretentious one. The earlier explorers, too, were not overscrupulous in this respect, and many cases of unnecessary, yet in the end successful, renaming may be cited.

Apart from this suggested new name, Munk more than once describes the great waterway as Lumley's or Hudson's Strait; and this use of the two names as synonymous has been characterised as a mistake of Munk's.[1] But it was, in any case, a mistake which Munk shared with everybody else at that time. It originated with Weymouth, and under the circumstances was very natural: nay, in a sense, it was no mistake at all. The facts are briefly these:—Davis, in 1587, gave the name of Lumley's Inlet to the same opening which had previously been named Frobisher's Strait, but which he, for reasons already explained, failed to identify. Of this inlet, he really only saw the opening from Davis' Strait, which he noticed in passing as he coasted southwards. The name, therefore, in reality only applied to the opening between Lock's Land (as it is now called) and Resolution Island. After passing the latter, which he did not recognise as an island, but on which he noticed the eastern headland, by him called Warwick's Foreland, Davis passed the entrance of Hudson's Strait, but without examining or even properly naming this "gulfe or second passage", as he calls it; only he noticed in it an extraordinary action of the tide, which he describes as "a furious overfall". His next successor, Weymouth, in 1602, after passing Warwick's Foreland, northwards bound, found himself opposite Lumley's Inlet, and recognised it as such, but was then driven back by north-east winds to the "gulfe" mentioned by Davis, through which he succeeded after a long struggle in entering the passage afterwards called Hudson's Strait,

---

[1] See P. Lauridsen's edition of the *Navigatio Septentrionalis*, note 6.

but which at that time had no proper or accepted English name *Ref. to Page of Text.* at all. Frobisher, indeed, had entered the Strait on his third voyage in 1578, mistaking it for Frobisher's Strait, and in Best's Page 10 account of the voyage¹ it is referred to several times as the (*continued*) "mistaken strait" or "the same mistaken streights". It is likewise so described on the map. But this is a mere descriptive epithet—not a proper name, any more than Davis' "furious overfall" on the Molyneux globe. Even if the author of the narrative intended it as a name, properly speaking, it never was accepted as a name for Hudson's Strait, because all the world, from Davis onward, for nearly two centuries believed that some place on the east coast of Greenland was meant by it. Referring to Warwick's Foreland, Weymouth says: "We could discern none other than that it was an island [which, indeed, Frobisher had already ascertained, calling it Queen Elizabeth's Foreland], which if it fall out to be so, then Lumley's Inlet and the next southern inlet where the great current setteth to the west must of necessity be one sea, which will be the greatest hope of passage that way."² Weymouth's account was not published till 1625; but the results of his voyage became generally known long before then, with the consequence that Lumley's Inlet at once came to be looked upon as part and parcel of the great waterway extending towards the west, up which he had sailed 100 leagues, as he estimated, and to the whole of which the name of Lumley's Inlet, in the absence of any other, was naturally transferred. Accordingly, Hudson (who, moreover, was acquainted with Weymouth's journals) says in his account of his voyage in 1608:³ "I therefore resolved to use all means I could to sayle to the north-west, considering the time and meanes we had, if the wind should friend us, as in the first part of our voyage it had done, and to make triall of that place called Lumley's Inlet and the furious over-fall of Capt. Davis, hoping to run it an hundred miles and then return as God should enable us." It was so much the more natural that the name of

---

¹ See Capt. Best, *A True Discourse, etc., Third Voyage*, pp. 20, 24, and 25; also the Reprint by the Hakluyt Society (London, 1867), pp. 242 and 247.

² *Purchas his Pilgrimes*, vol. iii, p. 810.

³ *Purchas his Pilgrimes*, vol. iii, p. 580; see also Asher's *Henry Hudson*, p. 44.

Ref. to Page of Text.
Page 10 (continued)

Lumley's Inlet should be extended to the whole of the waterway, of which it was reckoned an entrance, as the existence of any other continuation of that opening westwards was so entirely overlooked that all trace of any such thing disappeared from the maps for more than 150 years, the continuation which Frobisher had explored having been erroneously transferred to Greenland. There is, therefore, nothing surprising, and—viewed in the light of that time, as it should be—nothing to find fault with either in the fact that the Strait, or at least the main entrance to it, bears the name of Lumley's Inlet on the map published in 1612 by Hessel Gerritsz (and which is generally admitted to be in the main Hudson's) or in Gerritsz.'s explanation, in which he says that Hudson tried to find a passage through Lumley's Inlet by the way found by Weymouth, though in reality neither the one nor the other entered the Strait by the Lumley's Inlet of Davis. Indeed, it may be confidently asserted that "Lumley's Inlet" would most probably have been the name of Hudson's Strait to this day, if the sensation created by Hudson's discovery of the Bay, and death there, had not caused his name to be so closely associated with it. As it happened, Hudson's Strait soon became the generally-received name for the Strait, though Weymouth's view that this and Lumley's Inlet were "one sea" continued to be held for more than 150 years. The name "Lumley's Inlet" came to be restricted to the opening originally so called, together with the strait between the mainland and Resolution Island, for which we now use Frobisher's name, Gabriel Strait, whilst the real western continuation of the Inlet, as already stated, was ignored. The whole of that waterway was spoken of as the "North Channel" leading into Hudson's Strait, whilst the proper entrance was called the "South Channel", Resolution Island being described and generally figured on the maps as an island situated in the wide opening of the Strait and dividing it into two channels of nearly equal importance. The maps published within the period mentioned—from Hessel Gerritsz.'s downwards—and the expressions used by navigators like Hawkridge, Baffin, Luke Foxe, and others, down to Robson, Coats, and the "Clerk of the *California*", amply bear this out. It was not till the latter half of the eighteenth century that it was re-discovered that Lumley's Inlet was the opening of a great bay penetrating far westwards into the Continent, independent of—though, by means of Gabriel Strait, connected with—Hudson's Strait. At the same time, however, the name fell altogether out of use ; for, when *Ref. to Page of Text.* it had been ascertained that the localities described by Frobisher were not situated in Greenland, it soon became apparent that Page 10 Lumley's Inlet was but another name for Frobisher's Strait. *(continued)* From all this, it follows that, although Munk may appear to us, with our more complete knowledge, to have made a mistake in using the two names, Lumley's and Hudson's Strait, as synonymous, this is far from requiring an apology when looked upon with due consideration of the knowledge of the time.

It is not clearly stated on what grounds Munk's party satisfied themselves that the great inlet of which *Munckenes* formed, so to speak, the northern gatepost, really was Hudson's Strait; but they seem to have done so at once, although the only island which they could find in the opening (doubtless the largest of the Button Islands) was, according to their observation, in lat. 60° 40′, instead of 62° 30′ as it was stated to be in Munk's instructions. Resolution Island they do not appear to have recognised as an island, although several earlier explorers had done so—a circumstance which seems to militate against the supposition that any of them had been there before.

Munk prefaces his experiences in Hudson's Strait with some advice to future navigators ; but in this place a misprint or clerical error again renders the printed text meaningless, the words *vider end* (*i.e.*, "further than"), having been substituted for *under* (that is, "below"), which appears in the MS. Translated as it stands in the printed text, the passage would be to the effect that the navigator should always shape his course so as not to get further than $61\frac{1}{2}°$, which conveys no meaning ; whereas "below $61\frac{1}{2}°$", as in our translation, is quite intelligible. Munk's intention was to warn navigators against sailing too near the southern shore, and thus running the risk of being driven out of their course by the strong currents that would be encountered there. Munk's statements concerning the strength of the current, the height of the tides, and the great depth of the sea in these parts are confirmed by all subsequent writers.

Munk commenced his exploration of the Strait by sending his Page 11 lieutenant, Mauritz Stygge, on shore near *Munckenes* on the 12th of July, partly to fetch water, partly to examine the locality. In this place, too, the printed text is unintelligible on account of the word *haffner* (*i.e.*, "harbours") having been omitted after *finding*.

Ref. to Page of Text.
Page 11 (continued)

In our translation, we have inserted it in accordance with the MS. It appears that Munk wished to give his men some rest, and to wait in some convenient place for the ice, which so seriously impeded the navigation, to pass out of the Strait. No anchorage, however, could be discovered near Munkenes—at least, none offering sufficient shelter; and Munk was obliged to continue his voyage as best he could. In so doing, he followed the northern shore (that of Meta Incognita); but it does not appear whether he did so because he thought it best at the time, or because he was instructed to do so. Very likely it was merely a natural consequence of his having come down to the Strait from the north. At any rate it was in keeping with his advice to navigators above mentioned not to come below $61\frac{1}{2}°$, the propriety of which is borne out by the testimony of later times, to the effect that, in the early part of the summer, the northern coast is the more free from ice. But he overdid it, as it were, keeping between the ice and the shore, in consequence of which he was imprisoned between the two and much delayed.

Munk's troubles commenced already in the evening of July 13th, that is, at the close of the first day's sail within the Strait, when the vessels were caught in the ice and further manœuvring became impossible. Munk seems quite to have realised their danger, remembering, no doubt, his experience in the year 1609, when his ship was crushed in the ice off the island of Kolguew,[1] he and his crew escaping with difficulty. It appears that he wished to give his readers some notion of the seriousness of the situation by means of an illustration; but the only representation there is of anything of the kind, *viz.*, that on the first woodcut (facing p. 14) farthest to the right, is very tame, and if meant for the events here related, contrasts almost ludicrously with the grand words of the printed text.[2] The MS. simply says, "as the figure shows"; and a page is left blank for the insertion of a drawing; but, as in most of the other cases, none such has been inserted. We may note that the Danish printed text refers to "the *Kort* accompanying this treatise", which may easily be misunderstood,

---

[1] See p. xv.

[2] It is, most likely, really intended to illustrate the situation just before entering *Haresund*, though it is not referred to in the proper place in the text (see pp. 17 and 83).

because *Kort* ordinarily means a map; but there is nothing on the map illustrating this incident. Elsewhere, too, Munk uses *Kort* as synonymous with *Thaffle* (a plate). *Ref. to Page of Text.*

Having at length, at daybreak on the 15th of July, escaped from the grip of the ice, Munk was able during that day to make further headway, though sometimes reduced to tacking between the ice and the shore; but in the evening his progress was again arrested by the ice, which had accumulated round some islands. Munk does not supply any indications by which these may be identified, and we are in that respect left to conjecture. Considering, on the one hand, that Munk had had two days' sailing in the Strait before he came to these small islands, and, on the other hand, that after having got clear again of the ice which stopped him there, he was able to make progress only during few and short intervals before he reached *Haresund*, at least 140 English miles up the Strait, it is evident that the islands in question must have been a considerable distance within the entrance to Hudson's Strait. Mr. Lauridsen is of opinion that they must have been the Middle Savage Islands;[1] and this identification is not open to objection on the score of the considerations just adduced. But Munk's statement that they were "small islands which stretched away from the mainland in a more westerly direction", and that they stayed outside them for a considerable time, does not seem applicable to the Middle Savage Islands, which according to Coats[2] are situated six or seven miles from the main. On the Admiralty map, some nameless islands are marked between the Lower and the Middle Savage Islands, and much nearer to the shore, which might with greater probability be identified with those spoken of by Munk. There is, however, not the slightest necessity for supposing that the islands in question are amongst those which have been named by navigators or geographers, or have been put down on our maps. Munk evidently kept very close to the shore; and, considering the expressions he uses, the probability is altogether that the small islands of which he speaks were merely rocky islets, such as abound in many places along these coasts. Page 12

At first sight, there seems to be some confusion with regard to Page 13

See his edition of *Navigatio Septentrionalis*, note 13.
Geography of Hudson's Bay, (Hakluyt Society, 1852), p. 14.

Ref. to Page of Text.
Page 13 (continued)

the dates in this part of the narrative. After stating that they had entered a harbour on the 17th of July, Munk commences a new paragraph with the words, "On the 17th of July, I ordered the sloop to sail before us and look for anchorage", apparently a different event from that mentioned just before under the same date. Again, after having told how they had found and entered a good harbour on the 17th, he says that "on the following day", which must be understood to mean the 18th, he sent out men to examine the country. Nevertheless, he commences the following paragraph, in which he relates his interview with the natives, with the words "On the 18th of July", as if he were going to narrate the events of a fresh day. As, however, the dates are given in the MS. in the same manner as in the printed text, neither the copyist nor the printer can be in fault, and the want of clearness has probably arisen simply from Munk having copied his notes too closely. One entry may have been made in the middle of the day on July 17th, stating what had happened until then; the next paragraph, commencing "On the 17th of July", probably corresponds to an entry concerning their finding another harbour in the afternoon of the 17th, and the sending out of an exploring party in the morning of the 18th; and this may have been put down soon after the men had returned, which they did about midday. Finally, the paragraph commencing "On the 18th of July" narrates what took place in the afternoon of that day, *viz.*, the interview with the natives. If Munk had broken up his notes and told what had happened on each day in a separate paragraph, there would have been no appearance of confusion.

The harbour which Munk entered on the evening of the 17th, and to which he gave the name of *Rinsund*, cannot have been very far from the islands where the ice stopped him in the evening of the 15th, because the distance was covered in the course of the 17th, of which day a portion must have been spent in the harbour which they had entered in the morning of that day, and from which the sloop was sent out to reconnoitre. It is not clear from Munk's description whether it was a sound between islands or between an island and the mainland; but the latter is the more probable, as the natives and the reindeer, of which he speaks, would be more likely to be encountered on the mainland. Moreover, on the woodcut facing p. 14, on which Munk's meeting with the natives (which happened at Rinsund) and the shooting of reindeer are represented, the ships are seen lying close under the main, inside some small islands. This was the only place where Munk met with the natives, with whom his intercourse was very friendly, whilst many of the early explorers complain much of the hostility of the Esquimaux. In Munk's case they seem to have held back in a rather remarkable manner, unless it be that those whom he met were only casual visitors, having their home far away. It is curious that on the woodcut just mentioned the natives are drawn as naked, whereas not only was this manifestly improbable, but several Greenlanders had at that time been seen at Copenhagen in their native costume.[1]

Munk loosed from *Rinsund* on the 19th of July to continue his voyage; but he was compelled to return to his anchorage, where he remained until the evening of the 22nd, when he again set sail, after taking possession of the land in the name of King Christian IV., in token of which he set up the King's arms and monogram — no doubt brought out on purpose. He hoped that the ice would by this time have diminished sufficiently; but on the very next morning he found himself again enclosed by the ice, which even lifted the sloop completely out of the water, so that one could pass one's hand under her keel. Munk appears to have been much surprised and even alarmed at this occurrence, which, however, is not infrequent in Arctic navigation, and often tends rather to preserve than to endanger a ship.[2] In this place the

Ref. to Page of Text.

Page 13 (*continued*)

Page 14

Page 15

---

[1] Munk's account of how, in the hope of attracting the natives, he caused all kinds of small objects to be deposited wherever their fishing-nets were found, has been retold in a manner which strikingly illustrates how statements often are transformed by passing from hand to hand. Isaac de la Peyrère says (*Relation du Groenland*, pp. 238-239) that the Danes, finding fishing-nets suspended along the shore, attached all sorts of presents to them, but that no natives came. The translator in Churchill's *Voyages* (vol. vi, p. 407), misunderstanding the French word "*filets*", says that the Danes suspended all sorts of objects to small ropes. Finally, "the Clerk of the *California*" (*Account of a Voyage*, etc., p. 37), writes: "That night the Danes sailed, but were forced to return the next day, when they found everything they had presented them with hung with a string on the shore, and the Esquimaux gone."

[2] We may refer to the recent experiences of the Arctic traveller, Dr. Nansen, in this respect, and the discussions which have taken place on the subject in the Royal Geographical Society.

Ref. to Page of Text.
Page 15 (continued)

printed text again refers to the *Kort* for an illustration; but no map is meant. The MS. simply says, "The figure shows," and two pages are left blank for a drawing; but there is none. Nor is there any representation of this incident on either of the woodcuts.

Page 16

For several days, the vessels continued beset with ice, sometimes immoveably fixed, at other times able to proceed a little, but all the time in great danger. They, however, put their trust in a merciful Providence. In mentioning this, Munk says, under July 26th, that on that day they all gave something to the poor, which seems a very peculiar proceeding in Hudson's Strait. If this incident has not been referred to a wrong date (for the 25th was a Sunday), it would seem that a special service was held, at which there was an offertory, the proceeds of which were

Page 17 destined for the poor-box on their return home. During these days, they remained quite near to the mainland, drifting about amongst the islets girding the coast, at times so close to the latter that under ordinary circumstances they might have brought a hawser on shore, but unable to find shelter from the ice, with which they had to battle unceasingly. At length, on the 31st of July,

Page 18 they reached a small cove or bay, where they were in comparative safety, and where Munk decided to wait until navigation should become possible. This place, which he called *Haresund (i.e.,* "Hare Sound"), is, we believe, represented by the river to the right on the woodcut facing p. 14, into which the ships are entering surrounded by ice.

During his stay here, Munk examined the country in order to ascertain its capabilites. It seems that, like many other Arctic explorers, he imagined himself to have found metalliferous rocks;

Page 19 but, as his samples were lost with the frigate, it is not known what they really were. However, the circumstance caused him, when a second voyage was in contemplation, to ask for some person skilled in such matters to be added to his staff. Munk also mentions the occurrence of much Talc, then known as " Russian Glass", a mineral likewise noticed by other Arctic travellers.

As they remained nearly a fortnight at *Haresund*, the question where it was situated is of no small interest. The direct information on this point given in the text amounts to this: that it was on the northern coast, in lat. 62° 20', distant not much less than 50 Danish miles from the entrance of the Strait, and near a large bay extending towards the north. Considering how Munk had been drifting forwards and backwards with the ice, no great weight can be attached to his vague estimate of the distance; nor is the latitude of much use in determining the position, as the main direction of the coast is east and west. As, however, in reality, there is only one place on the northern coast of Hudson's Strait which could be described as a large bay extending northwards, viz., the so-called North Bay, we must conclude that *Haresund* was situated not far from that. The question remains whether it was to the East or to the West of the opening of North Bay. In our opinion, *Haresund* was some place not far east of the point where North Bay branches off from Hudson's Strait—not unlikely Icy Cove, which Coats describes as a particularly safe harbour.[1]

M. Ravn,[2] on the contrary, and after him M. Lauridsen,[3] have suggested that Haresund might with probability be sought for near the Upper Savage Islands, to the west of North Bay, but without giving any reasons for the suggestion. As regards the latitude and the proximity to North Bay, some locality near those islands might answer the requirements of identification as well as Icy Cove, and, as regards the distance from the entrance of the Strait, even better. But we have already pointed out that no strong argument can be drawn from these circumstances. At the same time, other and very weighty considerations may be adduced in favour of seeking *Haresund* to the East of North Bay. In the first place, it should be observed that Munk could not have reached any place near the Upper Savage Islands without crossing the mouth of North Bay; but neither does he imply any such thing, nor does his narrative allow of the supposition that he did. Attentive perusal of his narrative will prove that, until he reached *Haresund*, he remained quite close to the shore; nor is there the smallest indication of his having left it, as he would have to do (and for a long time, too) if he had crossed North Bay. He says, moreover, that the large bay extending northwards was so full of ice that it was impossible in a boat to advance more than

---

[1] *Geography of Hudson's Bay*, p. 14: "Icy Cove is a most safe harbour . . . and good anchor-ground, where I sheltered our ship from ice when hard pressed."

[2] *Dansk Maanedskrift*, 1860, p. 90.

[3] *Jens Munk's Navigatio*, note 18.

Ref. to Page of Text.

Page 19 (continued)

an English mile into it, which well accords with the observations of Coats to the effect that in North Bay and White Strait there is such an abundance of ice "that it has been said all our iles of ice come from this streight".[1] The supposition that Munk had crossed the mouth of the Bay before arriving at *Haresund* is clearly not admissible. Far more probable is it that, after having, in the course of the short night, advanced a few leagues from *Rinsund*, Munk was arrested by the mighty stream of ice proceeding from North Bay and finally forced on to the shore (from which he had never departed far)—fortunately without suffering shipwreck, but being carried, almost miraculously, into a safe harbour east of the Bay. To this may be added, in the second place, that the subsequent action of Munk and his pilots, as we shall see presently, agrees very much better with the supposition that *Haresund* was Icy Cove, or some place in that neighbourhood, than with the supposition that it was some place at or near the Upper Savage Islands.

We should mention in passing that on Munk's map *Haresund* is marked to the East of a great Bay or Strait, which may represent North Bay—a circumstance which so far agrees with our view; but, as will be seen hereafter from our notes on the map, the argument which might be founded on this is not so conclusive that we should like to rest our opinion on it.

After a stay of nearly a fortnight at *Haresund*, during which time the crew found rest and refreshment, while the ice cleared away sufficiently to allow of unimpeded navigation, Munk started again on his voyage on August 9th, steering W.S.W.

Page 20 Early the following morning, he found himself opposite a coast, along which, to use his own words, "the pilots [*i.e.*, Gordon and Watson] steered a southerly course, supposing that we had arrived in a large bay". The only large bay in which it could be proper for them to follow the western shore in a southerly direction was, of course, Hudson's Bay; and the sequel shows that they really imagined themselves to have reached the latter, though how they can have made such a mistake seems well-nigh inexplicable. It is in looking for an explanation of the indisputable fact that they did so, that we come upon the point alluded to above as having a bearing on the whereabouts of

---

[1] *Geography of Hudson's Bay*, p. 16.

Haresund, and which we may, therefore, conveniently discuss first. The point is this: that they could not have come to the conclusion that they had already entered Hudson's Bay unless they had thought that, in leaving *Haresund*, they had left the western extremity of Hudson's Strait. Now it is true that, even if Watson had been there before, Gordon, who no doubt took the lead, was probably in Hudson's Strait for the first time in his life; nor had as yet much been published or become generally known concerning this waterway. But this much was known: that the distance from the entrance of the Strait to the Bay was considerably in excess of what they had sailed to *Haresund*, even on their own somewhat liberal estimate. This, therefore, they must have overlooked or disregarded; but it seems difficult to understand how they could have done so, unless the real situation of *Haresund* be such as to countenance, in some measure, the idea that it was near the western extremity of the Strait. It is easy to see both that this would be the case if *Haresund* was Icy Cove, or some place in that vicinity, and also that no place near the Upper Savage Islands could meet this requirement. Had *Haresund* been in the last-named neighbourhood, they must have known themselves to be still in the Strait, on or near the northern shore, and the mistake in question could not have been committed; but, if *Haresund* was near Icy Cove, the matter would stand very differently. Not far west of that locality the coast takes a somewhat sharp turn, and trends away to the north for a considerable distance into the North Bay, just as it might be expected to do at the western extremity of the Strait. If, therefore, *Haresund* was near Icy Cove, there would be nothing in their recollection of that place, to prevent them from entertaining the idea, that the coast which they discovered on the morning of August 10th was the west coast of Hudson's Bay. It is because that idea is compatible with the identification of *Haresund* with Icy Cove, but not with the supposition that it was at or near the Upper Savage Islands, that we find a strong confirmation of our view in the action of the pilots on the occasion in question.

In passing, we may notice a fact which at first sight might appear to indicate that already, while they were still at *Haresund*, they imagined themselves to be at the entrance of Hudson's Bay, *viz.*, that they sailed away from thence towards the west-south-west, just as they did afterwards when they had really reached that

Ref. to Page of Text.

Page 20 *(continued)*

Ref. to Page of Text.
Page 20 *(continued)*

point. As, however, Munk expressly says that the wind was N.W., and that they sailed as near the wind as they could, it follows that their intention then was to make their way as best they could westwards, as they had done before; and no such conclusion can be drawn from that circumstance.

In resuming now the consideration of the action of the pilots in steering south along the coast which they saw before them in the morning of August 10th, there is another consideration which renders it difficult to understand how they can have fallen into such an error as the one they committed. Very little had appeared in print concerning the west coast of Hudson's Bay; but Purchas had published at least this much: that Button had sailed 200 leagues across the Bay before reaching the opposite shore. Nevertheless the pilots imagined that they had crossed the Bay in a single day and short summer's night, sailing in the same direction as Button had done. It seems clear that either Munk's instructions and the personal information of the pilots must have been very imperfect, or else we must suppose that Gordon and Watson, when they, no doubt unexpectedly, saw that coast before them trending south, were so taken aback that they lost confidence in their instructions and the information at their disposal, and on a sudden impulse set them both aside in order to follow what turned out to be a false scent.

Whether Munk himself, at any time, or to any extent, shared the mistake of the pilots does not appear. An indication of his having done so might perhaps be suspected in the fact that in the printed text Munk describes the coast which they mistook for the West Coast of Hudson's Bay as "the western coast of *Fretum Christian*." But this is not the expression he originally intended to use. The MS. had originally "southern" (*Syndere*), which is correct, but which has been altered in the MS. into "western" (*Vester*); nor is it difficult to suggest considerations which may have induced Munk to make this change. The portion of the coast in question no doubt did trend from south to north, and was in so far a "western" coast, a circumstance which Munk may have wished to emphasise in order to explain to some extent how the mistake came about. Again, he may have considered that the epithet of southern, as applied to this coast, would ill agree with his subsequent statement that the pilots steered a southerly course along it. But, in any case, he plainly describes it as the coast of the Strait; and his language with reference to North Bay and the other bay further west, to which he alludes (perhaps White Strait), does not in the least imply that they were portions of Hudson's Bay, or anything else than inlets from Hudson's Strait. At the same time, of course, it must be borne in mind that Munk wrote his account after his return home, in accordance with the fuller and more correct information which he had by that time acquired. Munk evidently wishes to decline the responsibility for the mistake and its consequences, and rightly so. As the pilots, Gordon in particular, had been engaged by the King especially with a view to attempting the Passage, Munk could not have taken upon himself the responsibility of refusing to act on their suggestion, even if he doubted its wisdom.

Ref. to Page of Text.

Page 20 (continued)

The printed text simply says that the idea of their having arrived in a large bay turned out a mistake; but, in the MS., the following remarkable words are added: *som Derres Relatsion Derom Udviser* (that is, "as their relation concerning it shows"). On the face of it, this passage seems to imply that Munk, when he wrote it, had before him some statement drawn up by Gordon and Watson in which this incident was referred to; and this is in itself very likely. The chief pilots on voyages of discovery often prepared such reports; and Gordon and Watson may very probably have utilised their enforced leisure at Churchill Harbour for that purpose. Or Munk may refer to some special statement with regard to the digression into Ungava Bay, which he may have required of them for his own justification in respect of the great delay which was caused thereby; or, finally, it may have been only a journal of theirs, containing notes put down from time to time, in order to serve as material for a report. But, in any case, no such document is now preserved. If Munk, at the time when he wrote his book, possessed such a statement, it has shared the fate of nearly all his other papers, and we have no means of guessing its contents or of knowing whether any valuable information has been lost with it. At the same time, it is quite possible that Munk does not refer to any written statement before him when he wrote his book, but only to explanations given by them while on the voyage. In this case the present tense of the verb *udviser* ("shows") has simply been transferred from his notes to his MS. without being altered to the past tense, as is the case in several other places. On this latter

Ref. to Page of Text. supposition, it will be easily understood that the passage was omitted from the printed text, as it would have been misleading.

Page 20 (continued) There is nothing to show with any certainty where Munk's land-fall was on the southern shore of Hudson's Strait. A W.S.W. course, such as he says that they steered on leaving *Haresund*, would, supposing this to be at or near Icy Cove, carry them to some point near Stupart's Bay; but we do not consider it probable that they struck the coast so far west. It is true, that in that neighbourhood the coast does trend north and south, and might so far deceive them; but this direction is not maintained very far south. Between Stupart's Bay and Cape Hope's Advance the coast forms a shallow bay, so that Munk and his party could not have followed the coast into Ungava Bay without sailing for some considerable distance in a south-easterly, and—in order to round the Cape—even in a north-easterly, direction; and that is not very probable. That there is no mention of it in Munk's narrative does not prove anything in this respect, because, as we have already mentioned (see p. 63), that portion of it which treats of the voyage from *Haresund* to Ungava Bay and back again as far as to Hudson's Bay, is so much condensed that there would be nothing surprising in such a detail being omitted. But it is scarcely conceivable that the pilots would not have found out their mistake at once, if they had found the coast turning back eastwards and northwards, in the way it does. As already stated, there are no means of settling the point with any certainty; but, upon the whole, we consider it most probable that Munk's landfall was east of Cape Hope's Advance. Their course from Icy Cove must in that case have been rather S. of S.W., whilst Munk says that they steered W.S.W.; but, as the north wind with which they started increased into a gale of great violence, causing such a tremendous sea as no one on board had seen before, it would not be surprising if they had been set considerably to the south-east. In fact, we hold that what happened to Munk was very much the same which had happened to Hudson, who, setting out from the Isle of God's Mercy, somewhere on the northern coast of the Strait, and steering S.W., found himself embayed behind Cape Hope's Advance, and, following the coast southwards, came into Ungava Bay.[1]

---

[1] *Purchas his Pilgrimes*, vol. iii, p. 599.

Having reached the southern or south-western shore of the Strait, they sailed along it in a southerly direction unimpeded by ice, and came at last to what Munk describes as a large promontory in lat. 60°. Munk, who gives very few dates in this part of his narrative, does not say how long they were in reaching this point; but the expression which he uses in the MS., viz., *med tidens Længde* (literally, "with the length of time"), seems to indicate a certain impatience on his part, as if he had not looked hopefully on their proceedings at the time. From the printed text, it appears as if Munk had called this promontory *Alecke Ness Kap*, which would be a curiously-formed name, because *Nes* and *Kap* mean the same thing; but the last word is not really a part of the name finally intended by Munk for this headland. In the MS. a blank space is left for the name, followed by the word *Kap*, the original intention having evidently been to choose a name ending in *Kap*, like *Nordkap*. *Alecke Ness* having been selected, the word *Kap* ought to have been omitted, and has remained only by a blunder of the copyist. On the map, the name is simply *Alcenes*. The first part of this name (of which the proper spelling would be Alkenes) is no doubt derived from *Alk* (Auk), and was suggested by the occurrence of many birds of that or similar kinds. Besides giving the latitude of this promontory (60°), Munk states that near it a large bay enters into the land in a south-westerly direction; but the identification of it is, nevertheless, not free from difficulty, because the coast-line from Cape Hope's Advance southwards nowhere presents any feature that could be described as a promontory. Mr. Lauridsen has suggested[1] that *Alkenes* may be the eastern extremity of the Island of Ekkertaujok, which lies so close to the mainland that the island, being longer from east to west than from south to north, may very likely have presented itself to Munk as a huge promontory. The eastern extremity of the island, moreover, is situated in lat. 59° 50′, only ten minutes below the latitude ascribed to *Alecke Nes* Cape. The bay of which Munk speaks, M. Lauridsen identifies[2] with Hope's Advance Bay. But this suggestion, though plausible enough in itself, and, as it were, a step in the right direction, presents, if followed up, difficulties which seem to

Ref. to Page of Text.

Page 20 *(continued)*

---

[1] In his edition of Munk's *Navigatio*, note 22.
[2] *Op. cit.*, note 24.

Ref. to Page of Text.

Page 20 (continued)

demand a different solution. If the eastern extremity of the Island of Ekkertaujok be Munk's *Alkenes*, Munk must have passed through the Strait between it and the island of Akpatok without mentioning the fact, which is not at all likely, as the Strait is only a few English miles wide. Besides this, the configuration of land and sea would in that case have appeared to him so remarkable that he could not be supposed to have passed it over in silence. Akpatok extending, as it does, about 70 miles towards the east, would not have appeared to Munk as an island, and the water on which he would have found himself after passing the Strait would not have appeared to him as a part of the sea from which he came, but as a separate inland sea. Hope's Advance Bay, too, cannot be described as stretching inwards due southwest, its main extension being due west; nor could it by any

Page 21

means be named or described as *Synder Bogt*[1] (the South Bay) in reference to the main part of Ungava Bay. Mr. Lauridsen, indeed, is of opinion that Munk mentions Akpatok under the name of *Snee Öeland;* but this, again, will not be found to agree with Munk's statements. Of *Snee Öeland*, Munk says that its north-western extremity was very high land, whilst the southern was surrounded by much ice, which implies that the island had its main extension from S.E. to N.W.; but Akpatok is a long narrow island, of which the main extension is from S.W. to N.E. No part of it could possibly be described as its north-western extremity. Besides, Munk mentions *Snee Öeland* as having been approached on the return journey when they were five Danish (22½ English) miles out of *Synder Bogt;* but, if Munk, as M. Lauridsen thinks, sailed between Ekkertaujok and Akpatok into Hope's Advance Bay, he must have passed Akpatok quite close, both going in and coming out, and cannot possibly have sighted it when about twenty English miles out.

It seems to us, therefore, much more probable that Munk, following the coast of the Strait southwards from Cape Hope's Advance, at some distance from the shore, failed to observe both the very narrow sound between Ekkertaujok and the mainland and the strait between that island and Akpatok, which

---

[1] It is not quite certain that *Synder bogt* —which does not occur on the map—is intended as a name. It may be a mere descriptive epithet, but we have found it convenient to treat it as a name.

although broader is rendered almost as inconspicuous by a small island lying close to the south of the opening and dividing the channel. Munk would, in that case, have taken the northern coasts of both of the islands (Ekkertaujok and Akpatok) to be the continuation of the coast of the mainland round a large bay; and—very likely steering across this apparent bay at some distance from the land—he would have entered Ungava Bay by rounding the eastern point of Akpatok, which point lies in lat. 60° 10′, and would be Munk's *Alecke Nes*. In this case, Ungava Bay (Munk's *Synder Bogt*) would appear to him as a portion of the sea from which he came, stretching away to the S.W., as he says that his *Synder Bogt* did. Instead of identifying *Snee Öeland* with Akpatok, as M. Lauridsen prefers to do, we consider that the name is intended for Green Island, which is certainly placed in two different positions on different maps, but which in either of the positions assigned to it might very well have been approached by Munk at the distance mentioned by him, N.N.W. of the easternmost point of Akpatok. On the English Admiralty chart, it is expressly described as high land, and its main extension appears to be from S.E. to N.W., which perfectly agrees with Munk's statements.

On Munk's map, *Alkenes* is not drawn as projecting so far towards the east—almost cutting off Ungava Bay from the Strait—as it ought to have been if representing the two islands taken together; but no serious objection to our explanation can be based on this, as nothing is more likely than that Munk, not having penetrated sufficiently far into the western portion of Ungava Bay, did not know how far the coast receded on the south side of his *Alkenes*, and how great, therefore, the length of the supposed promontory was. *Snee Öeland* is placed on Munk's map far outside Ungava Bay, and can therefore not be meant for Akpatok. Least of all could it be identified with Akpatok if Ekkertaujok is identified with *Alkenes*, as in this case Munk must have known that the distance between his *Snee Öeland* and his *Alkenes* was only as much as a few English miles.

Munk's explanation of the name *Snee Öeland* (*i.e.*, Snow Island) is curious. He says that "inasmuch as there were many birds flying to and from the land, and as it appeared white, being covered with snow", they called it *Snee Öeland*, a name

Ref. to Page of Text.

Page 21 *(continued)*

Ref. to Page of Text.

Page 21 (continued)

which might naturally be suggested by the last-mentioned circumstance, but has no reference whatever to the abundance of birds. The presence of many auks or similar birds may, on the contrary, very likely have determined the choice of the name of *Alkenes* for the promontory on which he bestowed this name. There can therefore be little doubt that some confusion has here crept into the text; but, as the printed book in this respect agrees with the MS., the responsibility falls in this case on Munk himself. In the printed text, we further read that the shape or appearance of this land is shown in the accompanying *Kort*, which seems to imply that some special illustration of it was intended; but this appears to be only one of the "improver's" misleading alterations; for the MS. merely says *Besee Kortet* ("See the Chart"), which laconic sentence seems to refer to the whole of the preceding account. As no space is left in the MS. for any illustration of *Snee Öeland*, there can be no doubt that *Kort*, in this place, means the general map, which is inserted here, and in which the position of the island is indicated, but this conveys no information as to its appearance.

Munk says that, the "English pilot" (of course, Gordon) at first intimated that the land bordering on the South Bay was "the place which we searched for", but that he soon revoked that opinion. The exact meaning of these words we are left to guess. Nothing is said in Munk's account as to the grounds on which Gordon concluded that he had been mistaken—points on which it would be of the utmost interest to have had information. But Munk's account of this digression is much condensed, as if in disgust of the blunder which had led to it, and by which so much valuable time was lost.

. It was on the 14th of August that they passed *Snee Öeland*, after having left Ungava Bay, making no doubt the best of their way westwards; but on the 20th, they had not yet reached farther than a point which they might have reached already on the 10th if the pilots had not made the mistake which brought them into Ungava Bay. Munk says, with evident satisfaction, that they were then back in their proper course, and the point is determined by Munk's statements to the effect that they were in lat. 62° 20', and that in that part of the Strait the distance between the land on either side was not more than sixteen Danish miles. This is, in effect, the width of the Strait in its narrowest part, between Big

Island on the north and Prince of Wales's Island on the south; *Ref. to Page of Text.*
and the fact that Munk makes an accurate statement on the
subject is rather remarkable; for he says at the same time that, Page 21
on account of fog, they could not see land on either side. From *(continued)*
this latter circumstance, it follows that Munk must either have
inserted this statement when he wrote his book, on information
obtained afterwards, or else that he had been supplied with
the information at the time from some source other than his own
observation. Munk may have passed this part of the Strait on
the homeward voyage in 1620 in clear weather, and may have
guessed that this was the place where he had found himself on
the 20th of August the year before; but the passage reads as if
they knew, when they sailed up in 1619, that in that part of the
Strait the width was only about 16 Danish miles.

Upon the whole, it may be observed that, after the return from
Ungava Bay, no more mistakes were committed in navigation, and
they seem after that event to have proceeded on their business,
knowing what they were about. If that impression is true, it
would prove that the mistake committed in steering south on the
10th of August was caused, not by want of information, but by
an error of judgment, a neglect of the information which they
possessed, and by which they ought to have let themselves be
guided.

That they had employed six days in coming up from Ungava
Bay to the place in the Strait where they found themselves on
the 20th of August, was no doubt caused by adverse winds; for
Munk says that on that day the wind became easterly, and that
they accordingly set their course west-by-north, implying that they
had hitherto been unable to follow a direct course up the Strait.
At some later time, which is not indicated, they appear to have
changed their direction for a more northerly one—W.N.W. half N.
—on which course they continued until they reached lat. 63° 20',
the most northerly point specified in Munk's account of his
expedition. Here it must be inferred that they again changed
their course for a more southerly one; but there is no direct statement to this effect in Munk's narrative; nor is there any indication
of the date when they did reach the latitude of 63° 20'. As we
have already pointed out more than once, the whole account of
the sailing down to and up from Ungava Bay, until Hudson's
Bay was reached, is extremely condensed. In this portion,

Ref. to Page of Text.
Page 21 (continued)

Munk gives only such general statements as "*In Summa*, we sailed W.N.W., etc.," after which he introduces various *Items*, culled from his notes and very loosely connected with each other.

Page 22

Munk states that, on their way to the point where they reached the latitude of 63° 20′, they had been at several localities, of which he says that they "are not now named here, but will be found pictured and described with diligence in the sea-chart which has been prepared to show this, according to their dimensions, quantity, quality, size and shape." A small hand is inserted in this place as a mark of reference. There is, however, no map or plate annexed to the book showing any such thing, but only the general map already mentioned, which is marked with a hand. If anyone should conclude, from the absence of such a chart, that anything originally intended for the reader had been omitted or suppressed, a glance at the MS. would at once undeceive him. There is in the MS. no trace of this grandiloquent announcement, which is doubtless due solely to the literary "improver", whose handiwork we have met with in several places, more particularly in references to the illustrations. Munk's MS. simply says, "which are not now here described, [but] which are, nevertheless, indicated on the accompanying map number," after which a large space is left open. Accordingly, where Munk in the sequel speaks of *Iisver*, *Söster*, and *Digses Eyland*, there is in the MS. a "*N.*," and a blank space for the number to be inserted when the map should be ready. This plan, however, was not ultimately followed: the names were inserted on the map itself, and, numbers having thus become superfluous, there is no allusion to any such in the printed text. From Munk's words, in the MS. as well as in the printed text, one would expect to find not a few places indicated on the map which are not referred to in the text; but, whatever be the reason, this is the case with two only; and that Munk does not allude more particularly to them in his narrative is no doubt due to the fact that he had not visited these places, but only passed by them. The expression used in the printed text, *vare wi paa* ("were we at") is ambiguous; but the MS. says plainly they *mödte under* the localities in question, which signifies that they "sailed close by" them. Under these circumstances, Munk could not, of course, have much to say concerning them. One of them is *Sydernes* ("the South Cape"), which name applies to some headland on the southern coast which can scarcely be any other than that on Prince of Wales Island. The other name which occurs on the map, but not in the text, is *Koldenes* (the "Cold Cape"), on the northern coast, which clearly represents the southern extremity of Big Island, where the coast commences to trend northwards. It would appear that Munk followed this coast for some distance northwards, as some of its main features are represented on his map; and it was very likely near it, somewhere near Fair Ness, that he reached his highest recorded latitude.[1]

Ref. to Page of Text.

Page 22 *(continued)*

As it is evident that Munk entered Hudson's Bay near Digges Islands, it follows of necessity that at some point or other he must have substituted—as we mentioned above—a south-westerly course for the more northerly one which had brought him into lat. 63° 20'. But his narrative does not supply us with any direct information as to the navigation between the point from which he adopted a more southerly course and his arrival at Hudson's Bay. He only communicates one "*item*" of his observations, which has reference to certain high islands which he passed; and there is nothing whatever to show that he did not, on this part of his voyage, notice other localities, which for some reason or other, he did not mention in his account.

The first locality mentioned by Munk near the western extremity of Hudson's Strait is this group of "high islands", to which he gives the name of *Iisver*,[2] no doubt on account of their being surrounded or covered with much ice. He says that they are marked on the map; but this is not the case, the name only being found there, *viz.*, close to the southern coast, and just within the western extremity of the Strait. For the identification of these islands, we find, in this place, only the indirect information that a sail of somewhat more than ten Danish miles from them in a westerly direction brings one near to the entrance into Hudson's Bay; but, in his account of the return voyage, Munk states that he left them to starboard, and that they were

---

[1] On *Sydernes* and *Koldenes*, see our observations on Munk's map.
[2] This rather remarkable name seems formed in analogy with several words in Icelandic ending in *ver*, and indicating places near the sea where some animals or other objects abound.

Ref. to Page of Text.
Page 22 (*continued*)

situated close to the mainland. These data, taken together, apply to no other land in this neighbourhood than Charles's Island, which we must suppose that he took for a group of islands. That it does present this appearance from some points of view or under some circumstances may be inferred from Capt. Coats' statement that "Cape Charles are a cluster of islands 90 miles east from Cape Digges, the northernmost of which is in the latitude of 62° 55'."[1] As will be shown more fully in our observations on the map, we consider that Charles Island (Munk's *Iisver*) is represented on Munk's map by a portion of the southern coast of Hudson's Strait, just above the name. Next to *Iisver*, Munk mentions two islands which he calls *Söster* (on the map *Systerne*—"the Sisters"), no doubt on account of their being somewhat similar and close together. Unfortunately, these islands are not marked distinctly on Munk's map, any more than his *Iisver*, and the name is misplaced far to the north of Munk's track—apparently in order to make room for a representation of a ship. For the identification of them, we are, therefore, altogether left to inference from Munk's text. In this, he says that one sights these islands "after advancing about ten miles westwards", which, in the absence of any other indication, must mean westwards from the last-named locality, *viz.*, the *Iisver*. Looking merely at a map, one is tempted to suspect that Salisbury and Nottingham Islands may be Munk's *Söster*, though they are perhaps rather too far apart to merit the name of "Sisters". This is, indeed, Mr. Lauridsen's view;[2] but Munk's further statements concerning his *Söster* will not, we believe, allow of their being identified with any other islands than the two largest of the Digges Islands. Munk implies very unmistakeably that they were situated at the very entrance to Hudson's Bay, on the direct route, which is most emphatically the case with the Digges Islands, but not with Salisbury and Nottingham Islands. Munk further states that he sailed round the *Söster* sounding—a proceeding which, if the latter are meant, was as meaningless as it would be tedious, and even difficult, on account of the strong currents and the abundance of drift-ice round them. But it could easily be performed in the case of the Digges Islands, and would be quite

---

[1] *Geography of Hudson's Bay*, p. 31.
[2] See his edition of Munk's *Navigatio*, note 26.

intelligible, because it would be of interest to know whether, in entering the Bay, it was preferable to keep outside the islands or to pass between them and the mainland, as both Hudson and Button had done (of which, however, Munk was probably not aware), and as he himself afterwards did when homeward bound. Munk recommends the outer route, north of the islands, which is quite to be expected if the *Söster* are taken to be Digges Islands, but which would be a very strange piece of advice if the former are identical with Salisbury and Nottingham Islands--as a glance at any map showing their relative positions will prove. To this may be added that, according to Munk's subsequent statements, a westerly course from his *Söster* brings a navigator to Mansfield Island, which applies correctly to Digges Islands, whereas a westerly course from Nottingham Island would lead to a quite different place at the northern extremity of Hudson's Bay. We believe that Digges Islands (Munk's *Söster*) are represented on his map by the peculiar projection of the land at the junction between the south coast of Hudson's Strait and the east coast of Hudson's Bay. To this point, the name would have referred distinctly if it had not been moved towards the north.

Before proceeding further, we may notice a consideration which might be looked upon as presenting a difficulty in the way of our identifications—*viz.* that, if Salisbury and Nottingham Islands are not represented by Munk's *Söster*, we shall have to admit that he does not mention them at all, although he can scarcely be supposed not to have seen them. It is true that Salisbury Island appears to be rather low; nor does Nottingham Island, though more rocky, appear to attain any great elevation; but almost all navigators who have described a voyage through Hudson's Strait mention them; and it would not be reasonable to suppose that they were obscured by fog on both occasions when Munk passed them. In itself, this consideration would not be of sufficient weight to counterbalance to any extent the argument which we have adduced in favour of our view; but it would, nevertheless, present a difficulty in the interpretation of Munk's narrative, if this portion of it made any sort of pretension to completeness. This, however, as we have already pointed out, is by no means the case. If Munk had given a fairly full account of this portion of the voyage, stating day by day how they sailed, and what places they passed, and if nevertheless there were no

Ref. to Page of Text.
Page 22 *(continued)*

Ref. to Page of Text.
Page 22 (continued)

references to these two islands, it would certainly have been strange. But Munk does nothing of the kind. He gives no account at all of his sailing through the westernmost part of the Strait, but only an isolated statement about the *Iisver*, which seem to have attracted his particular notice. Under these circumstances, there is nothing extraordinary in the silence of the text concerning Salisbury and Nottingham Islands. There is the less occasion for founding any conclusions on this, as the two islands, if we mistake not, are marked on Munk's map, though wrongly placed, *viz.*, close to what represents the western coast of Meta Incognita. The only other islands which these could be supposed to represent, if not meant for Salisbury and Nottingham Islands, would be the Digges Islands; but the position of these islands, at the very entrance to Hudson's Bay, is so striking that Munk cannot be supposed to have misplaced them on the map so far inside the Strait. It is far more probable that Salisbury and Nottingham Islands have been pushed somewhat towards the east; nor is it difficult to suggest explanations of this error. The place where the two islands ought to have been marked is occupied by the figure of a ship; and it is quite possible that the two islands may have been crowded out by that figure, just as the name of *Systrene* thereby has been pushed up towards the northern coast, and as—in another part of the map—the name *Munckenes* has been displaced by the figure of a ship to such an extent that it seems to apply to the island in the entrance of the Strait. Or the fact may, perhaps, with more probability be explained by assuming that Munk, when he came to work up his notes, did not find them sufficiently explicit; and, more particularly, that, although he had seen Salisbury and Nottingham Islands, he was not clear about their position. This explanation we are so much the more inclined to adopt, as it would also go far to account for Munk's brevity in dealing with this part of his voyage, and particularly for his omitting all mention of the two islands in his text.

Before leaving the subject of these islands, we may mention that our identification of Munk's *Iisver* differs from that of M. Lauridsen, the only other writer who has approached this subject. According to him,[1] *Iisver* are the Digges Islands, an opinion which is as contradictory to his own identification of Munk's *Söster* with

---

[1] See his edition of Munk's *Navigatio*, note 26.

Salisbury and Nottingham Islands as it is with Munk's text; for according to the latter, the *Iisver* are to be sought for ten Danish miles east both of the entrance of the Bay and of the *Söster;* but Digges Islands are at the very entrance of the Bay, and situated to the south-west of Salisbury and Nottingham Islands.

Ref. to Page of Text.

Page 22 (continued)

Munk next states that, proceeding westwards from these islands, one comes to a large flat island, which he calls *Digses Eyland*. Munk's description of this, and his statements with regard to its position, leave no doubt of its being what we call Mansfield Island; and it has been recognised as such already by M. Ravn,[1] whom M. Lauridsen follows.[2] Munk's transfer, however, of the name of Digges Island to Mansfield Island requires an explanation. M. Lauridsen has suggested that Munk may have been misled by the fact that, on Hessel Gerritsz.'s map, Mansfield Island is marked, but not named, and, at the same time, placed so near to the Digges Islands as almost to form a group with them, and he thinks that Munk may have supposed that the name "Digges Ilandt" was meant for the largest of that group. This is, of course, quite possible; but it does not appear to us altogether probable; for the name in question is printed on the map above Mansfield Island, in a slanting position, pointing quite unmistakeably to the largest of the Digges Islands, and not at all to Mansfield Island. There are, moreover, circumstances which seem to indicate that Munk deliberately proposed what he knew to be an innovation as regards this name. Whilst the *Söster* are mentioned by name in the MS., space being left open only for a reference number, the space for the name, as well as for the number, of the long flat island to the west of them is left blank. From this we may infer that he named the former in his notes, but did not give a name to the latter till his book went to press. We may notice also that, where the name occurs a second time (see p. 23), the expression used in the printed text (not in the MS.) is, "that which is now called *Digses Eyland*". This is precisely the phrase which Munk uses elsewhere in introducing a new name— a phrase, besides, which would be meaningless if Munk employed the name as it had been employed by his predecessors. Taking these facts into due consideration, we find it most probable that

---

[1] *Dansk Maanedskrift*, 1860, p. 91.
[2] See his edition of Munk's *Navigatio*, note 27.

Ref. to Page of Text.

Page 22 (continued) when Munk came to consider finally the question of these names, he decided to retain that of "the Sisters", which may have appeared to him particularly appropriate, although he was aware that on Gerritsz.'s map the largest of them was named *Digges Ilandt;* and that he transferred at the same time the name of *Digges Ilandt* to the much larger island, not far off, which had so greatly attracted his attention, and which, as far as he was aware, was nameless. It had indeed been named by Button; but his account had not yet been published.[1]

Page 23 Concerning Mansfield Island, too, Munk states that he sailed round it sounding, as he had done in the case of "the Sisters"— presumably in order to compare the passages east and west of it.

When clear of the islands, near the western extremity of Hudson's Strait, Munk found himself at length in that mysterious inland sea which had been discovered (or rather *re-*discovered by Hudson) nine years before, and which was then and for long after confidently expected to lead to the much-sought-for Passage. Munk bestowed upon it the name of *Novum Mare*, or (as it is on the map) *Novum Mare Christian;* and he was perfectly justified in proposing a name for it, because at that time it had no name as a whole. The southern portion, which Hudson himself had explored, was called by his name, while the western portion went by the name of Button's Bay. Munk's book is the earliest in which this sea is found treated of as a whole, and his map is the earliest on which it is represented in its entirety. His name, therefore, has theoretically every claim to general adoption. In England, however, where Munk's book did not become known till long after, the name of Hudson's Bay soon came to be applied to the whole of it; and, as the land around it came under English dominion, the English name has prevailed. For the same reason, the name of *Nova Dania*, which Munk bestowed on the country round his wintering place, never came into general use and become obsolete, like several other names which have been proposed for it.

---

[1] The name given by Button was really Mansell Island, after his relative, Admiral Sir Robert Mansell. It seems, however, at a very early date to have been corrupted into Mansfield Island, which is now generally received (See Miller Christy, *Voyages of Foxe and James*, p. 188 *n.*).

Perhaps at no point in Munk's voyage do we miss the guidance which a knowledge of Munk's instructions would have afforded us, more than at his setting out on this "New Sea". Up to this point, they can scarcely have contained much of special interest, because Munk had, in any case, to make his way through Hudson's Strait; and it would be an object to reach the sea beyond as early as possible in the year. But, arrived at the western extremity of the Strait, Munk had more than one course to choose between, and it would have been of the greatest interest to know what he was enjoined to do, and why. Some light is thrown upon the question by the account of the diversion into Ungava Bay. On that occasion, as soon as they thought that they had arrived at the western coast of Hudson's Bay, they turned immediately southwards, following the coast while searching for a certain place. What sort of place this was, how it was to be recognised, with what object it was sought, we are not told. In regard to these and similar questions, we are left to form inferences from what was actually done afterwards; but, bearing those proceedings in mind, we need not feel surprise at seeing Munk, as soon as he really was in the Bay, unhesitatingly steer across it in a south-westerly direction in search of the southern portion of the opposite shore. *Ref. to Page of Text. Page 23 (continued)*

Of the crossing, Munk gives but few particulars. As we have already observed, the account of his voyage from August 20th to September 7th is a good deal condensed, in comparison with the earlier and later portions, and we have suggested that in a measure this may have been caused by some imperfection of his notes. Generally speaking, however, this brevity is probably to be explained simply by supposing that Munk did not think it worth while to recount day by day the incidents of the navigation between the two dates mentioned, during which time they do not appear to have set foot on land. He wrote, apparently, not so much with a view of narrating the voyage itself, as to give an account of the places visited and the fate of the expedition; nor can he have foreseen that these details would have an interest for historians centuries after his own time. The mere sailing with both the ships across the Atlantic, up the Strait and across the Bay, would not, of course, supply him with such materials for a stirring or even readable account as he found in their first experiences in Arctic travelling—their danger and adventures in

Ref. to Page of Text.

Page 23 (continued)

the ice, their meeting with the natives, of which we read in the first part of the narrative—or in the gradual succumbing of the crew, and the dangerous return voyage, afterwards told. The tragic fate of the expedition, and the responsibility which naturally would be laid upon Munk in this respect, would, besides, afford every inducement for him to give as detailed an account of their winter life as he could.

Munk says that the course from the north end of his *Digses Erland* (Mansfield Island) to the harbour where he wintered is S.W. by S. and S.W., and that, when one comes into 30 fathoms, one may steer more southerly until the land comes into sight. He also says that it is a sail of three days and three nights; but it is not quite clear whether this statement is meant to indicate the time actually consumed or the time which ordinarily would be required for the crossing, nor whether that space of time is supposed to cover the whole passage or only so much of it as should be sailed S.W. by S. and S.W. In any case, a glance at a chart indicating the depth of the water shows the correctness of Munk's direction, as far as it goes. Inasmuch as nobody is known to have been in the harbour of Churchill before Munk, and as he only once sailed straight across the Bay to Churchill, the sailing-direction in question cannot have been supplied to Munk from any other source, nor can it be the result of repeated experience on his own part. It is simply a statement as to how he came there. Acting, as it seems, on his instructions, he sailed across the Bay in a south-westerly direction, until the decreasing depth indicated that he was nearing the opposite coast. He then turned south to follow it, found himself embayed behind Cape Churchill, and accidentally discovered Port Churchill, into which he entered, being obliged to seek shelter.

Page 24

Munk says that it was with great difficulty that he got into this harbour, on account of the severe weather which prevailed, and which also, as he implies, was the cause of both ships not coming in together. He says that in the storm *Lamprenen* had strayed (*var forvildet*) from them; and, if nothing else had been said about the movements of the sloop, the natural interpretation of Munk's words would be that the two vessels had lost each other in the gale and fog which he mentions. But he says immediately afterwards that the sloop rejoined him on September 9th, and that she had been along the coast to the north, where an opening had been supposed to exist, which, however, turned out not to be the case. It is not in the least probable that the party in the sloop, if they had accidentally lost the other vessel in a violent gale, would have gone off on a voyage of discovery towards the north. They would most certainly have had other things to think of; nor would they have been able to do exploration work in such stress of weather as Munk describes. We consider it far more probable, therefore, that the separation of the vessels was not accidental but intentional, and that the word *forvildet* (*i.e.*, lost or strayed) does not refer to the departure of the sloop, but to her failing to rejoin the larger vessel as expected.

Ref. to Page of Text.

Page 24 (*continued*)

The point above raised is of considerable importance, because Munk's map is the earliest published on which the West Coast of Hudson's Bay is laid down. The only part of this coast which Munk can have known from his own observation, is that along which he sailed, on his homeward voyage, in order to round the ice-belt which held him to the shore; but much more than that is shown on his map, and that not very incorrectly. If Munk derived the knowledge by which he delineated the coast from observations made on his own expedition, it must have been from the explorations of Watson in the sloop. These would necessarily require more time and more favourable circumstances than is compatible with the supposition that the sloop was only accidentally separated from the larger vessel by stress of weather, shortly before the arrival at Churchill River. If, on the contrary, we suppose that the sloop had been sent away on purpose some time before, all difficulties in that respect disappear.

Our view of the matter is, therefore, that the party in the sloop had been sent off by Munk in a westerly direction when they first entered Hudson's Bay, with orders to explore, with special reference to the reported existence of a passage there, as much of the northern part of the west coast as they could manage to examine within a certain time, and that, after so doing, they were ordered to proceed southwards along the west coast, in order to rejoin the frigate in a certain latitude. We suppose that Munk meanwhile examined the localities near the entrance of Hudson's Bay; and after that crossed the Bay, making for the point where he had ordered the sloop to meet him. Finally, we take Munk's words that the sloop was *forvildet* to mean that, not seeing her in the appointed neighbourhood, he concluded that she had missed him on account of the bad weather.

If it should be objected that it would be a hazardous thing thus to separate the vessels and trust to their meeting again at some such distant *rendezvous*, we would observe that, although they cannot have known anything about Churchill Harbour, they most likely were well aware that Button had sailed right across the "New Sea" in a south-westerly direction, and had there found a coast stretching far towards the north. They may have known within what latitudes the coast which he had discovered was situated; and they may very reasonably have considered that they would not have any difficulty in finding each other on that coast again in a given latitude.

Munk says that the sloop had been *under det Nörreland* ("under the northern land")—which expression, of course, must mean that part of the west coast of the Bay which was north of Churchill River. But the *Nörreland* may perfectly well be understood as comprising what he called "the mainland on the north side", and which he came to on August 11th, 1620 (see p. 53).

It is, of course, much to be regretted that Munk does not give any account of the search for the Passage which was carried out by the sloop; but he may very naturally have thought it not worth while, as the search was fruitless. We shall refer again to this matter in our observations on Munk's map.

The Wintering at Port Churchill.

We have hitherto referred to Munk's wintering-place as if there were no uncertainty as to his having wintered at Port Churchill; nor is there in reality any occasion at all for doubt on the subject. Both the ample description which Munk gives of the locality in his text, and the bird's-eye view which is shown on the woodcut facing p. 23, apply so exactly to Churchill Harbour, and to that alone of all the places on the coast, as to exclude all uncertainty; besides which, the fact of Munk having wintered at Port Churchill had been demonstrated by the discovery of unmistakable relics of his sojourn there, even before the geographical features of the place became sufficiently known to admit of the coincidence of his description with the real configuration of Churchill Harbour being recognised. We shall have an opportunity hereafter for adverting to these facts more fully; but it will be proper here to mention that, in spite of the convincing nature of the facts advanced above, several writers and cartographers at different times have put forth very erroneous suggestions as to the whereabouts of Munk's wintering-place. These mistakes are mostly traceable—as, indeed, has often been stated before—to Isaac de la Peyrère, whose abstract of Munk's narrative (in his book *Relation du Groenland*) we have had occasion to mention more than once. Somehow La Peyrère failed to realise that Munk, after reaching the latitude of 63° 20', continued his voyage for a considerable distance towards the south-west; and he understood the matter as if Munk had wintered in that latitude. It is true that La Peyrère's words do not necessarily bear this interpretation, but that he really meant to say so is evident from his map, on which Churchill Harbour, with Munk's wintering-place, is shown in lat. 63° 20'. We shall explain this more fully in discussing Munk's map. Suffice it here to say that La Peyrère's error continued to be repeated without criticism in books and on maps, until it was discovered that Churchill Harbour is really situated in about lat. 59°. Afterwards another mistake arose. Some authors, who either did not know, or did not give due weight to the strong evidence connecting Munk's winter quarters with Churchill Harbour, allowed themselves to be misled by La Peyrère's indication of the latitude, separated these two localities, and placed Munk's winter-quarters high up on the western coast of Hudson's Bay far from Churchill River. It is thus shown on a few maps of the 18th century, but the earliest writer who has adopted this view is, as far as we are aware, Sir John Barrow,[1] who fixes the place at Chesterfield Inlet; and his example was followed by several writers and map-makers. On the other hand, Mr. Ravn,[2] though fully aware of La Peyrère's mistake, yet falls into error from not giving due weight to the evidence afforded by Munk's description of the locality and the subsequent discovery of relics of the expedition at Churchill; in consequence of which he is inclined to believe that

Ref. to Page of Text.

Page 24 (*continued*)

---

[1] Sir John Barrow, *Chronological History of Arctic Voyages* (London, 1818), p. 231.

[2] *Udsigt over de Reiser*, etc. (*Dansk Maanedskrift*, 1860, p. 91).

Ref. to Page of Text.
Page 24 (continued)

the Severn River was Munk's wintering-place. As these mistakes have now only a literary interest, we need not here enter into further consideration of them; but it must be pointed out that La Peyrère could hardly have made his unfortunate mistake if Munk had not, strangely enough, omitted to state in his text the latitude of his "winter-harbour", as he calls it. Mr. Lauridsen,[1] indeed, is of opinion that Munk most likely did so purposely, by order of the King of Denmark, in order to conceal the situation of the harbour, where the larger ship had been left behind, lest anyone should go in search of it and carry her away. But this theory does not appear to have any sound foundation, seeing that the suppression of the figure indicating the latitude would have been quite ineffectual to conceal the whereabouts of the vessel, as long as the other very ample information concerning the harbour in which she lay was not withheld. Following Munk's sailing direction from Mansfield Island, no navigator could fail to strike the south-western coast of the Bay within a moderate distance, north or south, of the harbour; and, though three or four rivers enter the Bay within the extreme points at which he might arrive, the outer approach of Port Churchill is so characteristic, and the description of it given by Munk (for the professed purpose of guiding future navigators to the port where he says that *Enhiörningen* was left) is so clear and accurate, that no one willing to devote a few days to the search could fail to find it. No one who wished to find the vessel, and had access to Munk's book, would be kept back for want of the figure of the latitude; and that so much the less, as the map, on which the relative position of the various localities is represented, of course indirectly gives the information which is not expressly conveyed in the text. We cannot, therefore, consider it probable that King Christian IV, who was himself a practical sailor, ordered Munk to suppress the latitude of the port for the purpose of concealment. To this we may add that, in 1624, when Munk's book was published, scarcely anyone can have expected that the ship would still be in such a condition as to be worth fetching home. For these reasons, we believe that the absence from the text of any indication of the latitude of Port Churchill is purely accidental.

---

[1] See his Edition of Munk's *Navigatio*, pp. xxvi-xxvii.

As far as is known, Munk was the first European who visited Port Churchill. Sir Thomas Button must have sailed by it in 1612 on his voyage from Hope's Check to Port Nelson, and again, in 1613, on returning to the former place; but, as we have no detailed record of the former of these voyages, and none at all of the second, it is not known whether he explored the locality, or even noticed its existence. The coast is low; and, as the river makes a sharp bend just before discharging its waters into the sea through a mouth not more than 1,100 yards wide, it would not appear as a river to anyone sailing by, but only as the entrance of a creek, which would not invite the attention of Button, who was in search of a passage into the Pacific. Under these circumstances, we are perfectly justified in claiming for Munk the discovery of Port Churchill; and, if priority of publication were to be strictly adhered to with respect to geographical names, it ought undoubtedly to bear the name given to it by Munk, or else that of Port Munk.

As soon as the adjacent land became frequented by Europeans, some fifty or sixty years after Munk, the value of Port Churchill as a commercial harbour was recognised. Maps of, as well as detailed information concerning, it are, therefore, now available, by means of which we may easily follow Munk's movements. There is a large and good map in J. Robson's book on Hudson's Bay.[1] The most modern (which is, however, in a great measure founded on Robson's) is the one which accompanies Mr. C. N. Bell's paper, *Our Northern Waters* (Winnipeg, 1884), and of which a reproduction is annexed. From these and other sources we extract the following details:—Churchill Harbour lies immediately within the mouth of the Churchill River. This is of about the same size as the Rhine, and has a very rapid course down to a point about seven and a half miles from the sea, where its bed suddenly expands, forming at highwater a lagoon about five miles long and four miles broad at the widest; whilst, at low-water, the river flows between stony flats on either side. At the lower end of this lagoon, the river again contracts; and, at the outlet, it is confined between two rocky ledges rising to a height of about 20 feet above the sea-level.

---

[1] J. Robson, *An Account of Six Years' Residence in the Hudson's Bay* (London, 1752).

That on the eastern side turns rather inwards, towards the north-

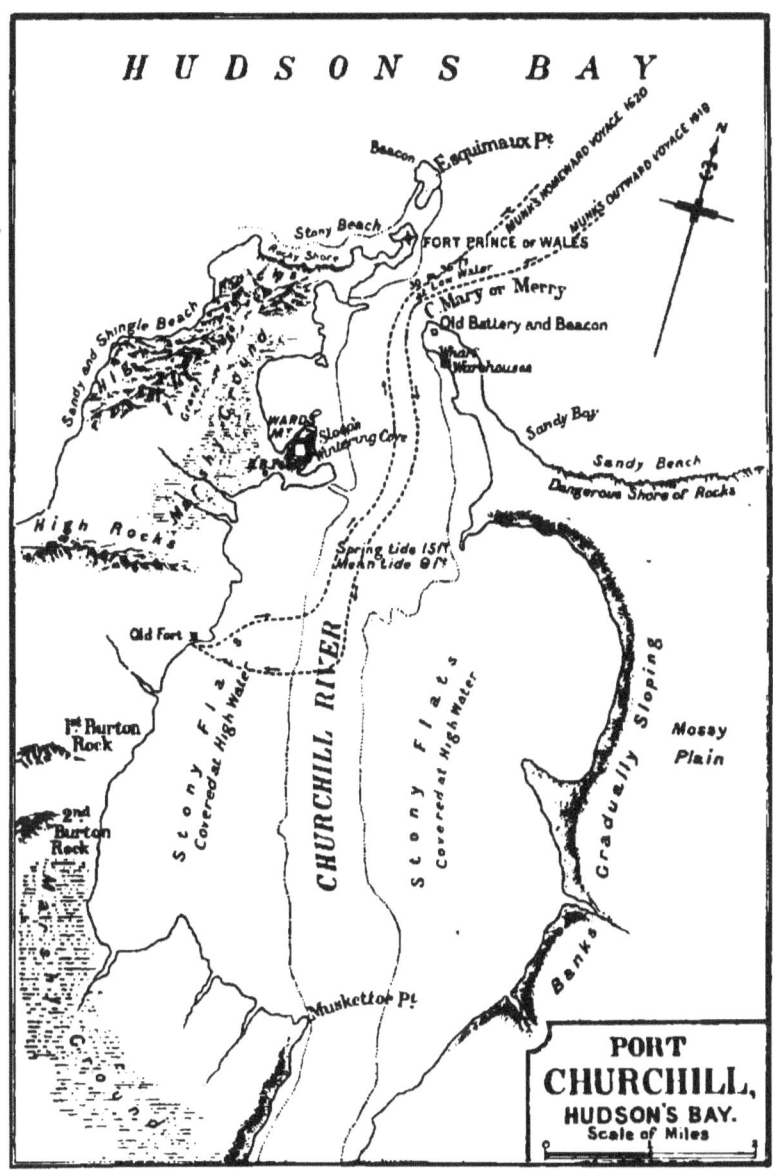

west; whilst the western ledge projects nearly a mile further into the sea, and at the same time bends towards the north-east, thus forcing the river (which, down to this point, flows almost due north) to take a decided turn to the north-east in entering the sea. The harbour is just within the eastern headland; and, as the western headland, by its shape and extent, protects the harbour from westerly and northerly gales, it is particularly safe. In this description, we easily recognise the long promontory on which Munk erected his beacons, and which would have to be left to starboard by anyone desiring to enter the harbour steering S.W. The width of the opening is only two-thirds of a mile, or less, but the depth is considerable—from seven to eight fathoms, as Munk says. The sunken rock in the entrance mentioned by Munk is not marked on the map, but is well known to exist, and is referred to by some writers-as St. Mary's, by others as Cap Merry's, Rock; but it is, as Munk says, easy to avoid. A comparison between the annexed map of Port Churchill and the bird's-eye view of the Port given on Munk's woodcut (facing page 23) will show that the main features of the locality, as well as the configuration of the adjoining parts of the coast, are unmistakeably, if somewhat rudely, reproduced in the latter.

Ref. to Page of Text.

Page 24 (continued)

It was on the 7th of September that Munk succeeded in bringing the frigate safe into harbour;' and his first care was to put together his pinnace, which had been brought out in pieces—a precaution of which we read in many accounts of Arctic voyages. Perhaps we may conclude from it that he intended, in any case, to remain some time in the place. In the night, fires were lit on the shore to warn the party in the sloop of Munk's whereabouts, lest they should pass the place by night and miss him. *Lamprenen* came in on the 9th from the north. Munk's next thought was for the health of his crews. He states that many of his men had fallen ill through overwork, caused by the unfavourable weather; but that the scurvy had already made its appearance amongst them, seems to be indicated by Munk's statement that they recovered as soon as they were, by his orders, brought on shore and had an opportunity of eating fresh fruit. It may be noted in passing that, although the kinds of fruit which he mentions are common in Denmark as well as in Norway, and are called by the same names, he speaks of their names as Norwegian, no doubt because his berry-gathering years had been spent in Norway. Another no doubt welcome change from

Ref. to Page of Text.

Page 24 (continued)

the salt diet of the ship was afforded by the White Whale, or Beluga, which occurs in such quantities in Hudson's Bay, and in the estuaries of the rivers which discharge into it, as to be the subject of a valuable fishery.[1] The remains of one of these animals attracted a Polar Bear, which Munk shot; and, at the request of the crew, it was utilised for the commissariat. Probably none of them had eaten Polar Bear before, although some parts of the Brown Bear are eaten in the North of Europe. By the Esquimaux (at least in Greenland), the Polar Bear is considered a great delicacy.

Page 25

Munk does not say whether, having reached the harbour to which they came on the 7th of September, they considered themselves to have arrived at "the place for which they searched", and for which they had looked in vain in Ungava Bay. Most likely his intention was merely to give the crew some rest and refreshment, to explore the neighbourhood, and after a while to proceed further, as they would naturally expect to have open sea for some time longer. But there happened to them what had happened to Button, who, fully three weeks earlier in the year, had entered Nelson River to repair, and had there been overtaken by the winter. The weather deteriorated so rapidly that the question of going into winter quarters had to be entertained within a week of Munk's arrival at Port Churchill. With a view to this, two boats were sent out—one towards the north, the other to the south—in order to ascertain whether better quarters were to be found within a distance of 30 or 40 English miles. It may be noticed in passing that Munk says that the boats were sent respectively to the West and to the East, which of course is founded on the circumstance that the portion of the coast on which Churchill River enters the sea, really does trend West and East, though only for a short distance. The two Danish mates, Brock and Petersen, who were in command of the boats, returned with the report that they had been unable to find any decent harbour where they had been; and no wonder, because Munk had had the good fortune to

---

[1] The Beluga (*Delphinapterus leucas*) enters regularly with the tide, and the Hudson's Bay Company derives a good income from the fishery. In former times, they were shot with rifles, but are now taken in trap-nets. The American whalers also take great numbers in the Bay.

strike—apparently by accident—by far the best harbour on the coast. As a matter of fact, Munk did not wait for the return of Brock, who was ten days away, but decided already on the 18th of September to remain where he was. Then followed a busy time in placing the vessels in safety and arranging winter quarters. Munk and his officers resolved for this purpose to take the ship behind some promontory, where she might have some protection against the drifting ice. The ships were at that time probably lying in what is now called Churchill Harbour proper—that is, in the deep pool of the river just inside Cap Merry, where the wharf and warehouses of the Hudson's Bay Company now are situated.[1] Though this place might be safe enough in other respects, yet the vessels were there too much exposed to the destructive action of the drift-ice, which was already then being carried up and down with great force by the strong current of the river and the tides, which run with an estimated velocity, at the mouth of the river, of six knots at half tide. Accordingly, on the 19th, they sailed up the river in search of a more suitable locality; but, after proceeding a certain distance, they found that they could ascend no further. Munk does not say how far they got; but, as he says elsewhere that *Enhiörningen* was left lying something like a Danish mile (*i.e.*, four and a half English miles) up the river, this would probably be the distance from the mouth to which they reached by sailing. On the next morning, it was found that the ice had cut into the sides of the vessels to the depth of about one inch and a half, proving the absolute necessity of speedy removal. They must have been lying in the permanent bed of the river, about a mile and a half up the lagoon above described; and the only way of bringing the vessels into comparative safety was to float them on to the shore at flood tide, across one of the flats which, as already mentioned, intervene between low-water and high-water mark on either side. Munk chose the western shore, no doubt partly because the flat there was much the narrower, partly because, opposite the spot where they must have been anchored,

Ref. to Page of Text.

Page 25 *(continued)*

---

[1] According to Lieut. A. R. Gordon (*Report of the Hudson's Bay Expedition of 1886*, pp. 8-9), this basin is 1500 yards north and south by about 1000 yards east and west, with a depth of over four fathoms at low water.

Ref. to Page of Text.

Page 25 (continued) it offers precisely such a locality as he desired to find, the coast receding somewhat towards the west behind a slight promontory. To this place, accordingly, the vessels were brought, though not without difficulty and danger, as Munk's narrative shows.[1] The flat which had to be crossed was not only—as all authorities describe it—covered with large boulders, but of considerable width. According to our map, the width is about one mile, with which Munk's estimate of "nearly 900 fathoms" agrees very well. The place is at a distance from the river's mouth of about four miles, as the crow flies, which agrees perfectly with Munk's statement; and that it really is the spot where Munk wintered is proved by the fact that one of his cannon was afterwards found here, in consequence of which the little bay in which it was found was called Munk's Cove. Sir J. Richardson, who mentions this fact (without, however, giving his authority), states[2] that the discovery in question was made when the Hudson's Bay Company established their fort on this river. The original fort of the company, which was erected in 1688, and rebuilt in 1718 (or, according to some, in 1721), was situated on the western shore of the estuary, in the place marked on the map "Old Fort", as the original fort came to be called after the erection of Prince of Wales's Fort at the entrance of the harbour in 1733.

Page 26 In this place, the vessels would not be affected by the current except when the tide was full, and the danger from drifting ice would, consequently, be very much less than in the permanent riverbed; besides which, the crews would be able easily to get on shore. The sloop was hauled on land with the assistance of a high tide, and the ship was moored securely and protected by various means, the description of which reminds one strongly of the measures taken by Button, with the same object in view, when he wintered on the Nelson River in 1612-13.[3] A part of the ships' stores

Page 27 was brought on shore, and huts or small houses appear to have been erected wherein to keep them safely. Munk does not

---

[1] We have indicated on the map of Churchill Harbour the course probably taken in bringing the vessels to their final station. The line representing the outward route of the sloop in 1620 is, however, purely conjectural.

[2] Sir J. Richardson, *The Arctic Regions* (Edinburgh, 1861), p. 107.

[3] See Luke Foxe's *North-West Foxe* (1635), p. 118; also Miller Christy's *Voyages of Foxe and James*, p. 187.

mention this in his account; but two such are seen in the woodcut, and remains of them are said to have existed not much more than a century ago.¹

In the next place, Munk adopted various measures for the comfort of the crew, with regard to which two points may be noticed. He distributed winter clothing, but no mention is made of fur garments, which in that climate are indispensable. That Munk afterwards recognised the lack of such garments as a grave defect in his outfit, is evident from his having (as already mentioned) placed fur-lined clothing in the forefront of his requirements for the proposed second voyage. The other point is that he was careful to make arrangements whereby the crew obtained the fullest possible amount of space to move about on board—an important matter as regards their health. No doubt, with the same view of enabling them to be out of the cabin as much as possible, he had three large fireplaces arranged on deck. One of these was on the so-called *Styrepligt*, a portion of the deck astern, principally intended for the working of the helm. It corresponds, we believe, to what was anciently called the "steerage" in English ships, which term we have therefore used in our translation, though it is now obsolete except in the combination "steerage passenger." At the same time, the men were employed a good deal on shore, in providing fuel and food and in other occupations.

Munk at once set to work to explore the country, particularly in order to establish intercourse with the natives; but in this he did not succeed, though he found traces of their presence everywhere, from which he concluded that they came there only in the summer time. He tried first, on the 7th of October, to ascend the river—to which he did not give any name—in a boat; but he found it unnavigable beyond a few English miles from where he was lying. This agrees with the statements of later authors, according to whom the lowest rapids are just above the head of the tide, a short distance above the upper end of the lagoon above referred to, and about eight miles from the sea.² The *Dieffuels Hug* ("Devil's Promontory") which Munk mentions in his account of this expedition, may very likely be Musketo

---

¹ See *post*, p. 135.
² Chas. N. Bell, *Our Northern Waters*, p. 45.

Ref. to Page of Text.
Page 28
(*continued*)
Page 29
Page 30

Point, situated where the ridge bordering the valley of the river on the west side terminates, and where the river expands as before described.

For some time, Munk and his men were much occupied in securing the ship against the drifting ice, which more than once shifted her position, and carried away breakwaters, etc.; but, when the ice lay firm along the shore (as it did after the 22nd of October), no further trouble arose from this source, and the men were free to employ themselves otherwise. Munk states that, after that time, and as long as the weather permitted, the men were much on shore, which he evidently encouraged for their healths' sake. His statement that they were mostly employed in the forest, cutting wood for fuel or in pursuit of game—both of which occupations are illustrated in the woodcut facing p. 23—would appear incredible to a modern traveller in that district, which is now almost treeless; but it appears from all accounts that, in the seventeenth century, and even in the middle of the eighteenth, the country was covered with forest, which in course of time has been destroyed. So notorious was the fact, that one writer[1] at the last-mentioned period appeals to it as an argument against La Peyrère's erroneous statement that Munk wintered in lat. 63° 20', and in favour of the view that he wintered at Port Churchill, because in that latitude no forest would have been found, whilst it existed at Port Churchill. Pines no doubt constituted the main growth; but poplars, willows, and juniper are also mentioned as growing in the forest.[2] Game was killed partly for food and partly for fur—no doubt intended for sale at home. There were many Norwegians amongst the crew; and, amongst the methods employed, Munk mentions especially one

---

[1] *An Account of a Voyage to Hudson's Bay, . . . by the Clerk of "The California"* (London, 1748), p. 105.

[2] See E. Umfreville, *The Present State of Hudson's Bay* (London, 1790), p. 24. He states that the forest had then been cleared for some miles from the fort, and that the remaining trees were but small. Dr. Robert Bell's "Map showing the Northern Limits of Forest Trees in Canada" (*Report of Canadian Geological Survey, 1881*) shows that the White Spruce (*Abies alba*), the Black Spruce (*Abies nigra*), the American Larch (*Larix americana*), and the Balsam Poplar (*Populus balsamifera*), all have their northernmost limit in the immediate vicinity of Port Churchill.

used in Norway, and called *at ligge for Glug*, which means lying in ambush behind a window or similar opening (called *Glug* both in Denmark and in Norway) in order to shoot animals attracted by a bait, or to mind traps, for which purpose small huts are erected in suitable places. The food-game consisted mostly of ptarmigan and hares. The former, belonging to the same species as the European Common Ptarmigan, are still very abundant in the country, where great numbers are killed annually by the servants of the Hudson's Bay Company. The early English explorers (Hudson, Button, Fox, James) spoke of these birds as White Partridges; but Munk and his Norwegian sailors of course easily recognised the *Rype*, familiar to them at home, and called it by its right name. Ref. to Page of Text.
Page 30 (continued)

As the winter increased in severity, much snow fell, often rendering locomotion across country impossible. A second attempt of Munk's to penetrate into the interior was frustrated by a violent snow-storm. Unfortunately they had no snow-shoes, nor did any of them know the use of them, which is quite an art and requires special training. This was one of the defects in their outfit which Munk was desirous of avoiding when a second expedition was thought of in 1621. Pp. 31-32

In many places, Munk expresses his astonishment at the extraordinary severity of the frost; and one day—the 3rd of December—he examined the ice on the estuary and found that, in the permanent bed of the river, it had attained a thickness of about 3 feet 7 inches English measure, which thickness it retained until long after Christmas. Where the water was still, he found the ice much thicker; but there is nothing in his narrative corresponding to the statement of La Peyrère[1] that they found the ice to be 300 to 360 feet thick. It does not, however, appear that the winter of 1619-20 was unusually early or severe. Munk says that, on October 22nd, the ice became firm near the shore; and, on the 30th, it covered the whole estuary, which—considering that his dates are all Old Style—corresponds to the experience of subsequent observers to the effect that Port Churchill does not freeze up till November.[2] On the 21st of Page 33

---

[1] *Relation du Groenland*, p. 256. The statement was reproduced by Forster, *Geschichte*, etc., p. 538 (Engl. trans., p. 470).

[2] C. N. Bell, *Our Northern Waters*, p. 46.

Ref. to Page of Text.
Page 33 (*continued*)

November, the sea outside was still open; but on February 6th they could see no open water, probably because the sea was obscured by fog, as the ice-belt along the shore is never very broad.[1]

In connection with this matter, Munk sets forth his view on the formation of icebergs, which, as readers conversant with the subject will have observed, contains all the germs of the true explanation, and prove him to have been an intelligent observer, anticipating (as he does) the results of much more recent scientific investigation. Had Munk said that the snow, sliding down the mountain sides, solidified into ice before reaching the water, instead of after, there would have been little or no fault to find with his description.[2] It may be noted in passing that, although Munk speaks of icebergs in connection with his observations on the ice at Port Churchill, he certainly did not observe any there, as they do not occur in that part of Hudson's Bay. His experience of them had been gained in Davis' and Hudson's Straits, where he had met many of them.

Other phenomena also attracted his attention. Thus he notices that, on the 23rd of November, there was an appearance in the sky as if there had been three suns on the heaven—a phenomenon of a kind which is not unfrequent in those lands of fog and mist. In the MS., there is a very rough indication of how these three "suns" partially covered one another, but no attempt at a drawing; nor is there any illustration in the printed book. Something similar he also noted under the date of January 20, 1620.

Page 34

A phenomenon of the same class appears to have been observed on the 10th of December with regard to the moon, simultaneously with the occurrence of an eclipse. Munk, however, seems to have mixed up the two phenomena, and his description is far from satisfactory. He expresses himself as being well aware that the hours of the commencement and the end of the eclipse might be made use of for the determination of

---

[1] C. N. Bell, *Our Northern Waters*, pp. 20 and 25.

[2] Capt. Luke Fox, when passing through Hudson's Strait ten years later, formed a somewhat similar theory of the formation of icebergs, which, though less correct than the above, is nevertheless interesting (See Christy, *Voyages of Foxe and James*, pp. 288 and 293).

the longitude of the locality; but his statements on these points are manifestly erroneous. The conditions under which he observed may have been unfavourable; but it is very probable that it was only after his return that he learned how the eclipse could be used for the purpose indicated. He had himself no means of taking longitudes on the voyage, and probably did not at all know how to do it. In this place, too, there is some difference between the MS. and the printed text, which should be noted. In the former, the above-mentioned phenomenon is described in the same terms as in the printed text; but, after the words in which it is stated that the eclipse ended at ten o'clock, the MS. has these words: "See the figure here following"; and after the figure there is a reference to the *Ephemerides*, in terms similar to those of the printed text, the paragraph concluding with these lines: "inasmuch as I am no Latin scholar, I cannot so well choose the expressions as I ought; but I hope that the well-disposed reader who has understanding will accept all in the best meaning." The figure in question (which occupies nearly a full page) consists of two concentric circles divided into quarters by a horizontal and a vertical diameter forming a cross, another line being drawn across them above the former. It is doubtless an imperfect copy of the drawing in Origanus' *Ephemerides* above quoted, representing this very eclipse.[1] Of course, the straight lines in question have their significance in connection with the manner in which the effect of eclipses are shown in that work, and have nothing to do with any cross appearing in the moon, which Munk seems to have thought to be part and parcel of an eclipse. The truth probably is that, at the time of the eclipse, the weather was misty, producing something in the nature of a halo, and that Munk, not knowing exactly what to pay attention to, took some random notes, which he himself afterwards misunderstood, as he did Origanus' figure. Not knowing much Latin, or having the assistance of an astronomer or competent mathematician, he found himself incapable of working out the problem, so he left it to the kind reader, pleading in excuse that he was no scholar.

As it is quite certain from other data that Munk wintered in the estuary of the Churchill River, and as the longitude of that

---

[1] *Ephemerides novæ 1599*, fol. Ccc. 3*b*, or *Annorum priorum 30 .... Ephemerides .... 1609*, fol. AAAA 1.

Ref. to Page of Text.

Page 34 (continued) place has long since been determined, the question whether the longitude can be calculated from Munk's statements on the eclipse has now no practical interest. But it was otherwise in Munk's time, when the West Coast of Hudson's Bay had only just been discovered, and no better *data* existed for determining its longitude. It was, therefore, natural for Isaac de La Peyrère to attempt, in his *Relation du Groenland*, to utilise Munk's *data* for this purpose; but (as we shall see when we come to discuss Munk's map) he did so in an arbitrary manner, so that his result would have been valueless even if it had happened to be correct, which it was not. M. Ravn[1] has, as a matter of curiosity, attempted the calculation on the basis of Munk's statements, with the result of finding much too westerly longitudes, proving that Munk incorrectly observed or wrongly recorded the elements of the eclipse.

Thus the long Arctic winter commenced without any much more serious mishap than that they had (as Munk expresses himself) to content themselves with ptarmigan, instead of goose, on the feast of St. Martin. On that day, roast goose is an obligatory item of the bill of fare in Denmark, apparently for no other reason than that the geese about that time are in good condition, having fattened on the corn dropped amongst the stubble—"stubble-geese", as Chaucer has it, though in England these are due at Michaelmas. Things seem to have gone on *Page 35* fairly well until Christmas, which, according to Munk's account, was celebrated not only with all due solemnity but also with all due jollity, and perhaps a little too much of the latter, the feasting commencing (as the Danish custom is) on Christmas Eve. From Munk's statement that there was a sermon and "Mass", it must not be concluded that they were Roman Catholics, the word *Messe* in Danish (in post-Reformation times) simply meaning Divine Service in the morning. The usual morning service on Sundays and festivals is called *Höimesse* (High Mass), the early service *Fromesse* (Early Mass), whether there be communion or not. In this case, no doubt, there was; and with that there would naturally be an offertory (*Juleoffer*) for the *Præst*, as the clergy are called in Denmark. The duties of

---

[1] *Udsigt*, etc., in *Dansk Maanedskrift*, 1860, p. 92.

religion observed, they had their Christmas dinner and amusements, and thus they "spent the Holy Days with the merriment that was got up," as Munk says in the printed book, expressing himself therein rather more cheerfully than in the MS., where the sentence reads, "and then we passed the Holy Days, according to our poor ability at the time." *Ref. to Page of Text. Pp. 36-39*

Howbeit, *Anno Domini* 1620 had barely commenced when sickness appeared among the crew to an alarming extent. Some of the men appear to have been ailing a long time, and a couple of deaths are recorded in 1619; but, with the New Year, the sick list soon began to swell. The same is recorded of Button's crew, and the reason was probably the same in both cases—*viz.*, that the continuance of the extremely severe cold prevented the men from taking sufficient outdoor exercise, whilst the ice and the deep snow diminished the supply of fresh meat and of vegetable food. That the disease was scurvy is evident from Munk's description of the symptoms, and he employs the name, but seems to apply it more particularly to the affection of the gums, speaking of the affection of the stomach as a kind of dysentery. Probably he had not before witnessed or heard of the disease in so acute a form, for he speaks of it as a rare and extraordinary disease. This is particularly the case in the entry under May 28, 1620 (see p. 47). With regard to this, however, it should be noted that, in the MS., the whole paragraph is very much shorter, and only mentions as remarkable the contraction of the limbs. Scurvy was well known at the time, and the importance of fresh meat and vegetable food was recognised. The *Cochlearia officinalis* went even then by the name of Scurvy Grass. But Munk does not seem to have been aware of the disastrous influence of alcohol on patients or persons beginning to ail from it. The people of Scandinavia were in former times hard drinkers, the Norwegians being surpassed in capacity for drink only by the Icelanders; and nothing would seem to the common man more natural than to counteract weakness by a liberal use of wine and spirits. There can be little doubt that this circumstance considerably aggravated the evil; but the want of fur clothing, which confined the men to the close quarters on board, had probably as large a share in it. At any rate, it would not be just to blame Munk for his liberality towards his crew in the matter of alcoholic drink, for

Ref. to Page of Text.

Pp. 36-39 (*continued*)

there is nothing to show that he acted otherwise than in ignorance of the bad effects to be expected.

That Munk can have had but little leisure and little inclination for either observing or noting down anything that happened outside while the state of things on board was so critical, is a matter of course, and only three remarks on such events occur in 1620. One has reference to the appearance of a parhelion on January 24th. Another concerns the variation of the needle at Port Churchill, but Munk's statements thereupon are not self-consistent. He says

Page 40 that, on the 11th of March (O.S., as are all his dates), the Spring Equinox, the sun rose in E.S.E. and set in W.N.W.; but he adds that the sun set at seven o'clock, though, says he, "it was not really more than six o'clock, on account of the variation." These statements do not go together. The points of the compass indicated refer, of course, to the magnetic north, and imply a variation of two points; but, if the hour is taken from the position of the sun by means of the compass dial, reckoning it to be noon when the sun stands over the south point, the variation would cause an error of only three-quarters of an hour for two points. If the sun really set in W.N.W. by compass, the variation was $22\frac{1}{2}°$ W., and the apparent time 6 hours 45 minutes. For the apparent time to be seven, the variation would have to be 30°, and the points of sunrise and sunset would be nearer S.E. by E. and N.W. by W.

The third remark refers to the return of migratory animals at the end of winter. In the entry for May 22nd (p. 47), he enumerates the birds which had at that time appeared; but in the MS. he adds that they did not include Auks nor Puffins, nor were there any four-footed beasts.

The long and melancholy tale of the progress of the disease, of the frequent deaths, and of the increasing difficulty of having the bodies properly buried, calls for few remarks. Unlike the skilful surgeon who managed to keep Capt. James's sick sailors in such condition that they could move about and do some work during his wintering in 1631-32, the surgeon of *Enhiörningen*

Pp. 41-42 could render no assistance at all. The vessel had been supplied with a store of medicaments, such as herbs, waters, medicines, etc., but the surgeon did not in the least know what use to make of them. They had been selected by physicians; but it was no part of their duty to supply information about the use of them—

indeed, it would have been against the etiquette of their profession so to do. Although, therefore, Munk's complaint that there were no "directions for use" accompanying the many bottles and packets was well enough founded from the point of view of common sense, nothing else was, under the circumstances, really to be expected. *Ref. to Page of Text.* Pp. 41-42 (*continued*)

At first Munk tried to honour the dead with proper burial, but it became more and more difficult; and, as his two falconets— small pieces which had not been taken into the hold with the heavier cannon—had come to grief when discharged in honour of Hans Brock, he could not have given his lieutenant a proper salute, even if his chief gunner (*Arkeliemester*, literally, "master of the powder magazine") and his mate had not both been dead before. At last, the survivors were obliged to drag the bodies unceremoniously to the grave on a little sledge which had been used for the transport of fuel, until even this could not be performed, and no burial at all could take place. Page 43

In the MS., Munk has noted down with each entry the number of the dead up to that date; but these notes have been omitted from the printed text. Below the date of February 20th is written "21 corpses"; below the 25th, "22 corpses"; and so on until the 4th of June, below which date is written "61 dead." By the end of March, half the crew were dead, and most of the others were suffering to such a degree that almost all there was to do had to be done by Munk himself. He had to be doctor, nurse, cook, and chaplain too—for the Good Friday homily (which only four others had strength enough to sit up and listen to) was no doubt read by himself. There is almost a touch of grim humour in his entry for Easter day (when 47 men had already succumbed) to the effect that he bestowed the office of the skipper, who had just died, on another man, although he was ill, in order that he might be of some use to him as far as his strength went. Munk himself was then quite ill, which is probably the meaning of the term *elendig* ("miserable") which he applies to himself. It does not appear that Munk tried any of the medicines he found in the surgeon's box, but he utilised the herbs to prepare baths for himself and the men. This, he says, did them good, very much as, according to Capt. James's description, his sick men, by means of baths in the morning, were enabled to work through the day. Pp. 44-46

Miserable as the state of things must have been for a long time on board *Enhiörningen*, the pitch of horror was reached when Munk himself, last of all, was struck down, and there was nobody left either to nurse the sick or to get the dead bodies out of the way. It appears that none were buried in the ground after the 12th of May, after which time the dead bodies had been thrown overboard, or dragged on deck and left there. In the entry for May 28th and following days, Munk says that three dead bodies (amongst which, evidently by mistake, he mentions the cook's mate) were lying on the steerage, and that only seven were left alive, waiting mournfully for the snow and ice to disappear, and (adds the MS.) for the green to begin to sprout from the ground. Amongst these seven, he counts two men who had gone on shore and remained there, and with whom perhaps the survivors remaining on board were able to communicate by shouting. On Whit Sunday, besides Munk and the two men on shore, only the sailmaker was left alive, and he apparently in a dying condition. In the printed text, it is stated that he died after Munk had left the ship; but in the MS. the passage to this effect does not occur, and his name (Martin) is entered, presumably as dead, just below the words " 61 dead " under the date of June 4th.

What hopes Munk can have had that his last Farewell—written down, it must be supposed, in his log-book or daily note-book, which is not now in existence—would ever reach Denmark is difficult to imagine. Of course, the words towards the conclusion about his family obtaining some benefit from his miserable death, amount to an appeal for a pension in their favour. How, by a last desperate effort, he succeeded in leaving the ship (now not much better than a charnel-house), and how he recovered so far as to be able to attempt the return to Europe in the sloop, with the assistance of the two men who recovered with him, Munk's own narrative sufficiently explains.

Munk says that, before leaving the place, he " drilled two or three holes in *Enhiörningen*, in order that the water which might be in the ship might remain when the ebb was half out, so that the ship should always remain firm on the ground, whatever ice might come." This statement does not seem very clear, because if Munk wished any water that already was in the ship to remain there, the drilling of holes in her sides would defeat, not further, that object. The meaning seems to be that he wished the hold of the ship to be to some extent filled with water, in order to steady her in the dock which he had constructed for her, and in which she had been lying all the winter. He drilled the holes in order that the water might pour in at full tide, but placed them so high up that whatever water was in her at half tide would remain. The breakwaters, etc., which he had caused to be made were probably still in good condition, and he thought that, by thus steadying the ship, she might remain safe, and able to withstand the attacks of the ice in the following winter. *Ref. to Page of Text.* Page 50 *(continued)*

Before concluding his account of his stay at Port Churchill, Munk says that he called it after himself—Jens Muncke's Bay. This is rather remarkable, because the name is distinctly English, not Danish. "Bay" is not a Danish word, and has never been used as an appellative, though *Bayen* ("the Bay") at one time was (and perhaps still sometimes is) used of the Bay of Biscay, as in English, from which language this use of it undoubtedly has come. It looks as if the name had been suggested by Gordon or Watson, perhaps in the report to which Munk in one place seems to allude (see p. 89). In this connection, too, it may be mentioned that the language of the *Navigatio Septentrionalis*—that of the MS. to a greater extent than that of the printed text—abounds in what a reader acquainted only with the Danish of modern literature would describe as Anglicisms. The greater number of these peculiarities find their explanation in the fact that, at the time when the book was written, the dialect of Jutland was still predominant in Denmark, which dialect to this day exhibits numberless points of resemblance to English, which do not occur in the present language of Danish literature. But there are some expressions which cannot be accounted for in this way, and which one is tempted to derive from Munk's intercourse with his English pilots, such as *fadoms* (in the MS.) for *Favne* (or *Fauffne*, as it was then spelt), and the participles *finding* and *entring* (in the entries for July 9th, 11th, and 12th), which have never been in use in Danish. Page 51

The Homeward Voyage.

With regard to the remaining portion of Munk's book, it must be noticed here that the manuscript preserved at the University Library of Copenhagen ceases with the words "whatever ice might come". There is, however, no reason whatever to suppose that the last part of the book, which treats of the return voyage, was not written by Munk himself. To a great extent, it has a meagre appearance and seems to be little more than a transcript of Munk's original notes; but this is only what naturally might be expected. Sailing, as Munk did, from the Churchill River to the coast of Norway without setting foot on land, what could he have to record, except short statements about wind and weather? Wherever there is the least occasion for it, he is as full and circumstantial as in any other part of his narrative.

Munk gives no details of their leaving the harbour,[1] nor does he indicate either the direction of the wind or the course steered after leaving it; but, as he would naturally try to sail home as straight as he could, in order not to be stopped by the early winter, he may safely be supposed to have steered N.E. as nearly as he could. However, the omission is not of great consequence, because, already in the evening of the first day he was caught in the ice, which formed (as usual in those waters) a broad belt not far from the shore, very difficult and hazardous to penetrate. Three days after, in relating how he lost his dog—probably the ship's dog, which had come out with them—he says that according to his guess, they were 40 miles (Danish) from land. But this must be an error of some kind; because that would imply that they were about one-third across the Bay, whereas they were still battling with the ice not far from the west coast. What is really meant cannot be even guessed, in the absence of the MS. That they were practically at a standstill—at any rate relatively to the ice—may be inferred from Munk's further statement that for two days they heard the dog howl.

After eight days, they escaped from the ice, but on the inner side, so that they were still prisoners. That they had not advanced much is evident from their falling in again with the boat of *Enhiörningen*, which Munk in starting had taken in tow, thinking that it might be useful, but had been obliged to abandon when caught in the ice ten days before. He does not say whether he again took possession of it. If he did, he probably lost it again in one of the severe gales which he experienced on the

---

[1] See above, p. 114, *note*.

homeward voyage; for, when he reached Norway, he had none. *Ref. to Page of Text.* After trying in vain to find an outlet in an easterly direction, he turned and sailed N.W., between the ice and the land. In so doing, he was well advised; for it appears to be an ascertained fact that the southern part of Hudson's Bay continues embarrassed with ice when the northern part is free, so that ships bound for York Factory are obliged, in order to avoid the ice in the centre of the Bay, to steer for Cape Churchill until within 60 leagues of land, when they may steer direct for the Nelson River.[1] *Page 52 (continued)*

For some days after having abandoned his attempt at getting through the ice east of Port Churchill, Munk's main direction was north-west, after which he seems to have sailed north. His expressions in the entry for August 4th are somewhat ambiguous. He says that he sailed between the ice and the land *vestvart op* (literally, "westwards up"). As he cannot have sailed westwards, it seems that the *vestvart* must apply to the land, and indicate that this was to the west of him; whilst "*op*" must apply to the sailing and mean northwards. How far he was obliged to follow the western coast northwards before he could get out from between it and the ice, he does not state; but he says that, at the last, he was forced so far towards the land as to come into 12 fathoms. As soon, however, as he was free, he chose an E.N.E. course, from which it may be inferred that he judged himself to have reached a point considerably north of Port Churchill. In all probability, it was near Cape Esquimaux, in lat. 61° 10', that Munk got clear of the ice. *Page 53*

The point on the northern coast of Hudson's Bay which he calls *Kolde Hug* (the Cold Cape) is not named on the map, but is doubtless represented by the point of land projecting into the *Novum Mare*; this is placed in the same latitude as *Haresund*, which agrees with the figures given in the text, 62° 30' and 62° 20' respectively. It is, however, quite possible that the absence of the name of *Kolde Hug* in its proper place may be due to the person who executed the map having by mistake placed the name, altered into *Koldenes*, against a similar point in Hudson's Strait, in about the same latitude. *Kolde Hug*

---

[1] E. Chappel, *Narrative of a Voyage to Hudson's Bay*, p. 173.

Ref. to Page of Text.
Page 53 (continued)

can scarcely be identified with anything else than Cary's Swan's Nest, on the southern coast of Coats' Island, so named by Button—a circumstance of which Munk, of course, cannot have been aware. Munk's latitude is about 20' too high; but, in other respects, his description agrees perfectly with what is known of the place from other sources. That it is situated on an island he could not know; and he naturally assumed that it was a part of the mainland to the north of the Bay—as which he represents it on his map.

After leaving *Kolde Hug*, Munk appears to have followed the south coast of Coats' Island for some distance, but gradually drawing away, steering E.N.E., which course brought him to a point north of Mansfield Island—by him, it will be remembered, called *Digses Eyland*. Had he not been stopped by ice, he would no doubt have proceeded direct into Hudson's Strait. As it was, he was obliged to beat forwards and backwards in front of impenetrable masses of ice.

At this point, Munk's statements are rather puzzling in some respects. He says that, on the morning of August 13th, he found himself off the north-east extremity of *Digses Eyland;* and, directly afterwards, he says that the eastern end of that island was in lat. 63°. A glance at the map shows that Munk, approaching the island from a place in about lat. 62° 20' by an E.N.E. course, would not naturally sight the north-east corner of it first, and that no point on the island could be properly described as the east end of it; nor does any part of the island reach a higher latitude than 62° 35'. The probable explanation is that Munk, in the dim light of the morning, perhaps on account of fog, did not observe the island, which lies low, until he was off the north-east corner of it. "East end" is probably a slip of the pen for north-east end; and, as regards its latitude, we may observe that the error is of about the same amount as in the case of *Kolde Hug*, and has probably the same cause. It is evident that Munk can have had but little chance of obtaining a tolerably accurate observation from the sloop's deck. At the same time, it is right to note that, on his map, the northern extremity of Mansfield Island is placed in about the same latitude as *Kolde Hug*, which he puts in 62° 30'—very nearly the right figure for Mansfield Island.

Munk says that for a "night and a day" (which would have been more correctly expressed "a day and a night") he had to beat about, being unable to get through the ice. He does not *Ref. to Page of Text.* say in what direction he tried to penetrate it; but the circumstance that he here speaks of the appearance of the southern part of Mansfield Island seems to indicate that he sailed southwards for a considerable distance on the eastern side of that island in order to find a way through. This is confirmed by Munk's statement that, on the morning of the 14th, he found himself surrounded by ice, with land close to him on both sides. This situation would be impossible anywhere in that neighbourhood, except in the bay formed by the Digges Islands and the mainland, near the southern opening of the channel separating the islands from the latter. It does not, however, appear with certainty whether Munk purposely tried for this channel, or had only come into this position by accident. Howbeit, he says that, finding himself so situated, he let down his mainsail and hauled himself through where the ice was "thinnest", which probably is to be taken in the sense of least packed. His "hauling" was no doubt accomplished by throwing the grapnel on to large pieces of ice and working up to it. Munk does not say expressly that in this way he passed through the sound or strait in question; but, as he afterwards says that he passed the *Söster* (the Digges Islands) to port on his return voyage, and as he could not possibly do so except by sailing through that strait, the context, all taken together, leaves no doubt on the point. Nor is this view of the matter weakened by the circumstance that, after describing how he got through the ice and into clear water, he states that he then sighted some high islands (two in number) to starboard, and at the same time to the south-west, which were the *Söster* or the Digges Islands. Nothing is more likely to have happened than that the islands were so much enveloped in mist while he passed through the strait that he did not recognise them, but that the fog cleared and revealed them to him when he had got into clear water, some distance to the north-west of them, and had turned eastwards, as he naturally would do, as soon as he could. In such a position, he would have them to starboard, and at the same time to S.W. In fact, the suddenness with which he appears to have got a sight of these islands would be inexplicable, except on the supposition that they had been obscured by a fog, which suddenly lifted. Munk's expressions admit, on the face of them, the interpretation that "the high islands" which he saw to

Page 53 *(continued)*

Page 54.

Ref. to Page of Text.
Page 54 (continued)

starboard comprised the *Iisvr;* but his statements in the place where they are first spoken of, to the effect that the latter were ten Danish miles or more to the east of the *Söster,* preclude such an interpretation of the passage before us. He cannot have seen both these groups to the south-west at the same time. The expression "some high islands" cannot therefore be taken to comprise more than the "two islands" mentioned afterwards. The ambiguity arises from the expression "other islands", which he applies to the *Iisvr;* but the use of the word "other" may very naturally be explained as a consequence of Munk having recollected, when he wrote this, that in a former place (in his account of the outward voyage) he had mentioned them together.

Being thus assured of his position, Munk set his course E.S.E. through Hudson's Strait. We may notice as remarkable that he does not here mention Nottingham and Salisbury Islands, any more than he does in his account of the outward voyage. One is tempted to suppose that, on the return voyage, they were hidden by fog; and that this may be a reason why he is altogether silent upon them. If, as we have suggested, his notes concerning these islands taken on the outward voyage were not sufficiently clear, and if he did not see them on his way back, he would probably consider it more prudent not to say anything about them. Munk says that he steered E.S.E. when he found himself inside the western entrance of Hudson's Strait; but he does not say whether it was by compass or by a true course. Most likely it was the latter; for it was not till two days later that, having passed his *Iisvr* to starboard, he approached the northern coast of Hudson's Strait. Thereupon he altered his course to E. by S., which, as he expressly says, was S.E. by E., allowance being made for the variation. It was high time that Munk should get away from these cold countries, as he no doubt was well aware, because he mentions, under August 15th, that there was much snow, that the wild geese were again flying briskly southwards, and that there was a good deal of ice in the strait, though scattered. He says it was nothing but *Loff an* and *hold Dregen* words of command which we have translated according to their sense, and which no doubt refer to the mode of progress thus described by Jérémie[1]: "On se *grapine,* c'est-à-dire, on saisit les

---

[1] In Bernard's *Recueil de Voyages au Nord,* tome VI (Amsterdam, 1720), p. 4 (2nd ed., tome V, 1724, p. 397; 3rd ed., tome III, 1732, p. 306).

Navires contre ces glaces comme contre une muraille, & lorsque *Ref. to Page of Text.* par la force des vents & des courants, qui sont très-violens dans ces endroits-là il se fait quelqu' ouverture au travers des glaces, Page 54 alors on met les voiles lorsqu'il est favorable, pour se faire passage *(continued)* avec de longs bâtons ferrez." Chappell also describes this mode of working by grappling, and says[1] that a main point is to get to lee of these large floes, where one is in quite smooth water; for which purpose it is, of course, necessary to luff.

On the fourth day after having cleared the Digges Islands, Pp. 55, 56. Munk passed *Munkenes*, in noting which he takes the opportunity of adding some details about the trending of the coast on both sides of the Cape, which prove that it must be the southernmost point of Resolution Island. It took them 33 days to cross the Atlantic, whilst on the outward voyage 20 days had sufficed from the coast of Norway to Cape Farewell; but on the homeward voyage they suffered severely from heavy gales. They were too few to work the sails to advantage, particularly as they had to pump incessantly. Munk's laconic entries, which day by day describe their progress, do not call for any special remark.

It was not till the 21st of September 1620, that the sloop in a Page 57. a "flying gale" (as the phrase goes in Denmark) shot *inden Skers*, that is, inside the belt of rocky islands which girts almost every part of the coast of Norway, forming the so-called *Skjærgaard*, and inside which they were safe from the fury of the Atlantic. They did not at the time know what place they had come to; but Munk gives—no doubt from information afterwards acquired —the name of one of the outermost islands which they passed, *viz.*, Allen, generally spelt Alden, one of a group called Böland, outside the entrance to Dalsfjord, which no doubt was the large fjord on which Munk found himself. On his frequent voyages to the north of Norway, Munk must often have passed and repassed this locality, and would very likely have recognised the outer islands if the weather had been favourable; but he does not seem to have known Dalsfjord itself. Dalsfjord is to the north of Sognefjord, so well known to tourists, and cuts into the district of Sönderfjord, which Munk spells Sundfjord. Having neither a boat nor an effective anchor, Munk could not come to a mooring Page 58.

---

[1] *Narrative of a Voyage to Hudson's Bay* (London, 1817), p. 121.

without assistance; and, as the outer part of Dalsfjord is rather
desolate, he waited in vain the whole day for somebody coming
out. At last he espied a man in a boat, whom he induced, in a
rather high-handed fashion, to bring a hawser on shore and to
convey him to the principal official of the district, in order to
demand the assistance to which he was entitled as being on
the King's errand.

Relics of Munk's Sojourn at Port Churchill.

With Munk's arrival at Bergen in September 1620, his narrative ends, though (as we have mentioned in our sketch of his life) he did not reach Copenhagen until Christmas. But, as a fitting supplement to Munk's account of his voyage, we may here relate what is known about the fate of the ship and its belongings which Munk left behind at Port Churchill.

It is evident from Munk's expressions that he expected a fresh expedition to be sent out ere very long, which might have fetched home *Enhiörningen;* but this was never done, and would have been useless, as far as fetching the ship was concerned. For more than fifty years after, no Europeans are known to have visited Port Churchill; and, even after the country had been occupied by the Hudson's Bay Company, founded in 1670, little attention was for some time bestowed upon Churchill River, though a small fort or station was erected. But the importance of the place was speedily recognised by the French, who, during the last decade of the seventeenth century, ousted the Company from most of its establishments in Hudson's Bay, of which they remained in possession until the Peace of Utrecht in 1713. The French officials, having heard from the natives of the earlier visit of strangers, and combining these reports with La Peyrère's well-known story, readily recognised that these strangers who had come by sea and had wintered and died at the River Manoteousibi, were none other than the members of Jens Munk's Expedition. Accordingly they named the river *Rivière Danoise,* or *Rivière de Monc.* It is in a memoir entitled *Relation du Detroit et de la Baie de Hudson,*[1] which gives the earliest geographical

---

[1] In Bernard's *Recueil de Voyages au Nord,* tome VI (Amsterdam, 1720), p. 3 (2nd ed., tome V, 1724, p. 396; 3rd ed., tome III, 1732, p. 305).

description of the country, that we find the report of what happened after Munk's departure. It is written by M. Jérémie, who was employed in the country, with short interruptions, from 1694 to 1714, first as lieutenant, afterwards—from 1708—as Governor, and who consequently had the best of opportunities for obtaining reliable information. The memoir opens with the following passage :—

"Pour prendre les choses dans leur origine, & pour mieux donner l'intelligence de ma Relation, je dirai que les Danois navigerent dans ces Pays, il y a quatre-vingt-dix à cent ans."

After an account of the country round Hudson's Strait, and its inhabitants, he continues :—

" Il faut présentement revenir à notre premier dessein, et dire que les Danois, après avoir passé tout le Détroit dont je viens de faire la description, continuant toûjours leur route vers le Nord, aborderent enfin la Terre ferme à une Riviere que l'on a nommée *Riviere Danoise*, & que les Sauvages nomment *Manoteousibi*, qui signifie Riviere des Etrangers. Là, ils mirent leurs Vaisseaux en hyvernement et se logerent aussi du mieux qu'ils purent, comme gens qui n'avoient nulle experience de ce Pays, & qui se défioient pas du grand froid qu'ils avoient à combatre : Enfin, ils essuyerent tant de misères, que la maladie s'étant mise entr' eux, ils moururent tous pendant l'hiver, sans qu'aucun Sauvage en eut connoissance.

" Le Printems venu, les glaces déborderent avec leur impetuosité ordinaire, & emporterent leur Vaisseau avec tout ce qui étoit dédans, à la reserve d'un canon de fonte d'environ 8 livres de balle, qui y resta, & qui y est encore tout entier, excepté le tourillon de la culasse que les Sauvages ont cassé à coups de pierres.

"Les Sauvages furent bien étonnez l'Eté suivant, lorsqu'ils arriverent dans ce lieu, de voir tant de corps morts, & des gens dont ils n'en avoient jamais vû de semblables. La terreur s'empara d'eux & les obligea de prendre la fuite, ne sachant que s'imaginer en voyant un tel spectacle. Mais, lorsque la peur eut fait place à la curiosité, ils retournerent dans le lieu où ils auroient fait, selon eux, le plus riche pillage qui jamais ait été fait. Mais, malheureusement, il y avoit de la poudre, dont ils ne savoient pas les proprietez ni la vertu ; ils y mirent imprudemment le feu qui les fit tous sauter, brûla la maison & tout ce qui étoit dedans; de manière que les autres, qui vinrent après eux, ne profiterent que des cloux et autre ferremens, qu'ils ramassoient dans les cendres de cet incendie."

Jérémie's description of the river in question leaves no doubt as to its being the Churchill River, which, as a matter of fact, retained the name of *Rivière Danoise*, or Danish River, for a long time. It may be specially mentioned that a confusion with the Seal River is excluded by the fact that Jérémie describes this separately under the name of *la Rivière du Loup-Marin*.

From this account (which must have lived as a tradition amongst the natives for a long time), it seems to follow that, although Munk did not succeed in coming into contact with the natives, some of these must have observed the arrival of the ships, or at any rate have seen the frigate before its destruction, or they could not have known anything about those strangers having come by sea. That the ship had not been carried off by the ice, as they probably concluded from not finding it when they came down to the place, but had been destroyed in the place where she was left, is to be inferred from the fact of one of the larger cannon having been found, which we know that Munk caused to be put in the hold. As Munk left *Enhiörningen* safe on July 16th, where she would not any more be exposed to drifting ice, and as he does not allude to any natives having shown themselves before his departure, it is perhaps the most probable conclusion, that it was only in the next following spring that the event related by Jérémie took place, when the ice of the second winter had destroyed the ship. At the same time, it should be noticed that a statement to the effect that the natives had obtained copper "from the brass guns of a Danish wreck, which they found on some coast," indicates the existence of a different version of the story.[1]

As the French took possession of the place in 1694, the piece seen by M. Jérémie was probably the same as that of which Sir John Richardson[2] speaks as having been found when the Hudson's Bay Company established themselves at Port Churchill, which they did in 1688, and the same to which the Clerk of the

---

[1] See J. Robson's *Account of a Six Years' Residence at Hudson's Bay* (London, 1752), p. 69.
[2] *The Polar Regions*, p. 107.

California alludes in proof of Munk having wintered at Port Churchill. He says it was marked C.4.[1]

The discovery of another piece, evidently one of the falconets, is mentioned in a valuable manuscript work entitled *Observations on Hudson's Bay*, written about 1770, by Thomas Hutchins, a surgeon, and chief factor in the service of the Hudson's Bay Company, in whose library the manuscript is now preserved. The passage referred to (fol. 245) is as follows:—

"Munk wintered in Churchill River. I have seen the bricks and other marks where he had his house, & two of his cannon has been found, one of which in my time at Churchill, about the size of a three-pounder, and marked Christian the IVth of Denmark, etc."

To the above may be added that the natives are reported[2] to have supplied themselves with metal from the wreckage, etc. It has even been contended that they never possessed any before; but, although this may be true as regards iron, it is not so as regards copper, which is found in the country and has been worked since time immemorial. Not to speak of that, Munk's cannon were of brass, and not of copper.

What became of these cannon does not appear to be known; but it does not seem quite impossible that some relics of Munk's Expedition may yet be found.

---

[1] *An Account of a Voyage to Hudson's Bay* . . . (London 1748), I, p. 105.

[2] See J. Robson's *Account of a Six Years' Residence at Hudson's Bay* (London, 1752), p. 69.

II.—OBSERVATIONS ON MUNK'S MAP, AND ON THE GEOGRAPHICAL RESULTS OF HIS VOYAGE.

On Munk's Instructions.

HAVING in the foregoing pages critically examined Munk's account of his voyage, we are now in a position to consider what were the results of that enterprise as regards the solution of the problem for the sake of which it was undertaken, as well as regards the advancement of geographical knowledge.

In approaching this matter we are naturally led back to the question of Munk's instructions. As stated above (p. xcvii), no copy or extract of the letter of instructions given to him in his capacity of commander of the expedition is now known to exist. Instead, therefore, of being able to refer to such a document for the better understanding of the narrative, we are left to infer from the latter what that document may have contained. In the course of our observations on Munk's report, we have accordingly drawn attention to the indications—direct or indirect—which it contains, as to how he was instructed to proceed; and we may now conveniently place together and supplement what has thus been advanced, in different places, on this subject. We may so much the more safely base our conclusions with regard to what he was to do, on his report of what he actually did, as Munk repeatedly affirms that he had obeyed his instructions as closely as he could.

To begin with, we notice that Munk's direct course from Karmsund on the west coast of Norway, where he had put in on account of the sloop having sprung a leak, would have been almost due west, between the islands of Orkney and Shetland, south of Cape Farewell, straight on to the coast of America. Munk, however, steered north-west after leaving Stavanger fjord, as far as the northern extremity of Shetland, from whence he took a westerly course, passing closely to the south of the Færö group, with the result that he struck the coast of Greenland somewhat to the north of Cape Farewell—according to the MS. in lat. 60° 25′, according to the printed text in lat. 61° 25′. Munk does not say whether this was intentional or not; but the former appears the more probable. As he evidently took some trouble to approach Cape Farewell, and to start from thence across

Davis' Strait, we can scarcely doubt that he had been directed to do so; and, in that case, it would be very natural for him to approach the east coast of Greenland purposely, in order to drop down to Cape Farewell with the Arctic current which sets southwards along the coast. He may have done so from his own knowledge, or by the advice of his pilots, but he may very well have been ordered to do so, just as was the case with Captain Button when he sailed for Hudson's Bay in 1612. In the seventh paragraph of the letter of instructions given to Captain Button it is stated : " We think your surest waie wil be to stand upp to Iceland and soe over to Groinland in the heighte of 61, soe to fall downe with the current to the most southerlie cape of that land lying in about 59°, called Cape Farewell," etc.[1]

Munk implies plainly that he was directed to cross Davis' Strait in order to seek the entrance to Hudson's Strait in about lat. 62° 30', and that, in order to recognise the latter the more readily, he was instructed to look for an island situated there, in lat. 62° 30'. He does not say, however, whether this island was supposed to lie in the entrance itself or on one side, either south or north of it. This point in Munk's instructions is rather remarkable. The question arises: From what source can those who drew up those instructions have derived the information on which they based that direction for Munk, that he was to recognise Hudson's Strait by an island situated in lat. 62° 30'? That the entrance of Hudson's Strait is bounded by an island on the north side (Resolution Island) had been recognised already by Frobisher, and afterwards by Weymouth and Button; but the localities visited by the former were (as we know) at the time believed to lie on the east coast of Greenland, and neither Weymouth's nor Button's reports had yet been made public. Hudson had not recognised Resolution Island as such, though the southern end of Gabriel Strait is indicated on his chart as published by Hessel Gerritsz. On the latter map, however, a group of three islands are figured to the north of the entrance—no doubt a duplicate of Resolution Island.[2] The instruction to look for an island marking

---

[1] See Miller Christy, *Voyages of Foxe and James*, p. 637.

[2] Accordingly, on some French maps they are called *Iles de Resolution*. It would be perhaps more correct to say that they represent Resolution Island and the Lower Savage islands.

the entrance to Hudson's Strait may, therefore, have been taken from Hessel Gerritsz.'s map, and may really refer to Resolution Island. But the indication of the latitude in which that island was to be found must have been taken from another source, because, on the map in question, the entrance of Hudson's Strait is placed fairly correctly between lat. 60° 30' and 61° 35'. It can scarcely be doubted that the figure 62° 30' for the latitude of this island is founded on Davis' account of his voyage, in which he ascribes the latitude of 62° to his Lumley's inlet. As we have explained before, the latter was, in Munk's time, looked upon as part and parcel of Hudson's Strait, so that on Gerritsz.'s map the name of "Lomlies Inlet" is placed against the main entrance to Hudson's Strait. The instruction to look for an island at the entrance of the Strait, and the figure for the latitude of the island, were thus, as it would seem, derived from two different sources: it being overlooked, or not understood, that these two items referred to different places.

It is remarkable that Button's instructions not only direct him to approach Hudson's Strait from Cape Farewell very much in the manner as Munk appears to have been ordered to do, but also contain the same mistake, which we have just pointed out, as regards the latitude. The document in question continues from the last word of the passage just quoted, thus: "wch pointe [Cape Farewell], as the ice will give you leave, you must double; and from thence, or rather from 20 or 30 L. to the Northward of it, if you shall fall ouer Davis his streights to the western Maine, in the height 62 Degrees or thereabouts, you shall finde Hudson's streights, wch you maie knowe by the furious course of the Sea and Ice into it, and by certaine Islandes to the Northerne side there of as your carde [doubtless Hudson's] shows." Striking, however, as this coincidence is, what we have adduced in the foregoing sufficiently explains how the error in question may have the same origin in both cases, independently of one another.

As regards the navigation through the strait, there is nothing in the narrative to suggest that Munk had any particular instructions. We may note, however, that he at once took to following the northern shore as far as *Haresund*, opposite Cape Hope's Advance (called by Hudson Cape Prince Henry); for, if he acted thus under instructions to that effect, these must have been founded on information obtained from England, where it was known at that time that the northern shore was the more free from ice. In this case we should have another coincidence between Munk's and Button's instructions, of which latter the eighth paragraph commences thus: " Being in [Hudson's Strait] We holde it best for you to keepe the Northerne side as most free from pester of ice, at least till you be past Cape Henry", etc. At the same time there is no necessity for supposing that Munk, in this particular, acted in obedience to orders, for, as he came from the north, he would naturally follow the northern shore.

Having passed through Hudson's Strait and arrived at the entrance of Hudson's Bay, Munk appears to have crossed the latter without hesitation in a south-westerly direction; and, as he does not state his reasons for so doing, we may fairly conclude that he did so in obedience to his instructions, as Button had done before him. In the letter of instructions given to the latter, we read in the eighth paragraph the following: "Therefore, remembering that your end is West, we should have you stand over to the opposite Maine, in the latitude of some 58 degrees [which implies a south-westerly course] etc." Indeed, it does not seem too much to say, that if Munk had sailed under Button's instructions he could scarcely have acted very differently from what he did. There is not, however, on that account any necessity for thinking that Button's instructions were known in Denmark; for in this case, as in the others we have mentioned, there is another and quite natural explanation of the coincidence between the modes of action of the two commanders. The fact that Button had crossed the Bay, sailing south-west, and thus had reached the western shore, had been published by Purchas, and may therefore be supposed to have been pretty generally known.

With regard to the exploration work to be done by Munk in the Bay, it should be observed that, as we have stated before (p. xcv to p. xcvii), the shores of the Bay had, previously to 1619, been examined so far, that there remained only four points towards which future expeditions in search of a North-West Passage could reasonably be directed. As regards two of these, Roe's Welcome and what we now call Fox Channel, there is no indication that Munk was charged with the exploration of them; but that he was enjoined to examine the south-western and southern coasts of the Bay seems to be clearly indicated by the fact that Gordon and Watson, when they—shortly after leaving

Haresund—mistook a portion of the south coast of Hudson's Strait for the western shore of Hudson Bay, at once steered southwards along the coast, examining it as they went.

Nor was, in our opinion, the question whether a passage might not still be found somewhere in the west coast overlooked in Munk's instructions. We have already (p. 105) propounded the view that the sloop was sent away on purpose, when the expedition had entered Hudson's Bay in order to explore a portion of the northern and western coast before rejoining the frigate farther south on the west coast ; and we are of opinion that it was not a random search which was thus instituted, but that it was undertaken in consequence of some distinct injunction in Munk's instructions. Munk's statement that during the separation of the two vessels the sloop had been "under the northern land, where an open passage was supposed to exist but there was none", may —we admit—be understood as importing merely that the party in the sloop, while near the coast in question (whether accidentally or purposely), had observed what looked like a passage, but on examination found that it was no such thing. But this does not seem to us a natural interpretation. If that was all, Munk would scarcely have alluded to it, or he would have expressed himself otherwise. It is far more agreeable to his simple diction to understand those words as meaning that the sloop had been under the "northern land", because an opening was supposed to exist there, and in order to ascertain whether it was so or not. This interpretation implies that in some quarters there was an idea that a passage was likely to be found in that neighbourhood, and that Munk had had his attention drawn to it. As regards the former of these points, we have already stated that, at that time, the notion was very generally entertained in England, that a passage would be found on the western shore of Hudson's Bay, more particularly in a place with which the name of " Hubbart's Hope" was associated ; and, as regards the latter point, it must be admitted, that though in 1619 nothing had as yet been published concerning " Hubbart's Hope", information concerning it had most likely reached Denmark—if through no other channel, through Gordon and Watson. In our opinion, therefore, the sloop was dispatched on purpose to "the northern land", there to look for the opening, the existence and position of which was connected in men's minds with "Hubbart's Hope". As, however, this view does not agree with what has hitherto been accepted concerning "Hubbart's Hope", we must enter a little more fully into the matter in order to show that, although "Hubbart's Hope" has been very generally taken to be only another name for Churchill Bay, or even Churchill River, it had originally little or nothing to do with that locality. The facts are the following :—

Although Button, on his return in 1613, could not claim to have discovered any passage or any channel which might be looked upon with probability as the eastern opening of a passage, he had by no means abandoned the hope of a passage being found, as appears both from his own statements and from other contemporary evidence,[1] notably from the statements of Purchas.[2] The account of this author, to whom we owe our principal information on "Hubbart's Hope', is the following : "Once he [Button] was very confident in conversation with me of a passage that way, and said that he had therein satisfied his Maiestie, who from his discourse in private inferred the necessitie thereof. And the mayne argument was the movement of the Tyde." After stating what Button had observed concerning the direction of the tide at Nelson River during the winter 1612-13, Purchas continues: "The summer following he found about lat. of 60 degrees, a strong Race of a Tyde, running sometimes eastward, sometimes westward. Whereupon Josiah Hubert, in his Platt, called that Place 'Hubbart's Hope', as in the map appeareth." Neither Hubert's Platt, nor any copy of it, is now known to exist, but the map to which Purchas refers is the one prepared by Henry Briggs, which accompanies Purchas's discourse on the probability of a Northwest Passage, from which we have been quoting. On this map we find the name "Hubbart's Hope" in lat. 60°, which we must infer from Purchas's words to be the same place in which it appeared on the Platt. The expressions used by Purchas, just quoted, plainly convey that "Hubbart's Hope" originally meant that place in Hudson's Bay where the tide was observed to come sometimes from the west, or, as they sailed near the west coast, the nearest point of the latter. It is evident that Hubert called the place by that name, not because he there observed anything

---

[1] See Miller Christy, *Voyages of Foxe and James*, pp. lxv-lxvii and lxxi.

[2] *Purchas his Pilgrimes*, iii, p. 848.

that looked like the opening of a passage, but because he founded fresh hopes of finding a passage on the consideration that the flood tide could not come from the west in that place unless there existed a passage admitting it from the Pacific; though that, of course, might be some distance off, particularly as the tide did not invariably come from the west. Nevertheless it is equally plain from Briggs' Map that "Hubbart's Hope" had, somehow or other, come to be misunderstood, at least by some, as if it meant some insufficiently explored bay or inlet, which Hubert was supposed to have looked upon as likely to lead to a passage. The opening of such an inlet in lat. 60° is marked on Briggs' Map. Both Foxe and James took the name of "Hubbart's Hope" in that sense, and on their voyages in 1631 (coming from the north) sought for such an inlet in lat. 60° and further south, until they were close to the southern shore of what we now call Churchill Bay. Finding nothing else that answered to their ideas of "Hubbart's Hope", they appear to have concluded that what was meant by this name was that very bay, and this view has ever since been generally accepted.

Purchas's statement, however (which is decisive, being the original and only authentic source of information on the subject), shows that Hubert did not apply the name in question to any opening supposed to be connected with the passage. Nor is he in the least likely to have thought that a passage would be found in Churchill Bay. When Button and his party observed that strong flow of tide from the west they had only just left that locality, and if they had thought that it came through Churchill Bay, surely they would have returned at once and sought there for the passage, to discover which they had come all the way from England. The fact of their not doing so clearly proves that they did not at the time imagine that the opening of the passage was in Churchill Bay: nor are they likely to have formed such an idea afterwards. The low-lying coast round that open and comparatively shallow bay is not at all of such a character that anybody, knowing so much of it as Button's party must have done, could reasonably suspect a passage between two mighty oceans to be, as it were, lurking there. In a mountainous country, the opening of such a passage might well be a narrow one, but, in a flat country, the waters would have made a way for themselves that could not be overlooked. It is not to be supposed that Button, or anyone who had been with him there, could afterwards have imagined that they had twice passed the opening of a channel admitting the tide from the Pacific, in a place like that, without noticing it. Still less probable is it that they should have noticed the Churchill River, and that this should be meant by "Hubbart's Hope"; or that they should afterwards have bethought themselves that this might be the looked-for passage. Not only does its insignificant size preclude this latter notion, but there is no indication whatever of their having particularly noticed or even observed the mouth of the river. Even if the name of "Hubbart's Hope" had reference to some particular bay or inlet, there is, as far as we are aware, no evidence at all connecting it with Churchill River. On the contrary, the mouth of the latter is in lat. 59°, but the race of tide was observed in lat. 60°.

The mistake that has been committed in the matter of "Hubbart's Hope" appears to us to have been mainly this: that it has been taken for granted that if the passage, of which the course of the tide at "Hubbart's Hope" apparently gave evidence, was not found in lat. 60°, it would be found south of that place. In reality there is nothing to prove that such was the idea of Josias Hubert; on the contrary, there is a strong piece of evidence pointing in quite the opposite direction, but the bearing of which on this question has hitherto been overlooked. We refer to Josias Hubert's answer to Capt. Button's "second demand", as related by Luke Foxe.[1] This writer relates how Button, while in winter quarters at Nelson River, set the more intelligent of his men to work out problems of navigation for exercise, and he publishes some of their answers. One of the questions—the one referred to by Josias Hubert as the second demand—appears to have been to the effect, how they had better proceed in their work of exploration when the milder season should set them free again. Hubert's words are as follows: "My answer to the 2 Demand is to search to the Northward about this Westerne land, untill if it be possible, that we may finde the flood coming from the Westward, and to bend our courses against that flood, following the ebbe, searching that way for the passage for

---

[1] *North-West Foxe*, 1635, p. 120; Miller Christy, *Voyages of Foxe and James*, pp. 171-172.

this flood which we have had from the Eastward. I cannot be persuaded, but that they are the veynes of some headlands to the Northwards of the Checks, and by the Inlets of Rivers which let the flood tides into them, which Headlands being found, I do assure myselfe that the tide will be found to come from the Westward."

We do not see any way of interpreting this statement otherwise than that Hubert, while at Nelson River, after having passed Churchill Bay on his way down from "Hopes Checked" (in lat. 60° 40′), was of opinion that the passage would be found north of those headlands, which, he expected, would be discovered north of "Hopes Checked": that is, not in Churchill Bay, which is south of lat. 60°, but some way to the north of 60° 40′.

This, then, was the idea which was in Hubert's mind when, on going north next summer, he observed a strong tide flowing sometimes from the west, in about lat. 60°. It is easy to understand that he and others looked upon this fact as strongly confirmatory of his views; and it is equally easy to understand why Button, who appears to have shared Hubert's ideas, did not turn back to look for the passage in Churchill Bay, but on the contrary pressed on and sought for it north of "Hopes Checked", about the inlets in the north-west corner of Hudson's Bay. Their search was in vain; but as the coast is much indented and girt with islands, there is, under the circumstances, nothing remarkable in the fact that they, nevertheless, clung to their preconceived notions about the movement of the tide, and what might be concluded from it; and that, rather than abandon their hopes, they considered it probable that they had somehow overlooked the opening of a passage. This, we believe, they expected to be found somewhere north of lat. 60° 40′, far from Churchill Bay, and we believe that the representation on Briggs' map, whereby Foxe and James were misled, rested on a mistake. Of how old date this mistake may be we cannot tell; we do not hear of it till 1625, when Briggs' map appeared in Purchas's *Pilgrimes*, that is, twelve years after Button's return. But it is not unreasonable to suppose that in 1618-19, when the King of Denmark and his advisers obtained the information on which they acted in sending out an expedition, and when Gordon and Watson came to Denmark in order to take part in it, the mistaken notion of Hubert's ideas which we have been criticising had not yet supplanted the true one, which, if we are not in error, may fairly be assumed to have been current for some time.

Taking all this into consideration, we have little or no doubt that Munk was instructed to search for a passage in that part of the bay where Hubert, as we think, had hoped to find one; and that for this purpose the sloop was sent out to "the northern land." Whether the dispatching the sloop by herself on this errand was part of the original plan, we cannot guess. That this was the case may, perhaps, be inferred from Munk's silence as to his motive; at the same time it is quite possible that that step may have been decided upon on the voyage, for when they arrived in Hudson's Bay, the season was so far advanced that it may have been thought advisable thus to divide the work.

As we have already stated, Munk was doubtless instructed to cross the Bay in a south-westerly direction, in order, first, to examine that part of the opposite coast to which such a course would bring him, and from which he might afterwards proceed northwards, if necessary, whenever the season permitted. But it appears that he was not merely instructed in a general way to explore the coast. Munk says that, while in Ungava Bay "the English pilot" (that is, Gordon) at one time intimated that the low wooded land which they found to the south of that bay was "the place which they searched for." After a time, however, Gordon convinced himself that it was not so. From these statements we may infer that Munk's letter of instructions directed him to look for some particular place, the description of which answered, in some measure, to the character of the low wooded land forming the south coast of Ungava Bay. At the same time, the letter of instructions must also have given information which enabled them to conclude from their examination that this land was not, after all, "the place" in question. For what purpose this place was sought is not stated; but, as the passage to the Pacific itself is evidently not meant, the only other reasonable interpretation seems to be, that a halting-place was intended, from which exploring trips might be undertaken, and, probably, also where the expedition might winter: for Munk's expressions leave no doubt of such an eventuality having been foreseen. Some definite place was, it would seem, indicated by his instructions, and one is tempted to think that it was none other than Port Nelson, where Button had wintered.

Here, however, we meet the serious question: From what source could those who drew up Munk's instructions have obtained information about any locality whatever on the west coast of Hudson's Bay? No one had been there except Button, and his report had not been published, nor did the short notice in Purchas's *Pilgrimage* supply any such information. There seems to be no other alternative than to assume that special unpublished information on Button's voyage was at the disposal of the Danish authorities, and the most reasonable view seems to be that it was obtained through Watson—supposing that he had served under Button. If so, it might also account to some extent for his being entrusted with the exploration—at any rate, the preliminary exploration—of the northern portion of the West Coast Bay, as he would have been present at "Hubbart's Hope," when that famous tide, coming from the west, was observed; and would know more than anybody else in the expedition what precise expectations were founded on it.

In Munk's account of his wintering and return journey there is no allusion to his instructions, and we have no clue whatever to his ulterior orders. We cannot, therefore, pursue this subject in further detail, but in addition to the above, we may say that the care with which Munk examined courses, passages and harbours everywhere, and which did not seem to be called for by his immediate necessities, seem to indicate that he was especially directed to investigate all such matters: as we have seen that the commanders of the expedition to Greenland in 1605-6-7 were.[1]

Munk's Map.

With regard to the geographical results of Munk's voyage we have principally to consider his map, which is worthy of much more attention than its appearance may bespeak for it at first sight. It is but coarsely cut in wood, which is so much the more unfortunate, as it is drawn on a small scale. The names are put in rather carelessly, upside down, and in some cases far from their proper places; several of them, too, are badly misspelled. No degrees are indicated; moreover, some features of it are certainly not based on actual observations. Nevertheless, there is no reason for doubting that it is, upon the whole, as faithful a repre-

---

[1] See Book I, pp. xlv, xcvi.

sentation of Munk's ideas of the countries he had visited as his own (or his draughtsman's) skill in drawing, and the resources of a Copenhagen printer of that period, could produce; and—making due allowance for circumstances—we believe that when properly examined (which has never yet been done) it will be found to be no mean performance for its date, in spite of its obvious shortcomings.

In comparing Munk's map with others, it cannot but be felt as an inconvenience that no degrees of latitude or longitude are indicated on it; and their absence is so much the more to be regretted, as Munk, if he had marked them, would have avoided some serious misunderstandings on the part of others. At the same time, however, it must of course be assumed that the different localities are put down (or, at any rate, are intended to appear) in their proper positions relatively to each other, according to Munk's conception of them; from which it follows that the indications of the geographical position of certain places given in the text indirectly determine that of others. Nor is there any great difficulty in supplying the defect in question : if not with perfect accuracy, at any rate with sufficient approximation to accuracy to render a comparison with other maps possible.

Of Munk's statements in the text concerning the position of various localities, only one refers to longitude; but there are several references to latitude; and if the places in question had been put down on the map accurately in the relative positions assigned to them in the text, we should of course have had a secure basis for laying down both parallels and meridians; but this has not been done, and parallels drawn through these localities would mostly not be in their proper distances from one another, according to Munk's figures. A sufficiently near approximation may, however, be arrived at in the following manner. Amongst the latitudes mentioned by Munk, four refer to well-defined points, *viz.*, Cape Farewell in 60° 30′, *Munkenes* in 61° 20′, *Haresund* in 62° 20′, and *Kolde Hug* in 62° 30′. If we measure the distances from south to north between each of these points and the others on the map, and compare them with each other and with the figures given in Munk's text, we find that *Kolde Hug* is placed somewhat to the south of *Haresund*, instead of north of the same ; but that the other distances, of an average, correspond very nearly to a scale of a quarter of an inch to a degree of latitude; none of them much exceeding or falling much short of that measurement. We shall, therefore, probably be sufficiently near the mark, if we ascribe to Munk's map, as we have it, a scale, based on a distance of a quarter of an inch between the parallels of 60° and 61°, and of an eighth of an inch for each degree of longitude; the map being no doubt intended to be drawn on Mercator's projection. As any inaccuracy in the distance between the parallels quickly betrays itself in the longitudes, if these are calculated from it, we may notice the fact that if the scale indicated is applied to Munk's map, both the distance from the west coast of Hudson's Bay to the westernmost point of Digges Islands (represented, in our opinion, on Munk's map, by the extreme western point of the south coast of Hudson's Strait), and also the distance from this latter point to Cape Farewell, turn out to cover just the proper number of degrees: a fact which appears to us strongly to confirm our view that Munk's map really is drawn on the scale we have suggested. It may be objected that, although it appears from this that Munk correctly estimated the proportion between the distances in question, it does not follow that Munk himself considered the two distances mentioned to cover just the number of degrees, which happens to be correct. That Munk, however, really intended the degree of longitude to be as we have indicated, seems to be confirmed by the following very remarkable fact. A striking peculiarity of Munk's map is the proportionately excessive length of Hudson's Strait: a feature to which we shall have to revert again, but of which we may say at once that it was undoubtedly borrowed from Hessel Gerritsz.'s map. This being so, it is reasonable to suppose that Munk intended the Strait to occupy, on his own map, the same number of degrees of longitude as it does on Gerritsz.'s map. On this latter, the distance between the extreme western point of the Digges Islands and the northernmost point of Labrador covers 20 deg. 45 min., or very nearly 21 degrees; whilst on Munk's map the corresponding distance covers two inches and five-eighths, which, divided by 21, give the same results as we found before, *viz.*, one-eighth of an inch to a degree of longitude.

It must be admitted that it is probably quite accidental that these coincidences are so close as they really are, but they can scarcely be looked upon as in the main fortuitous. We have, therefore, no hesitation in basing our comparison of Munk's map with others on the assumption that it is drawn to the scale above indicated. At the same time, it should, of course, be noted that we have no means of guessing the size of Munk's original map, which probably was very much larger than the reproduction of it in his book ; and that it is probably quite accidental that it has been reduced to a size in which the proportions of the degrees can be expressed so simply, in English measure, as we have indicated.

In numbering the degrees of longitude we ought, in strictness, to go by Munk's figure for the longitude of Cape Farewell, the only one he mentions. *viz.*, 60° 30', which, as we have already explained, must be understood as counted from Frankfort on the Oder. As this place is situated in long. 14° 34' east of Greenwich, Munk's figure for Cape Farewell would be equivalent to 45° 56' west of Greenwich, provided that his calculation started from the true longitude of Frankfort; and as the true longitude of Cape Farewell is 43° 53', his figure is, on that supposition, 2 deg. 3 min. too high. For the whole of this error, however, Munk can scarcely be held responsible. We have already stated that he does not appear to have determined any longitudes by astronomical observation. He was doubtless in that respect reduced to calculation by dead reckoning, which he probably started from Copenhagen. According to Origanus,[1] the clock difference between the latter place and Frankfort on the Oder is 13 minutes, corresponding to 3 deg. 15 min. of longitude, whereas the true difference is only one deg. 59 min. Assuming, therefore, that Munk obtained his figure for the longitude of Cape Farewell by adding 3 deg. 15 min. to the result of his dead reckoning from Copenhagen, we find that out of his total error as much as one deg. 16 min. is due to his being misled by Origanus, which leaves a fault of his own of only 47 min. too much.

On Hessel Gerritsz.'s map Cape Farewell stands in about longitude 344° 30' east of St. Miguel, Azores, which corresponds to 40° 40' west of Greenwich. As, however, longitudes in those days were reckoned from several different starting-points, it would be tedious to compare Munk's figure for the longitude of Cape Farewell with those of other cartographers, but we believe it would be found more correct than that on most maps of the

---

[1] *Novæ Motuum Coelestium Ephemerides* .... Francofurti in Viadrum. Anno 1609, p. 105.

seventeenth century. Nor would such a comparison be of much interest for our present purpose, because the main question before us is not whether Munk correctly estimated the difference in longitude between Cape Farewell and any other point to the east of it, not shown on the map, but whether the different localities shown on the map are in their proper relative longitude; and for this purpose we must measure their distance from some point on the map, which can be none other than Cape Farewell. How Munk himself would have numbered the meridian of Cape Farewell, if he were to have counted from Greenwich, we have no means of knowing. This, however, is indifferent for our purpose, and in order to compare the longitude of any place, as shown on Munk's map, with the longitude of the corresponding place on a modern map, we need only add the figure for the true longitude of Cape Farewell to the figure indicating the difference in longitude between the place in question and Cape Farewell, according to our scale. For simplicity's sake we shall count from the meridian of 44° instead of from the Cape itself, which is in long. 43° 53'.

In order to facilitate a comparison between Munk's map and modern ones, we have caused a copy of the former, with the degrees of latitude and longitude marked according to what has been explained in the foregoing, to be here inserted[1]. As the writing on Munk's map is put on, looking south instead of north, we have inserted one set of the figures for the degrees in keeping with the writing on the map, whilst the other set corresponds to the usual practice. Owing to the small size of Munk's map, and the clumsiness of its execution, smaller differences than five minutes of latitude or ten minutes of longitude cannot be estimated with certainty, nor is any greater accuracy required for our purpose.

Thus prepared, we may now proceed to compare Munk's map, on the one hand with modern ones, in order to test its accuracy, on the other hand with those of an earlier date, in order to ascertain how far he may have been influenced by them or improved upon them. Of the latter class, practically only one comes into consideration, and that only as regards Hudson's Strait, viz., the

---

[1] The copy having turned out a trifle too large, the degrees very slightly exceed the measurements given on p. 145; but this, of course, does not affect our argument. The marking, too, of the degrees is not quite even, but accurate enough for our purpose.

one published in 1612 by Hessel Gerritsz., in order to illustrate Hudson's discoveries. Hudson's Strait and Bay (the former, at any rate) had indeed been known for more than half a century before Hudson's time, having been visited by Portuguese, afterwards by French and others, who resorted in great numbers to the Newfoundland Bank for fishing. The Strait, in some cases apparently the Bay also, are accordingly marked on numerous maps of the 16th century, generally under the Portuguese name of *Baia das Medaus*; but although the general outline and the position of these parts—mostly near the proper latitude—exclude all doubt as to what is meant by the designers of these maps, the representations of the coasts in question generally exhibit so little resemblance to reality in detail, that a close comparison with more modern maps is out of the question. These earlier maps need not, therefore, be further noticed.

During the time between the publication of Gerritsz.'s map and that of Munk others are known to have been executed, notably those of Josias Hubert and William Baffin, but they were not published at the time. Henry Briggs' map, published in Purchas's *Pilgrimes* in 1625, was no doubt founded on these two, and may have existed before Munk's map was published in 1624, but there is no indication of Munk having known any of them. Hessel Gerritsz.'s map, which Munk certainly made use of, is therefore the only earlier one that we need here consider.

The first particular of Munk's map to which we would draw attention is the southern extremity of Greenland, which is drawn much narrower and more true to nature than on that of Hessel Gerritsz., and many other maps of that period, no doubt in accordance with Munk's own observations. A deep inlet is shown on the west coast about sixty miles north of Cape Farewell, and another less deep on the east coast in the same latitude; but there is no indication at all of any strait penetrating from the east coast into Davis' Strait corresponding to the Frobisher Strait of the Molyneux Globe, etc. Nor is there any indication of this Strait higher up on the east coast of Greenland, which, however, is not shown on this map further north than 65° 30'. Some portions of the west coast of Greenland Munk may have seen, but for the most part he must have borrowed his representation of it from his predecessors. The same holds good of the American coast north of lat. 63°, and the coast of Labrador, all of which

James Hall's Expeditions 1605, 1606 (Hakluyt Society, 1897) one published in 1612 by Hessel Gerritsz., in order to illustrate Hudson's discoveries. Hudson's Strait and Bay (the former, at any rate) had indeed been known for more than half a century before Hudson's time, having been visited by Portuguese, afterwards by French and others, who resorted in great numbers to the Newfoundland Bank for fishing. The Strait, in some cases apparently the Bay also, are accordingly marked on numerous maps of the 16th century, generally under the Portuguese name of *Baia dus Medaus;* but although the general outline and the position of these parts—mostly near the proper latitude—exclude all doubt as to what is meant by the designers of these maps, the representations of the coasts in question generally exhibit so little resemblance to reality in detail, that a close comparison with more modern maps is out of the question. These earlier maps need not, therefore, be further noticed.

During the time between the publication of Gerritsz.'s map and that of Munk others are known to have been executed, notably those of Josias Hubert and William Baffin, but they were not published at the time. Henry Briggs' map, published in Purchas's *Pilgrimes* in 1625, was no doubt founded on these two, and may have existed before Munk's map was published in 1624, but there is no indication of Munk having known any of them. Hessel Gerritsz.'s map, which Munk certainly made use of, is therefore the only earlier one that we need here consider.

The first particular of Munk's map to which we would draw attention is the southern extremity of Greenland, which is drawn much narrower and more true to nature than on that of Hessel Gerritsz., and many other maps of that period, no doubt in accordance with Munk's own observations. A deep inlet is shown on the west coast about sixty miles north of Cape Farewell, and another less deep on the east coast in the same latitude; but there is no indication at all of any strait penetrating from the east coast into Davis' Strait corresponding to the Frobisher Strait of the Molyneux Globe, etc. Nor is there any indication of this Strait higher up on the east coast of Greenland, which, however, is not shown on this map further north than 62° 30′. Some portions of the west coast of Greenland Munk may have seen, but for the most part he must have borrowed his representation of it from his predecessors. The same holds good of the American coast north of lat. 63°, and the coast of Labrador, all of which seem to have been filled in for the sake of completeness without any pretension to accuracy.

The first locality explored by Munk on the west coast of America was his *Iisefjorde* (Frobisher's Strait or Lumley's Inlet), and his representation of it is evidently quite independent. Although Davis had already described this inlet, which is indicated on the 'New Map', it is quite absent from Hessel Gerritsz.'s map, and the name is there transferred to what was afterwards called Hudson's Strait. The coastline between what is really Resolution Island and the country north of Lumley's Inlet is interrupted—as if it were still unexplored—but there is no indication of anything like an inlet. Close outside is an island called the Island of Good Fortune, Gerritsz. having, as it seems, thought that the island spoken of by Weymouth as lying near Lumley's Inlet might be the *Ilha de Fortune* of the Portuguese, which, however, on the old maps is placed south of the entrance to *Baia dus Medaus* (Hudson's Strait). Of this there is nothing on Munk's map, where we simply find two deep inlets, of which the larger more northerly one—no doubt Frobisher's Bay—trends south-east to north-west, whilst the more southerly one, which we identify with the northern end of Gabriel's Sound, has a more east-westerly direction. Had Munk's map become generally known it would have served to preserve the real Lumley's Inlet in its place in the maps, from which it disappeared for 150 years. The coast north of the inlet was not explored by Munk, and is put down by him too far east.

Resolution Island is not represented as such either on Gerritsz.'s or on Munk's map, though the southern entrance of Gabriel Sound is shown on the former, the northern entrance—as we believe—on the latter. Outside it, Gerritsz. has placed three small islands to which we have alluded above as being collectively a duplicate of Resolution Island. As they do not exist, Munk cannot have observed any islands in that place. Nevertheless, we find three such marked on his map, though very indistinctly, between the coast of what really is Resolution Island, and the representation of two ships. If they are meant for the same islands which are shown on Gerritsz.'s map, we must suppose that they have been put on in deference to the authority of the latter; but as the coast is not very accurately laid down in this place it is difficult to decide the question.

A fact which strikes one at once, on comparing Munk's map with a modern map, is that the distance between Cape Farewell and the entrance of Hudson's Strait is much too small. If we take a line between the northernmost point of Labrador and Cape Resolution to mark the entrance of Hudson's Strait, we find this to be on Munk's map, according to our scale, 13 deg. and 20 min. distant from the meridian of 44°, from which we count instead of from Cape Farewell. In reality, the line indicated coincides almost accurately with the meridian of 64° 30′ west of Greenwich, and the distance in question is 20 deg. 30 min., or 7 deg. 10 min. more than it appears to be on Munk's map. In this respect Gerritsz. is nearer to the truth, as on his map the distance between Cape Farewell and the north point of Labrador covers about 22 deg. 45 min. As it is not in the least likely that Munk should have made so great a mistake in estimating the distance, the fact that on the map it is represented as occupying seven degrees of longitude less than it really does requires a special explanation. At first sight it might be thought that perhaps it had been caused by a wish to bring Cape Farewell within the compass of the map without giving the latter an inconvenient size. But against this must be put the consideration, that after all but very little would be gained in point of expense or otherwise by such an expedient; and also the important fact, already mentioned, that on Munk's map the proportionate distance between Cape Farewell and the western extremity of Hudson's Strait is correctly indicated, which seems to show that Cape Farewell has not been moved out of its proper place. There remains only the alternative of supposing that the eastern coast of America has been moved towards the East, and this explanation is in perfect keeping with the fact that an excessive length has been attributed to Hudson's Strait. As already mentioned, this feature is, in our view, borrowed from Hessel Gerritsz.'s map, on which the Strait extends through nearly 21 degrees of longitude instead of 13 degrees and 40 minutes, measured from the northernmost point of Labrador to the westernmost point of the Digges Islands. It is not only, generally speaking, very improbable that two different persons should have fallen into such an error independently of one another; but there subsists, besides, as we shall see, so close an agreement between the two maps as regards the manner in which the excessive length of the Strait has been produced, that we are debarred from any other conclusion than that this feature has been transferred to Munk's map from the earlier one of Hessel Gerritsz. Indeed, this error of the latter cartographer reappears, more or less pronounced, on many maps of the seventeenth and early part of the eighteenth centuries. Hessel Gerritsz. did not possess any independent information by which he could check his (or Hudson's) calculation of the length of the Strait, and he therefore simply extended it sufficiently far westwards. Accordingly, we find on his map that, whilst the northernmost point of Labrador stands in long. 321° 45', according to his numbering, equal to long. 63° 25' west of Greenwich, the westernmost point of the Digges Islands is in long. 301°, equal to long. 84° 10' west of Greenwich, that is six degrees too far west. Munk appears to have adopted a contrary proceeding. He seems to have felt sure that the westernmost point of the Digges Islands was not farther from Cape Farewell than a little over 34 degrees. Placing it accordingly in that position, he could not accommodate the great length attributed to Hudson's Strait by Hessel Gerritsz. otherwise than by shortening the distance between Cape Farewell and the entrance of the Strait by seven degrees. That is accordingly what we find done on his map.

Originally, this error with regard to the length of Hudson's Strait must of course have been caused by a miscalculation of the distance sailed, whether due to Hudson—of whose card Gerritsz.'s map is supposed to be a reproduction—or to Gerritsz. himself. But the question remains, what can have induced Munk to adopt it? The general impression produced by a careful study of Munk's work is that, whenever he had observations of his own to go by he trusted them more than the statements of others; the fact, too, that he estimated the distance between Cape Farewell and the western extremity of the Strait so accurately, proves that he was by no means without material for judging rightly in the matter, and cannot be supposed to have miscalculated the distance between Cape Farewell and the American coast. We therefore consider it probable that, in accommodating his map to Hessel Gerritsz.'s in this, as in some other particulars which will be mentioned, he yielded to some special consideration. It may be that he felt somewhat diffident in deviating considerably from a map of so much note; or, more likely, it may be that in designing the map he had the co-operation of some person to whom he felt bound to defer, or to whom by force of circumstances he was obliged to leave it, and who thought more of Hessel Gerritsz.'s map than of Munk's notes and sketches.

In examining more closely this matter of the length of Hudson's Strait, we find—what in fact is implied in the preceding remarks —that the error in question does not affect all parts of the Strait equally. It will be found that the easterly displacement is greater near the entrance than higher up, gradually diminishing as we ascend the Strait. At the entrance it amounts to 7 deg. 10 min., the northernmost part of Labrador being in about long. 57° 20' instead of 64° 30'; but the extreme western point of Digges Islands is in its proper longitude. It will also be observed that the lengthening of the Strait is not merely or principally brought about by drawing the various portions of coast which really had been examined by Munk proportionally too long, but mostly by insertion of pieces of coast which have no real existence at all. It is evident from Munk's narrative that he was not favoured with a continuous sight of the shore on either side, but had an opportunity of seeing only detached portions, which afterwards were connected by conjectural lines; and it is in these intervals that the interpolations to which the excessive length of the Strait is mostly due occur.

Coming now to details, we observe, first, that the width of the entrance, measured between the parallels of the northernmost point of Labrador and of *Munkenes* is, according to Munk's map, about one deg. and 30 min., which is about 45 min. too much, and is owing to the fact that *Munkenes* is placed about 10 min. more northerly than it ought to have been according to the text, and that the northernmost point of Labrador is placed about 35 min. too southerly. On Gerritsz.'s map the two points are in their correct latitude.

The island which is seen in the entrance is no doubt the largest of the Button islands, but it is drawn much too large; probably because Munk took it to be the one by which, according to his instructions, he was to recognise the opening, and wished to draw attention to it. It is shown on the map in the latitude given in the text. On Hessel Gerritsz.'s map no island is marked in that position, but many old maps show some islands in the same position, the largest of which is called *Ilha de Fortune*.

Turning our attention first to the south coast, we come at once inside the opening to the longest of the interpolated portions. On Hessel Gerritsz.'s map it is quite straight; at the eastern extremity a headland juts out from it, which represents the northernmost projection of Labrador; at its western extremity a quite similar prominent headland is observed, from which the coast trends away in a southerly direction into Ungava Bay. The second projection of land is, no doubt, a mere duplicate of that terminating in the northernmost point of Labrador, and its appearance on Gerritsz.'s map may be explained by supposing that Hudson, when he found himself forced southwards by the wind and the ice into Ungava Bay, and observed the headland to the east and the coast trending away from it to the south, failed to recognise it as the same which he had seen forming the south side of the entrance to Hudson's Strait, but imagined it to be another similar one situated further west. Munk, who like Hudson came into Ungava Bay unintentionally, may have been deceived in a similar manner; or he may have borrowed this feature from Hessel Gerritsz., and modified it according to his own observations. On Munk's map the interpolated imaginary piece of coast in question is much larger than on Gerritsz.'s map, nor is it straight as on the latter. The south coast of Hudson's Strait is on Munk's map seen to recede just inside the entrance—very much as it really does—though in a south-westerly instead of a southerly direction. This, however, is continued only for a distance of about seventy miles, after which the coast turns northwest, forming in this way a triangular bay, into which a broad river or inlet is seen to open. To the west of this bay another very similar but smaller one is marked, bounded to the west by what we consider the duplicate of the northern projection of Labrador, beyond which the coast definitely turns into Ungava Bay. Neither of these bays exists; but it is not difficult to understand how, having observed the coast to fall away to the south, just inside the entrance to the Strait, and supposing the headland which he saw to the east in sailing into Ungava Bay to be a different one, Munk may have been led to draw the coastline which he supposed to connect them, as he has done, though we cannot suggest the origin of the inlet at the bottom of the triangular bay.

The great expansion, or bay, on the south side of Hudson's Strait, just inside the entrance, is drawn more open, and, in so far

more true to nature on Gerritsz.'s map than on Munk's, where
it is encroached upon by the interpolated piece of land just spoken
of. At the same time, Munk's representation is superior in so
far, that Hope's Advance Bay and Akpatok are distinctly marked,
whilst there is no indication of them on Gerritsz.'s map. This is
a rather remarkable fact, considering that it is quite clear from
Prickett's account that Hudson penetrated quite as far into
Ungava Bay as Munk did afterwards, and that Hudson's party
observed that Akpatok was an island.[1] On Munk's map, Ungava
Bay is not so sharply separated from the Strait as it is in reality,
because Akpatok, the supposed promontory of *Alckenes*, is drawn
too short, and with a main direction a little south of east, instead
of north-east. In consequence of this, Hope's Advance Bay
appears not to be drawn deep enough, but the western extremity
of it is laid down one deg. and 30 min. west of the meridian of the
point corresponding to Cape Hope's Advance, which is only
10 min. out of proportion. The shallow bay formed by the
main land, and the islands of Ekkertaujok and Akpatok, to the
north of the latter, appears too deep and narrow (on account
of an incorrect projection of the coast south of Cape Hope's
Advance); on the other hand, the bottom of Ungava Bay is
in lat. 58°, only 25 min. too southerly. On Gerritsz.'s map it is
in lat. 59°.

Concerning *Snee Öeland* we can say nothing definite, on
account of the uncertainty still existing as to the true place of
Green Island, with which we have identified it. In any case, it
seems to be placed too northerly in proportion to some other
localities, but the receding part of the Strait in which it is situated
is drawn too narrow. *Snee Öeland* is not shown on Gerritsz.'s
map, where, however, another island is marked close to Cape
Hope's Advance, which Munk does not notice.[2]

The point on Munk's map corresponding to Cape Hope's
Advance is, according to the scale which we are applying, about
22 deg. 40 min. west of Cape Farewell, corresponding to long.

---

[1] See *Purchas his Pilgrimes*, vol. iii, p. 509; Asher, *Henry Hudson*,
p. 104 (Hakluyt Soc., 1860).

[2] It may be noted here that on the map this name is apparently
spelt *Snecer*, a corruption, which seems to show that Munk has not
revised the writing on the map.

66° 40′ west of Greenwich, whereas the promontory really lies in long. 70°. It is, therefore, about 3 deg. 20 min. too far east, but, as the displacement of the entrance amounts to 7 deg. 10 min., the error is considerably diminished in this part of the Strait. On Gerritsz.'s map this point is in long. 72° 20′ west of Greenwich.

The next point west of Cape Hope's Advance which admits of fairly certain identification is Munk's *Sydernes*, which, we believe, represents Prince of Wales's Island merged into the somewhat broader projection of land to the south of it, which in reality is separated from the island by a narrow sound. On Munk's map the prominent piece of coast against which the name of *Sydernes* is placed lies between long. 27 and 28 deg. west of Cape Farewell (corresponding to long. 71° and 72° west of Greenwich), whilst the portion of the coastline which it represents in reality only reaches from long. 72° 25′ to 72° 50′. The representation on Munk's map is, therefore, much too large; but similar exaggerations occur elsewhere on Munk's map, where localities are represented which he has especially noticed. As the figures just quoted show, the eastern limit of this portion of the coast is placed one deg. and 25 min. too far east; but, as compared with Cape Hope's Advance, the eastern displacement of the whole coast is here reduced by nearly two and a half degrees. This is mainly due to the fact that the coastline between the two last-mentioned points is laid down on Munk's map in its full length and straight: whereas in reality it forms two bays, one of which recedes as much as 20 miles; at the same time the direction of the coast on the map is almost due east and west (with a rise in latitude of only 30 min.), instead of north-west (with a rise in latitude of about one degree). This is particularly noticeable just east of *Sydernes*, between it and an inlet which is clearly marked on Munk's map, one deg. and 20 min. to the east of *Sydernes*, and at the same time 20 min. to the south of it; whilst on the Admiralty Chart the corresponding inlet is shown only 30 min. to the east, but at the same time 30 min. to to the south of Prince of Wales Island. On Gerritsz.'s map "The King's Foreland", which in our opinion corresponds to *Sydernes*, is in about long. 74° west of Greenwich.

As we have already stated, Munk's *Iisver*, which we identify with Charles Island, are, like Prince of Wales Island, not distinguished on his map from the mainland (close to which he says

that they are situated), but appear merely as a projection of it.
The name of *Iisver*, on Munk's map, is placed alongside the
coast, near the western entrance of Hudson's Strait, without distinctly referring to any special part of it; but, on the supposition
that Munk's *Iisver* is Charles Island, there is, we believe, no difficulty in recognising the particular part of the coast which represents *Iisver*. About three degrees of longitude inside the western
entrance of the Strait, the coast, on the south side, exhibits a
rather sharp salient point, which in appearance and position
corresponds so closely to the northernmost point of Charles
Island, that we can have no hesitation in identifying it with the
latter. They stand, within a few minutes, in the same longitude,
viz., about 75° west of Greenwich; and, like the northern headland of Charles Island, the promontory shown on the map is
flanked by a shallow bay on either side, with which it forms
a coast line resembling very much that of the north coast
of Charles Island, and of not much greater extent from east to
west. To the west of this piece of coast, in long. 75° 40', according to our scale, we observe, on Munk's map, a well-defined deep
bay, which we take to represent the western entrance of the
channel between Charles Island and the main land, which we
believe to have been omitted by the fault of the draughtsman
who reduced the map for publication. East of the same piece
of coast on Munk's map, a slight but unmistakeable indentation
or bend of the coastline indicates, in our view, the position of
the eastern entrance of the channel in question, and is situated
in the same longitude as the latter, *viz.*, about 74°. It will be
noticed that if this piece of coast really represents Charles Island,
it is very nearly in the right position as regards longitude.
The fact is, that the coastline between the two points which
we take for the west end of Prince of Wales Island and the east
end of Charles Island, is drawn so much too long that the
gradually diminishing easterly displacement which we have noticed
in other places lower down the Strait has here altogether disappeared. The oftmentioned piece of coast which represents
Charles Island reaches, in fact, a little too far west; as, however,
the remainder of the south coast of Hudson's Strait is drawn
as much too short, the result is that the westernmost point of it
on Munk's map (which in our opinion really represents the
westernmost point of the Digges Islands) is, according to the

scale we have applied, nearly 33 deg. and 10 min. west of Cape Farewell (or, more precisely, the meridian of 44°), corresponding nearly to long. 78° 10′ west of Greenwich, which is correct. On Gerritsz.'s map this point is in long. 301°, equal to 84° 10′ west of Greenwich.

The whole southern coast of Hudson's Strait is on Munk's map placed too low in point of latitude, but not uniformly so. The northern extremity of Labrador is 35 min., the Cape of Hope's Advance about one degree, *Sydernes* one deg. and 35 min., and the extreme point to the west one deg. and 30 min., too far south. This is not very surprising when it is remembered that Munk only sailed along the coast from east to west, and *vice versâ*, without landing and observing anywhere. The only point with regard to which he was in such a position that he could obtain the latitude of it is *Alkenes*, the east end of Akpatok, which the text places correctly in lat. 60°, but which on the map is quite 30 min. further south; probably owing —at any rate in a measure—to its being represented as pointing to the south-east instead of the north-east.

It does not appear that Munk borrowed any detail from Hessel Gerritsz. as regards the western half of the south coast of Hudson's Strait. The general north-west trend of the coast west of Cape Hope's Advance, and the configuration of the two wide bays between that promontory and Prince of Wales Island, and between the latter and Charles Island, are better represented on Gerritsz.'s map, on which also the latitudes, upon the whole, are more correctly given. But it will be seen from the foregoing that Munk's representation in several places bears evidence of much more careful examination of the coast, so as to render posible a very detailed comparison with modern maps. On Gerritsz.'s map, as on Munk's, Prince of Wales Island and Charles Island are not represented as islands, but as portions of the coast close to which they are situated. The Digges Islands, however, are drawn as islands on Gerritsz.'s map.

Concerning Munk's representation of the northern shore of Hudson's Strait, to which we must now turn our attention, we may first note that it agrees with that on modern maps in so far that the coast trends north-west for some distance inside the entrance, after which it assumes a westerly direction; a feature which is not shown on Gerritsz.'s map. Like the corresponding part of the southern shore of the Strait, this part of the northern shore is drawn too long, but the error in the longitude of the entrance diminishes gradually, though not evenly, towards the west. Cape Resolution stands on Munk's map, as it ought to, almost exactly north of the northernmost point of Labrador, and is like the latter misplaced, 7 deg. 10 min. too far east; but *Munkenes* is only six degrees too far east, *viz.*, in long. 59° instead of 65°, being fully one degree too far west of Cape Resolution. The point where the coast, as just mentioned, turns westwards is not very sharply defined, but it is shown on Munk's map about 18 deg. west of Cape Farewell, or in about long. 62°, whilst the true longitude is about 67° 30′, so that the initial displacement of the coast towards the east is at this point reduced from 7 deg. to 5½ deg. Partly on account of the coastline being thus unduly lengthened, partly because *Munkenes* is placed in lat. 61° 30′ instead of lat. 61° 20′ (as stated in the text), this lower portion of the north coast appears to trend west-north-west instead of due north-west. The principal defect of this part of Munk's map is that the southern entrance to Gabriel Sound is only indicated by a small bay. This is remarkable, not only because it is clearly indicated as an inlet on Gerritsz.'s map, but because Munk remained a whole day close to Resolution Island, and the opening of Gabriel Sound is too wide to be easily overlooked. As, however, we read in his account that they were much distressed at that time by the weather and the ice, this may account for Munk not having obtained sufficiently accurate material for his map.

From the bend of the coastline above mentioned, the latter trends westwards: on modern maps a little to the north, on Munk's map due west. On this part of the coast, as represented by him, we notice two deep inlets, one not far from the bend, the other fully two degrees farther west. Between them the name *Harsont*, which of course is meant for *Haresund*, is inserted in such a manner that it may apply equally well to either of these inlets, or to some point on the coast between them. The name, *Rensund* (of course the same as *Rinsund*, and in fact more correctly spelt than the latter) is inserted a long way to the east of these inlets, pointing to a place on the coast where the ships are represented lying close to land. As it appears from the narrative that *Haresund* was an inlet, and the last place of that kind visited on the north coast, it is most probable that the name on the map is intended for the westernmost of the two inlets in question, and it remains to decide what is represented by the other. At first, one might perhaps be tempted to take it for the southern entrance of Gabriel Sound—of course very much displaced; but this view is not tenable, because in that case the name of *Rinsund* (which certainly did not apply to any place on Resolution Island) would have been placed west of the inlet on the map, whereas it stands well to the east of it. Nor is it probable that the inlet in question is meant for *Rinsund* itself. As we have mentioned above (see p. 82), Munk's statements about their stay at *Rinsund* point to its being a sound between the mainland and some islands, rather than an inlet from the sea; and this view is corroborated by the representation on the woodcut facing p. 14, which seems to illustrate this part of the map. The two streams shown on the woodcut correspond most likely to the two inlets shown on the map; and, just as on the latter, the ships are represented lying close to the shore at the point against which the name of *Rinsund* is placed, east of the easternmost inlet, so, on the woodcut, the ships are represented lying east of the easternmost stream, close to the shore, inside some islands. We therefore consider it probable that the easternmost of the inlets on the map is intended for some locality of that kind, which Munk's party may have seen on their excursions from *Rinsund*, but which is not mentioned in Munk's narrative. As a matter of fact, a bay or short inlet similar to Icy Cove is found in this neighbourhood opposite the Middle Savage Islands, just west of the bend of the coastline above alluded to, which on the Admiralty Chart is named Jackman's Sound; and we consider it most probable that it is this bay which is represented by the easternmost stream or inlet on the woodcut and the map. We believe, accordingly, that *Rinsund* was a narrow sound between the mainland and some small islands close to the shore, not far east of Jackman's Sound; which, however, cannot be identified more accurately without a more detailed knowledge of the coast than we possess. It will be noticed that if these two inlets on the map represent Icy Cove and Jackman's Sound respectively, they are drawn out of all proportion large; there are, in fact, no inlets at all on this coast of a size corresponding to the representation on Munk's map. The distance between the two inlets, likewise, is four times the real distance between Icy Cove and Jackman's Sound. This, however, is only another instance of the exaggeration which we have noticed before in the drawing of localities which Munk had specially explored. Another instance of the same is afforded by the representation of two islands outside *Haresund*, which probably are meant for the rocky islets where they were hard pressed by the ice before they found a refuge in that harbour (see p. 17).

If *Haresund* is Icy Cove, as we suppose, it is in some respects not much out of its proper place on Munk's map. We may note particularly that its position, compared with Cape Hope's Advance, accords well with our view of their movements in Hudson's Strait. By the scale which we apply to Munk's map, the western shoulder of *Haresund* stands 21 deg. and 30 min. west of Cape Farewell, or in long. 65° 30' west of Greenwich, whereas the true longitude of Icy Cove is 68° 30'. If, therefore, our identification is correct, *Haresund* is only three deg. too far to the east, whilst the easterly displacement at the oft-mentioned bend of the coast amounts to five and a half degrees. This diminution is chiefly due to the fact that on Munk's map the two inlets of which we have just been treating, with the coast between them, cover three degrees of longitude, whilst Jackman's Sound and Icy Cove, with the intervening coast, only occupy 45 min. It may be noted that neither of the two inlets appears on Hessel Gerritsz.'s map. Munk states the latitude of two points on this part of the coast *viz.*, *Munkeness*, which in the text he places correctly in lat. 61° 20', but on the map reaches no further south than 61° 30', and *Haresund*, the entrance of which is placed on the map in lat. 62° 20', which is the latitude stated in the text, and also the true latitude of Icy Cove.

Munk's representation of the northern shore of Hudson's Strait, immediately west of *Haresund*, is very faulty. In reality the coastline turns northwards into North Bay, at a point which does not seem to be as yet accurately determined, but which is certainly situated within 30 min. west of Icy Cove, and the distance from Icy Cove to the southern extremity of Big Island, which bounds the north bay on the western side, covers only one deg. and 50 min.; but on Munk's map the coastline is continued west of *Haresund* through four deg. of longitude before it turns northwards, and the distance from this turning-point to his *Koldenes*, which no doubt represents the southern extremity of Big Island, is on his map equal to four deg. of longitude; making the total difference in longitude between that point and *Haresund* eight deg., or six deg. and 10 min. more than the real difference between Big Island and Icy Cove. Moreover, whereas the coast in North Bay recedes only 30 to 35 miles, Munk's map shows a great waterway branching off from Hudson's Strait east of *Koldenes*, and continued in a north-easterly direction for about 250 miles, ending blind near the head of Cumberland Inlet. As regards the excessive width of the opening, which represents the entrance of North Bay, it is not difficult to imagine how Munk may have fallen into error. It appears from his narrative that, when he left *Haresund* on the outward voyage, he did not cross North Bay, but was carried over to the southern coast of Hudson's Strait, and when he passed Big Island on his return from Ungava Bay the island was not visible on account of fog. He must have seen Big Island on the homeward voyage, since he has named it; but he may not on that occasion have seen the coast about Icy Cove; and he may, therefore, very well have been in uncertainty about the distance between these two points. Far more difficult is it to account for the long piece of coast intervening between *Haresund* and North Bay, because in the text Munk says expressly that the great bay to the west of *Haresund* was close to it; nor is there anything in the text indicating that Munk looked upon the bay in question as connected with such a great waterway stretching far towards the north-east, as is shown on the map. For an explanation we seem to be thrown back on the supposition that Munk himself was not wholly responsible for the map, except as regards parts which he had examined himself, but that the drawing of other parts was left more or less to a different hand. The representation in question on Munk's map is evidently conjectural, and may possibly be derived from Best's map, or be connected with the fact that on Gerritsz.'s map a similar great strait is shown farther west, though, on the latter, North Bay is indicated pretty accurately.

Whatever may be the true explanation of the error just discussed, it had the effect of causing Big Island, the southern extremity of which is represented by Munk's *Koldenes*, to be very much displaced towards the west. The difference in longitude between *Koldenes* and *Haresund* is on Munk's map over eight deg., whilst the true difference between Big Island and Icy Cove is only one deg. and 50 min. As, however, *Haresund*—if it be Icy

Cove—is placed three deg. too far east on Munk's map, the result is that *Koldenes* is placed 3 deg. and 20 min. too far west. According to the scale we apply to Munk's map, the longitude of *Koldenes* corresponds to about 73° 50′ west of Greenwich, whilst the southernmost point of Big Island is in 70° 30′ west of Greenwich. Apart from this error, the west coast of Big Island and Meta Incognita is evidently laid down from actual observation. *Koldenes* is in lat. 62° 15′, only 15 min. too southerly for the southern extremity of Big Island. About 20 min. further north-west, a small bay seems to indicate the entrance of White Strait. Another, larger, bay to the north of this is drawn too deep, but a marked projection of the land between lat. 63° 10′ and 63° 30′, bounded by a small bay to the north of it, corresponds evidently to Fair Ness, which is really but little farther north, and presents quite a similar configuration. Munk says that he proceeded in this direction as far as lat. 63° 20′ before he changed his course to a south-westerly one for Hudson's Bay, and we have laid down his course accordingly on the track chart. To judge, however, from his map, he must have been far enough to gain a fairly true impression of the coastline as far as the land near King Charles Cape, with which we identify a projection of land pointing south in long. 79° to 79° 30′, and lat. 64° 40′. On this supposition, the place assigned to it by Munk is much too westerly (though not more than is the case with the whole of this coast), but is only about 25 min. too northerly. The direction of the coastline as far as Fair Ness is on Munk's map fairly correct, being only one point too northerly.

As we shall see, this westerly displacement of the north coast is maintained (though somewhat diminished) all through, as far as the north-west corner of Hudson's Bay; from which we may perhaps conclude that the map was originally nearly correct in this respect, and that, either by an error in the reduction or engraving, or by the interference of some person who imagined that he could improve upon Munk's drawing, the whole of this part of the map was shifted westwards. The latter supposition is by far the more probable one; because, if we mistake not, it is due to this displacement of the north coast that the south coast of Hudson's Strait is shown in a wrong latitude, particularly from Cape Hope's Advance to Cape Wolstenholme. The north-east point of Charles Island is really in lat. 62° 55′, and that of Prince of Wales Island in lat. 62° 12′, whilst *Koldenes*, the south point of Big Island, is in lat. 62° 30′; at the same time the difference in longitude between the latter point and the eastern extremity of Charles Island is only three deg. 30 min. From this it follows that if *Koldenes* and the west coast of Meta Incognita are laid down more than three deg. too far west, but in the proper latitude, Hudson's Strait would be reduced to a very narrow channel indeed, or even appear to be closed up altogether. It is very likely, in order to avoid this, that the south coast of the Strait has been brought down more than one degree below its proper latitude (s. p. 160).

In the next place we must turn our attention to the islands situated in the western opening of Hudson's Strait, and the first we come to are Salisbury and Nottingham Islands. On Gerritsz.'s map only one island is shown in their place, which is named Salisbury Island, but seems rather to be meant for Nottingham Island, which is nearest to Hudson's track, unless it stands for both of them. Munk's map is the earliest published map on which they are both shown, but the representation of them is not accurate: the more northerly one, which must be meant for Salisbury Island, is placed north-west instead of north-east of the more southerly one, which must be intended for Nottingham Island Moreover, they are drawn too small, and in a wrong position both as regards latitude and longitude. The islands are really situated between lat. 63° 10′ and 63° 50′, but appear on Munk's map between lat. 62° 20′ and 62° 45′. As regards longitude they appear at first sight most extraordinarily misplaced, being close to the west coast of Meta Incognita; but this is chiefly due to the fact above discussed, that the coast in question is laid down on the map fully three degrees too far west. The islands themselves are, therefore, not so much displaced as might be thought at first sight. Whilst the easternmost point of Salisbury Island is in long. 76° 30′, the easternmost island on Munk's map is no farther east than about 75°. In explanation of these islands being shown on Munk's map out of their proper place, we need not add anything to what we have stated on p. 99.

Concerning the representation of Digges Islands on Munk's map, we may refer to what has been mentioned on pp. 98-99. On the original map they must have been marked as islands; and that they appear merged in the mainland on the reproduction of the map in Munk's book is doubtless due to the small size of the latter, combined with the clumsiness of its execution.

In examining Munk's representation of Hudson's Bay, we need not bestow much attention on the eastern coast or James's Bay, which were not visited by Munk, or anybody of his party, and the detail of which he must, consequently, have borrowed from Hessel Gerritsz., though they are rendered with not a little freedom. It should be noticed, however, that whilst on Gerritsz.'s map the east coast of the Bay is placed about six degrees too far west, on account of the excessive length given to Hudson's Strait (see p. 154), the coast in question appears on Munk's map in its proper longitude. The point corresponding to the extreme western limit of Hudson's exploration (Cape Henrietta Maria) is, however, on Munk's map, placed in about the same distance west of the east coast of Hudson's Bay as on Gerritsz.'s map, in consequence of which the width of James's Bay is nearly the same on both maps.

Mansfield Island is shown on both maps, but Munk has no doubt drawn it from his own observations, though not more correctly. On his map it appears broader and shorter, and situated between lat. 60° 50′ and 62°, whilst on Gerritsz.'s map it is placed between lat. 60° 40′ and 62° 50′. As the real position is between 61° 35′ and 62° 38′, it will be seen that Munk gives the extension from north to south pretty accurately, but places the whole island half a degree too southerly. On Gerritsz.'s map the meridian of 300° east of St. Miguel (85° 10′ west of Greenwich), passes through the middle of the island (which on that map bears no name), whilst Digges Islands are in long. 301°. On Munk's map a meridian so drawn would be 36 deg. 10 min. west of Cape Farewell, about two deg. west of Digges Islands, corresponding to long. 80° 10′ west of Greenwich, which is the true longitude.

As regards the remainder of Hudson's Bay, we cannot compare Munk's map to any other previously published, because none such exists. Munk's map of these parts is, as far as we know, entirely original.

Munk, it will be remembered, sailed straight across Hudson's Bay to Port Churchill, which point, therefore, next claims our attention. As he appears to have kept a pretty direct course, he would have the means for a very fair computation of the longitudinal difference between the Digges Islands and the west coast of Hudson's Bay, and the map shows that he succeeded very well in computing it. The west coast of Hudson's Bay, at the bottom of Churchill Bay is, according to our scale, 50 deg. 30 min. west of Cape Farewell on Munk's map, which corresponds to long. 94° 30′ west of Greenwich ; that is to say, it is only 30 min. too far east. Port Churchill itself appears much displaced, the opening being between 47 deg. 30 min. and 48 deg. 30 min. west of Cape Farewell, and so wide as to occupy nearly one degree. These figures correspond to 91° 30′ and 92° 30′ west of Greenwich, whilst in reality the opening lies in about 94° 15′. This, however, is obviously caused by the inner portion of the southern coast of Churchill Bay being greatly lengthened, so as to make room for a disproportionately large representation of the harbour and its vicinity. The outline of the coast near the harbour is drawn sufficiently large to reproduce the configuration shown in the bird's-eye-view of the harbour on the second woodcut (facing p. 23), which could not possibly have been done without departing greatly from the general scale of the map. We have already noticed similar exaggerated representations of particular localities in other parts of the map. Munk, doubtless, had this done in order to show unmistakably where the harbour was, and to facilitate the finding of it ; but, of course, this part of his map is spoilt by it, as this portion of the coast occupies about three deg. in longitude, instead of about 50 min.

Between Cape Merry, which bounds the entrance to Port Churchill on the east side, and Cape Churchill, the coast is similarly lengthened, showing the shallow bay between them. As the distance between the two points mentioned on Munk's map covers one deg. 10 min. instead of 55 min., the result is that Cape Churchill is about 46 deg. 10 min. west of Cape Farewell, corresponding to 90° 10′ west of Greenwich, whereas that promontory really lies in long. 93° 15′. The coast from thence southwards to Port Nelson is consequently displaced eastwards to the same extent.

The latitude of Port Churchill is not mentioned in Munk's text, but on his map the entrance of it is placed in about lat. 58° 50′ to 55′, only a few minutes below the correct figure. It may be noticed that, on the map, the opening of Port Churchill faces north, a little to the west, whilst in reality it faces northeast, as shown on the woodcut.

According to Munk's narrative, he did not himself make any exploring expeditions along the coast, either to the north or to the south of Port Churchill, while he was there; but he must have seen a considerable portion of it, both in coming to and leaving the harbour, particularly on the latter occasion, when he spent several days sailing on both sides of the harbour, in order to double or penetrate the belt of ice which held him prisoner between it and the land. As regards the coast east and south of Port Churchill, which we will consider first, there is no evidence to show how far he went; and it is not at all probable that he ever came within sight of Nelson River, or the bay in which it discharges. Nevertheless, the bay and the river are unmistakeably laid down on his map. An explanation of this remarkable fact may, perhaps, be found in Munk's statement that Hans Brock, the Danish mate on board *Enhiörningen*, was sent out on Sept. 13th, 1619, in order to explore the coast southwards of Port Churchill, but only returned on Sept. 23rd. It is true that he was not ordered to proceed further than nine miles Danish, which would be only one-third of the distance to Port Nelson, and also that he was only in an open boat. But it is difficult to understand what he can have been doing all that time, if he had not gone further. It is, therefore, probable that he advanced far enough along the coast to have a sight of the bay, if not actually to explore it. If so, he must be supposed to have reported his observations to Munk. If, furthermore, as we think not unlikely, Watson had been with Button when he wintered at Port Nelson in 1612-13, Munk may have learnt from him various particulars, by means of which he may have been able to identify the place of which Brock reported with the place of which Watson had told him; and the representation of these parts on Munk's map may be the result of a combination of these reports. At the same time, if Munk was directed to make for the place where Button had wintered (which we consider not improbable) he may have been supplied with some information concerning the configuration of the land near Port Nelson. In any case, the information he received was not very complete, as, on his map, Port Nelson stands fully two degrees too low in point of latitude. As regards the direction of the coast beyond Port Nelson, it is evident that Munk was informed that it trended north-east, but not that this direction was maintained only for about fifty miles, after which, at Cape Tatnam, it turns southwards again, as it does at Cape Churchill. Thus, no doubt, it came about that Munk filled up the still unexplored part of the coast of Hudson's Bay by continuing the coastline from the mouth of Nelson River in a north-easterly direction, far enough to meet the extreme point reached by Hudson (Cape Henrietta Maria), as shown on Gerritsz.'s map. According to Hessel Gerritsz. this point was in lat. 60°, and the result of Munk resorting to the expedient indicated was the appearance on Munk's map of an enormous projection of land filling up the southwestern part of the bay. Owing to the fact, already mentioned, that Port Nelson is placed fully two degrees too far south, the bay at the head of which it is situated is converted into a very deep funnel-shaped inlet, in consequence of which the projection of land in question appears to encroach on Hudson's Bay even more than would otherwise be the case. This projection of land is quite fictitious. Cape Henrietta Maria is not situated farther north than lat. 55° 10', and the coastline which connects it with Cape Tatnam, near Nelson River, is so far from forming a projection of land, that, on the contrary, it curves gently round in a south-easterly direction forming a very flat bay. With the informformation Munk possessed, it was very natural for him to fill up the gap between the points mentioned in the manner adopted by him; and the unsatisfactory result was due to his having been misled by Gerritsz. as to the latitude of Cape Henrietta Maria, and to his not knowing at what distance east of Nelson River the coast resumed its southerly direction. The configuration of this projecting piece of land is, of course, quite conjectural, and we cannot account for the detail of it. More particularly is this the case with regard to the large island shown close to the north of it, and which should perhaps be looked upon as forming the northern portion of it, because it is this island which approaches to the latitude of 60°, which Hessel Gerritsz. ascribes to Cape Henrietta Maria. It seems that in order to make the western coast of James Bay meet his coastline east of Port Nelson, Munk altered the former; but as the whole of this representation is conjectural, it is not worth further consideration.

With regard to the coast north of Port Churchill the case stands differently. Munk, no doubt, sailed along this coast for some distance on his homeward voyage, but, as he took a north-easterly course for Hudson's Strait when he was able to leave the coast, he cannot have been farther north than lat. 61°, if indeed so far. Nevertheless, the representation on Munk's map of the coast north of that latitude shows, in several respects, such a remarkable agreement with its real configuration, that it must have been laid down from actual observation. Nor would it suffice, with regard to this, to fall back on the supposition that Munk had received information, directly or indirectly, from persons who had been with Button's expedition. The manner in which Port Nelson is marked on Munk's map agrees so far with what we find on Briggs's map, that it would not be unreasonable to conclude that they had their information from the same source; but Munk's map of the west coast of Hudson's Bay exhibits important features of which nothing is to be seen on Briggs' map. From this we conclude that Munk had special and more direct information; nor is there any difficulty connected with this view if we adopt the opinion above propounded, to the effect that the sloop was despatched expressly to investigate this coast.

As we have already stated, the west coast of Hudson's Bay in Churchill Bay is on Munk's map very nearly in the true longitude, according to our calculation, *viz.*, in long. 94° 30′ instead of long. 95° west of Greenwich. Instead, however, of curving gradually round towards the north-east, from long. 95° in Churchill Bay to long. 90° in Daly Bay, as the coastline really does in the main, it turns on Munk's map sharply to the east in about lat. 60°, and continues in this direction through nearly five degrees of longitude before it again turns northwards, thus converting Churchill Bay from a very open round bay into a comparatively long and narrow inlet. From the rocks at the mouth of Port Churchill, the coast in question may very likely have presented such an appearance, particularly if the variation of the compass was not duly considered, and this may explain how it has come to be drawn thus on Munk's map. At the northern shoulder of the bay thus formed, in lat. 60°, the coastline on Munk's map turns due north, but it turns westerly again in lat. 62° 10′. On this portion of the coast, a little north of lat. 61°, a deep inlet is shown, which in position corresponds to Nevill Bay, but in point of shape much more resembles Ranken Inlet.

In lat. 62° 10′ the coastline on Munk's map turns, as already stated, westwards into a great inlet, of which the western extremity is not shown on the map, although the piece which is represented has a length of fully 120 miles. This can scarcely be meant for anything but Chesterfield Inlet, though the opening is placed between lat. 62° 10′ and 62° 45′, instead of between lat. 63° and 63° 25′. This identification is strengthened by two circumstances: viz., the fact that two islands are marked as situated in the opening, corresponding to Promise Island and Fairway Island of the Admiralty Chart, and that the northern headland is placed much more westerly than the southern headland. This, indeed, is not their true relative position; rather the contrary is the case. But the localities would, nevertheless, appear in the positions given to them on Munk's map to a person sailing by who mistook the trend of the coast to be due north, as on Munk's map, instead of north-east as it really is.

As is implied in the foregoing statements, Munk's map is the earliest on which the features just discussed, and particularly Chesterfield Inlet, appears.

A little north of the 63rd parallel the coastline on Munk's map forms a sharp little bay pointing north-west, from the head of which it turns back and is continued in a south-westerly direction through six degrees of longitude to a headland projecting into Hudson's Bay in lat. 62° 10′. The identity of the small peculiarly-shaped bay—where the coast turns westwards on Munk's map—with Daly Bay, which forms the extreme north-west corner of Hudson's Bay—is unmistakeable, and the latitude of the northernmost extremity, about 63° 40′, is correct within about 30 minutes. Whoever originally drew that must have been there, and Munk must have had a sketch of it, whether done by Watson or anybody else. Munk's map is the earliest known on which it is marked. A well-marked promontory on the north coast, just out of Daly Bay, represents clearly enough Cape Fullerton, but there is no indication either of Roe's Welcome or of Fisher's Strait, which were both observed by Button's expedition. The entrance to the latter seems to be indicated by a small bay behind the headland in lat. 62° 10′ abovementioned, which unmistakeably represents Cape Southampton.

As regards longitude, the entrance to Chesterfield Inlet, inside the islands, is placed about 48 deg. west of Cape Farewell, which corresponds to a true longitude of 92° west of Greenwich, whilst the entrance really is in 91° to 91° 15′. The innermost corner of Daly Bay, however, is wider of the mark, being in long. 92° 10′ instead of about 89° 50′. This is in keeping with the fact above alluded to, that the northern shoulder of Chesterfield

Inlet is set back towards the west fully two degrees, and that from this point the coast is drawn trending north instead of north-east. At the same time it must be borne in mind that, as we stated above (p. 165), a corresponding displacement towards the west is observable through the whole northern coast of Hudson's Bay and Strait as far as *Koldenes*, the southern extremity of Big Island.

The promontory, which in our opinion represents Cape Fullerton, is placed in long. 90° and lat. 63° 10', instead of long. 88° 30' and lat. 64°; Cape Southampton is shown in long. 86° instead of 83° 40', and in lat. 62° 15', which is only 3 min. too northerly. It will be seen from these figures that the difference in longitude between Daly Bay and Cape Southampton is nearly correct on Munk's map. The coast between Cape Fullerton and Cape Southampton was evidently not actually observed on the voyage, but the headlands which have been seen were connected on the map by a conjectural coastline. The party in the sloop probably passed Cape Southampton, and steering north-west approached Cape Fullerton and Daly Bay, from which they followed the coast southwards. The representation on Munk's map of the northern coast from Cape Southampton to Cape Fullerton reminds one not a little of Baffin's and Briggs' maps, but the similarity is not greater than would naturally be expected between maps of the same localities.

Munk's *Kolde Hug* we have identified with Cary's Swans' Nest, and the correctness of this cannot be subject to any reasonable doubt, as Munk expressly states that the coast eastwards of the promontory trends north-east, which is really the case east of Cary's Swans' Nest. At the same time Munk's statement excludes the only other possible identification of *Kolde Hug*, viz., with Cape Southampton, because east of this latter the coast does not trend north-east, but mainly east, forming a round bay between Cape Southampton and Cary's Swans' Nest, which is clearly marked on Munk's map. *Kolde Hug* is on Munk's map in lat. 62° 15' (in the text 62° 30'), a couple of minutes more northerly than Cary's Swans' Nest, and in long. 85°, whilst the latter promontory is in long. 83° 10'. As regards longitude it is, therefore, somewhat less out of place than Cape Southampton, which is owing to the circumstances that the bay between the two promontories is drawn twice as wide as it really is.

From Cary's Swans' Nest Munk steered an easterly course,

gradually drawing away from Coats Island; and he does not appear, on the return voyage, to have been near any part of the coast to the north between Coats Island and his *Koldenes*, which we identify with the southern extremity of Big Island. On the outward voyage he, no doubt, observed pretty closely the coast between *Koldenes* and Fair Ness, and also noticed some of the high headlands to the north; but the coastline on his map from Cary's Swans' Nest round to Fair Ness must nevertheless in the main be conjectural, and formed by connecting the different headlands by means of conjectural lines. North-east of *Kolde Hug* (Cary's Swans' Nest) two bays or inlets are marked close together, of which we take the westernmost to mark merely some land, west of Cape Pembroke, which either was too low to show above the horizon or otherwise was hidden. The sharp promontory to the north of it we believe to be Cape Pembroke, which for some reason has appeared separated from the rest of Coats Island. The next bay on Munk's map, between lat. 63° and 63° 15′, we believe to mark Evans Inlet, which opens between lat. 63° and 63° 20′. North of this inlet a broad projection of land is shown on Munk's map, between lat. 63° 10′ and 63° 30′, which we believe to represent Seahorse Point, with which it agrees very nearly in latitude, as the latter really stands between lat. 63° 30′ and 63° 40′. On Munk's map this projection is about 38 deg. west of Cape Farewell, corresponding to long. 82° west of Greenwich, whilst Seahorse Point stands in long. 80° 5′. As, however, on Munk's map the whole northern coast is displaced towards the west to the extent of a couple of degrees, the position of the projecting land in question corresponds really to that of Seahorse Point. Munk did not know of the existence of Foxe's Channel, and as he found the coast trending north-east from Cary's Swans' Nest, and doubtless from his northernmost point on the outward voyage had seen the coast curving round to the north-west and west from Fair Ness to King Charles Cape, he would naturally conclude that the sea between these points formed a round bay such as he has drawn on his map. In fact, if a line be drawn from Cape Pembroke by Seahorse Point to King Charles Cape; and, further, round Gordon Bay to Fair Ness and the southern extremity of Big Island, as shown on any good modern map, the configuration resulting would be very like the representation on Munk's map.

We have thus made a complete round of Hudson's Strait and Bay as represented on Munk's map, and we have not hesitated to go into great detail, because, in any case, Munk's map occupies a distinct historical position in the cartography of these regions, being the first published map of the entire Bay and the second published map of the Strait; whilst at the same time a fair judgment on Munk's achievement cannot be arrived at without a careful and detailed examination. As the result of this, it appears to us that we may justly claim for it an honourable place amongst the early maps of the seventeenth century: not only on account of the large number of geographical features which are represented on it for the first time—as far, at any rate, as published maps are concerned—but also on account of its remarkable fidelity in many details.

As we have stated already, Munk's book has never until now been translated into any other language from the original Danish; and its contents would probably have remained unknown to the world at large, but for the abstract of it which Isaac de la Peyrère incorporated with his book, *Relation du Groenlande*. Unfortunately this abstract is full of mistakes, some of which are very serious. The mischief thus caused would, however, have been counteracted in a great measure if Peyrère had reproduced Munk's map as he found it in the *Navigatio Septentrionalis*. Unluckily, the French writer imagined that he could improve on Munk's performance; and accompanied his book with a map which certainly, as he says, is in the main a reproduction of Munk's, but in which he has introduced considerable alterations, in order to make it agree with his own misunderstandings of Munk's text— a fact of which the reader is not made aware. As it is chiefly through this second edition (if we may so call it) that Munk's map has influenced the subsequent cartography of this region, we cannot avoid entering on a circumstantial examination of it. It appears that La Peyrère, in the first place, addressed himself (as indeed was natural) to the task of supplying the system of parallels and meridians which did not appear on Munk's map. For this purpose he very properly made use of the data which he found—or imagined were found—in Munk's text; but, unfortunately, he did not choose the most reliable ones, nor did he proceed in a self-consistent manner. La Peyrère explains in a particular notice how he set to work.[1] His map comprises the whole of the North Atlantic, from the coasts of Norway and of Scotland to North America. He says that he has laid down the parallels by means of what he knew from other sources concerning the latitude of Iceland, Spitzbergen, and Cape Farewell, and what Munk says concerning the latitude of his winter-harbour. The two first-named have no bearing on Hudson's Strait or Bay. Cape Farewell is placed by La Peyrère in lat. 60°, which is more nearly right than Munk's figure, 60½°; but under the circumstances this makes little difference, and there is no reason at all for thinking that La Peyrère was aware that Munk in his text had mentioned the latitude of Cape Farewell. As regards Munk's winter-harbour, we have already discussed the fact that, although it is shown on Munk's map in the correct latitude, the latter is nowhere mentioned in the text. Hereby a door was opened to mistake; and, as it happened, La Peyrère appears to have been

---

[1] J'ay dressé cette Carte sur quatre Eleuations qui m'ont èsté particulierement connuës, du cap Faruel, de l'Islande, du Spitsberg, & de cét endroit de la Mer Christiane, où les glaces arresterent le Capitaine Munck, qui est icy marqué, & nommé, Port d'hyuer de Munck.

J'ay pris les longitudes de tous ces lieux, sur le Meridien de l'isle de Fer des Canaries, par l'aduis de Monsieur Roberual Mathematicien de grand nom, & de Monsieur Sanson, excellent Geographe que jay consultez pour la construction de cette Carte.

La longitude du port d'hyuer de Munck, m'a esté plus precisément connuë que les autres, par une Ecclypse de Lune, qui est rapportée dans la Relation mesme de ce Capitaine, qui dit l'auoir veuë estant à ce port, sur les huit heures du soir, du vingtième Decembre, [N. S.] de l'année mil six cent dix-neuf. Elle dut paroistre à Paris, suiuant les Tables des mouuemens celestes, sur les trois heures du matin, ou enuiron, du 21. du mesme mois. Mais parce que cette Eclypse dura trois heures & plus, & que le Capitaine Munck ne dit pas s'il la vid, ou à son commencement ou à son milieu, ou à sa fin; Monsieur Gassendy à qui j'ai eu recours touchant cette difficulté, & dont la suffisance est connuë de tous ceux qui font profession d'aymer les belles lettres, m'a conseillé, pour la vraysemblance de la conjecture, & pour ne pas tomber dans l'vn, ou l'autre extreme, de poser que cette Eclypse fut apperceuë au port de Munck, entre son commencement, & sa fin; c'est à dire, vers le milieu du temps qu'elle dura, & a l'heure ou environ, qu'ell dût paroistre à Paris, etc.—
Relation du Groenland, pp. a ii b—a iv a.

misinformed, or to have misunderstood his informant, to the effect that Munk found his progress arrested by ice when he had reached the latitude of 63° 20′, and was obliged to winter there. With this idea he seems to have been so strongly impressed that, when he found it was not in keeping with Munk's map, he did not conclude that he had been led into error himself, but assumed that Munk had grossly misplaced his winter-harbour on his own map. Acting on this extraordinary and unwarrantable notion, he took upon himself to alter Munk's map, so as to make it harmonise with his own erroneous ideas. For this purpose La Peyrère first moved the whole of Hudson's Bay and Strait (at least, the western portion of the latter) a couple of degrees towards the north, so as to bring the point representing the Digges Island into lat. 64°, the north end of Mansfield Island into 65½°, etc.; after which he brought the west coast up an additional two degrees, as compared with the east coast. By this process of distortion the mouth of Churchill River, with Munk's harbour, is carried into a latitude of about 63° 30′, between four and five degrees further north than the place assigned to it on Munk's own map.

With regard to the longitude La Peyrère does not appear to have learnt or noticed that Munk gives the longitude of Cape Farewell, but he imagined that he had an excellent means of determining it in Munk's statement concerning the eclipse. It is, however, evident from his expressions that his knowledge of Munk's statement was very imperfect, and he made up for their defects by quite arbitrary assumptions. The consequence was that he obtained a longitude for Port Churchill of 81° 30′ west of Ferro, or 99° 10′ west of Greenwich: nearly four and a half degrees too westerly.

Although La Peyrère's map is founded in the main on Munk's, it differs considerably from the latter in many other respects than those mentioned. The detail of the coastline is not reproduced with any approach to fidelity, and the north coast of Hudson's Strait is entirely imaginary, apparently founded on ideas borrowed from the map in Best's account of Frobisher's voyages. The representation of Greenland is borrowed from Hessel Gerritsz.'s map. Only three of the names on Munk's map appear on La Peyrère's, of course translated into French, *viz.*, *Destroit Christian*, for Hudson's Strait, *Port d'hyver de Monck*, for Port Churchill, and Munk's name for Hudson's Bay. With regard to this, however, La Peyrère has made a mistake. Munk's name for the whole bay is *Novum Mare Christian*, but this La Peyrère has, as it were, divided into two: *Mer Christiane* for the northern part, and *Mer Nouveau* for the southern part—an error which has survived to our days, being still found on M. Lauridsen's map, in his edition of Munk's *Navigatio Septentrionalis*. Besides the three names mentioned, La Peyrère has inserted that of *Nouveau Danemarc*, which he has taken from Munk's text.

If La Peyrère had not taken upon himself to "improve" Munk's map in the manner described, instead of reproducing it as it was, geographical science would have been considerably advanced; whereas his composition caused great confusion in the cartography of Hudson's Bay, the traces of which can be followed down to the end of the last century. His proceeding, moreover, was unjust to Munk, because he nowhere states in what respects he had deviated from Munk, who consequently got the blame for his imaginations when their true character was discovered.

On the Continent, where La Peyrère's book obtained great notoriety, both in the original and in the numerous translations, cartographers naturally availed themselves of the information contained in it, particularly as regards Hudson's Bay, not suspecting its untrustworthiness. On very many if not most of the maps published on the Continent, in the latter half of the seventeenth century, the representation of Hudson's Bay is more or less founded on La Peyrère's. The maps of this series, commencing with Sanson's map of North America (Paris, 1650), are all characterised by the great projection of land in the south-west corner of the bay, bounded by a deep funnel-shaped inlet to the west of it. As these geographers do not seem to have known anything about Port Nelson, or the rivers which there enter Hudson's Bay, and of which there is an indication on Munk's map, some of them appear to have imagined that a communication with the Polar Sea existed there. On all these maps we find the west coast of the bay drawn as on Munk's map, or rather on La Peyrère's edition of it, exhibiting three deep inlets, on the southernmost of which Munk's winter-harbour is marked; and the name of New Denmark, translated into various languages, is found applied to the country around them. Several others of La Peyrère's names are met with on these maps.

More correct information became available for Continental cartographers when the French occupied the western portion of the Hudson's Bay territory, from the closing years of the seventeenth century to 1713, particularly through the paper of M. Jérémie already referred to, which was published in 1720. This was not accompanied by any map, but the data contained in it soon found place on French maps, and others founded on them. On the maps of this series, which commences with G. Delisle's map of North America (Paris, 1722), not only the great projection of land in the south-west corner of the bay is omitted (that was the case already, on a map published by Jaillot, 1719), but Nelson R., Churchill R., and Seal R., are laid down under the names of *R. de Bourbon, R. de Monc ou Danoise*, and *R. des Loups marins*. On some maps we find *Port de Monc* placed opposite Churchill River. It having been found that Munk's harbour was not, as La Peyrère had stated, in lat. 63° 20', but in lat. 59°, the whole of that part of his map was discredited, and the coast north of Churchill River drawn straight, whereby the early discovery and representation of Chesterfield Inlet and Daly Bay fell into oblivion. At the same time, some of the Continental cartographers must have obtained information from Munk's original work, because on several of these maps we find features which they cannot have derived from La Peyrère. We mentioned above that, on Munk's map, a peculiar (non-existing) triangular bay appears on the south side of Hudson's Strait, just inside the entrance, which La Peyrère has not reproduced. This bay is shown on several maps dating from the first quarter of the eighteenth century, variously modified, but unmistakeable, and the name of *Baye du Sud* is applied to it.[1] This circumstance, of course, shows that whoever first introduced this feature (we believe G. Delisle, or his informant) had misunderstood Munk's account; but as neither the bay nor the name is mentioned in the *Relation du Groenland*, it proves conclusively that he must have had the original account before him. Nevertheless we find on a map by d'Anville, of the middle of the eighteenth century, *Port de Monc* again placed in lat. 63½°, between Marble

---

[1] Maps showing these features were published by Delisle (Paris), Homann (Nürnberg), Schenck (Holland), and others.

Island and Chesterfield Inlet. This may, perhaps, be explained by supposing that the discovery (or rediscovery) of Chesterfield Inlet, so clearly shown on Munk's map, had suggested to the author of the map in question that, after all, the manner in which this part of the coast had been drawn by Munk contained more truth than it had lately been credited with: at the same time the author of this map may not have been acquainted with the strong evidence which connected Munk's winter-harbour with Churchill River.

In England, Munk's original treatise appears never to have become known at all; it is not, that we are aware, noticed by one single writer; nor does La Peyrère's book seem to have been known until a translation appeared in Churchill's *Collection of Voyages and Travels* in 1704.

The earliest published English map on which Hudson's Bay is represented appeared in 1625, in the third volume of *Purchas his Pilgrimes*. It was drawn by the celebrated mathematician, Henry Briggs, with a view of showing the geographical discoveries which had been made down to that time, and which had a bearing on the question whether a North-West Passage was likely to be found. Although it was published after Munk's map, there is no indication whatever of its author having known the latter, or indeed of his having been at all aware of Munk's expedition having taken place. Nevertheless, a comparison between the two maps is of no small interest. With regard to Hudson's Strait, we notice that on Briggs' map the long piece of coast interpolated on Gerritsz.'s and Munk's maps, immediately inside the entrance on the south side, is absent, and that Ungava Bay, with Akpatok, are clearly marked; but for the rest, Briggs' drawing of the coasts of Hudson's Strait resembles but very distantly the real configuration, and is upon the whole decidedly inferior to both Hessel Gerritsz.'s and Munk's, which largely rested on autopsy. Neither the east coast of Hudson's nor James's Bay had been visited by anybody since Hudson's time, and the representation of these parts on Briggs' map, as on Munk's, must, therefore, in the main be borrowed from Hessel Gerritsz. As regards the west coast of James's Bay, however, an important difference is noticeable. On Hessel Gerritsz.'s map the western shoulder of James's Bay (Cape Henrietta Maria, the extreme point reached by Hudson) is placed in about lat. 60: but on Briggs' map it is shown—of course conjecturally—in lat. 56° 30′; no doubt because Briggs had reason to doubt Gerritsz.'s accuracy in this respect. Even thus, however, the point in question is placed about 100 miles too northerly, and the consequence is that to the west of James's Bay we find on Briggs' map a very considerable, quite fictitious, projection of land similar to that on Munk's map. In both cases this error has the same cause, as explained above; but on Briggs' map the projection is much smaller, partly because he reduced Gerritsz.'s error by one half, partly because he had at his disposal more correct information derived from Button's expedition, whereby he was enabled to place both Port Nelson and Cape Tatnam very nearly in their right latitudes; with the result that the large funnel-shaped inlet leading to Port Nelson on Munk's map is on Briggs' map reduced to very much smaller and truer proportions.

We have suggested that Munk may have received some information, through Watson or otherwise, concerning Button's expedition, but a comparison between his map and Briggs' shows conclusively that Munk's representation of the west coast of Hudson's Bay was not founded on any information from that quarter. Purchas plainly intimates that Briggs' map, in a large measure, was founded on, or even a reproduction of, Hubert's Platt, but the drawing of the coastline bounding Hudson's Bay on Briggs' map is quite different from that on Munk's. On the former the opening of a wide inlet named Hubbart's Hope, which has no existence in reality, is marked in the place of Churchill Bay. To the north of this the coast curves round in a north-westerly direction, much as it does in nature; but there is nothing shown that resembles the two inlets shown on Munk's map, and of which the northernmost, no doubt, is Chesterfield Inlet; nor is Daly Bay marked on Briggs' map. On the north coast we find Button's Ne Ultra, and the entrance to Foxe's Channel (which was discovered by Baffin), both marked, whilst on Munk's map there is no indication of either of these features. If Munk had based his map of these parts on information derived from Button's expedition, we should have expected to find Chesterfield Inlet on Briggs' map and Button's Ne Ultra on Munk's; and the result of our comparison, therefore, must be to establish the originality of Munk's map.

This result is further strengthened by comparison with the two next following English maps, *viz.*, James's, published in 1633, and Luke Foxe's, which appeared in 1635, each of them founded on its author's personal investigation of the coast, 1631-1632. On both of these maps Cape Henrietta Maria is marked in its proper position, and there is no vestige of the fictitious projection of land which appears on Briggs' map, but which does not reappear on any later English map. On both of these, and all later English maps, Churchill Bay is drawn fairly correctly, but on neither of them is any deep inlet marked on the west coast, nor is Daly Bay marked. On neither of these maps is there any allusion to Munk, or any reproduction of features first shown on his map; nor have we found anything of the kind on any other English maps of the seventeenth century. It was not till the eighteenth century, after the appearance in Churchill's *Collection* of reproductions of La Peyrère's map, that allusions to Munk appeared on English maps. On a large map of North America, by Herman Moll (dedicated to Lord Somers), without a date, we thus find Churchill River under the name of "Munck R.". Nevertheless, the words "Here I. Munk wintered A.D. 1619" are placed against the coast in lat. 63°, and the name, "New Denmark," is placed here. Evidently the author, who probably borrowed these features from some Continental map, did not know why the French had given the name of Munk's River to the Churchill River. On a later map by the same author the name Churchill River is inserted instead of "Munck R.", whilst the legend just quoted stands in the same place. On a map of North America by R. W. Seale, the name "Munk's R." is applied to an inlet in lat. 65°. Here we also find the name of "South Bay", but misapplied to an inlet indicated considerably farther to the west than Cape Hope's Advance. In Th. Jeffery's *American Atlas* (1775) there is a map of Hudson's Bay (No. 5.6), on which we find the name of "Danish or Churchill River"; whilst the name of "South Bay" is applied to the whole of the great bight formed by Hudson's Strait inside Cape Chidley—a use of the name which might very suitably be revived in memory of Munk, as it would be convenient to have a name for this expansion of the Strait, which now is nameless. In the same Atlas there is a map of the British Empire in America, by Samuel Dunn (No. 8), on which the name "Churchill, or Danish R.", is followed by the words, "where Jn. Munk wintered in 1619."

On some maps Munk's names occur applied in a very arbitrary manner; for instance, on Middleton's Chart of Hudson's Bay (1743), whereon a piece of water near Baffin's Bay is inscribed " Christian Sea, so called by John Munk a Dane in the year 1691" [*sic*]. The name of "New Denmark" is sometimes found similarly misplaced.

The reoccupation of the Hudson's Bay territory by the English naturally had the consequence that the French, and upon the whole the older names for localities there, by degrees fell into disuse; though some of them survived for some time at the side of the English ones; and Munk's names gradually disappeared from the maps. We have mentioned that some of them occur on the map illustrating A. W. Graah's voyage to East Greenland; but this, of course, is easily explained, as Graah was a Danish writer who had specially acquainted himself with early Danish literature touching arctic geography. The latest instance of any of Munk's names being used that has come under our notice is that of *Süd Bay* as an alternative name for Ungava Bay, on C. F. Weiland's map of North America (Weimar, 1846).

In conclusion we may mention a point which should have been noticed before, but has been accidentally passed over. On Munk's map the name *Munkenes Winterhauen* is written alongside the west coast of what we have described as the funnel-shaped inlet, in such a way that persons unacquainted with the text and the woodcut of the harbour may easily mistake the name as meant for the inlet in question, particularly as the figure of a ship is placed in the mouth of the inlet. On La Peyrère's map the corresponding inscription is placed just below the true locality, but in such a way that it may easily be misunderstood as applying to some point near the mouth of the funnel-shaped inlet, where, moreover, two ships are depicted, whilst all the other figures of ships which occur on Munk's map are omitted. Whether La Peyrère himself was under a misunderstanding of this kind, we have no means of deciding. The place where the ships are shown is in lat. 63° 20′, according to his scale. The same want of precision is noticeable on the various reproductions of La Peyrère's map, excepting the one in the first volume of Churchill's *Collection*, on which the words *Here Munk wintered* are placed below the funnel-shaped inlet, clearly indicating that the translator had understood the harbour to be in that inlet. The map in question belongs to the translation of the 26th navigation of Hulsius (see pp. lxi and cxvi), but on the copy of La Peyrère's map, which accompanies the latter, the legend: *Haafen alwo Cap Munck überwintert* is placed as on the original.

INDEX.

Akpatok, 20 n., 91, 92, 93, 157, 160, 180
Aleckenes, or Alkenes, 20, 91, 92, 93, 94, 157, 160
Allen, 57, 131
Anville, d', 179
Asher, George, lxxii, lxxviii

Baffin, William, lxxxiv, lxxxv, 151, 173
Baia dus Medaus, 151, 152
Barrow, Sir John, lxviii n., cxvii, 107
Bay, Jens Munk's, 51, 125
Baye du Sud, 179
Bell, C. N., 109, 115, 117
Bell, Robert, 116 n.
Beluga, 24, 112
Best, George, 75, 77
Big Island, 163, 164, 165, 174
Briggs, Henry, lxxxvii, 141, 142, 151, 171, 180
Brock, Hans, xvii, cix, cxvi, 25, 26, 37, 112, 169
Bullock, Capt., lxxxvii
Button Islands, 79, 155
Button, Sir Thomas, lxxx, ciii, 109, 114, 137, 138, 142, 143
Bylot, Robert, lxxxiv, lxxxv

Cape Best, 75
Cape Charles, 98
Cape Digges, 98
Cape Farewell, 7, 8, 9, 67, 69, 70, 72, 73, 149
Cape Fullerton, 172, 173
Cape Henrietta Maria, 167, 170, 180, 182
Cape Hope's Advance, 90, 157, 160
Cape, King Charles's, 165, 174
Cape Merry, 113
Cape Merry's Rock, 111
Cape Pembroke, 174
Cape Resolution, 161
Cape Southampton, 172, 173
Cape Tatnam, 169, 181
Cape Tordenskjold, 68
Cape Warwick, 75
Cape Wolstenholme, 165

Cartier, Jaques, lxxv
Cary's Swan's Nest, 53 n., 128, 173, 174
Caspersen, Casper, surgeon, cvii, 36, 37, 38, 41, 122
Chamberlain, John, news-writer, cxiv
Chappel, E., 127 n., 131
Charles Island, 22 n., 98, 159
Chesterfield Inlet, 107, 171, 172, 180
Christian IV of Denmark, xv, xxvi, xlix, 64
Christy, Miller, 118 n., 137 n.
Churchill Bay, 141, 142, 144, 182
Churchill Harbour (see Port Churchill)
Churchill River, 107, 182 (see also Port Churchill)
Clerk of California, The, 69, 83, 116 n., 134
Coats Island, 128, 174
Coats, W., 81, 85, 98
Corte Real, Gaspar, lxxiii

Dalsfjord, 57 n., 131
Daly Bay, 172
Danish River, 182
Davis, John, lxxiv, 76
Davis Strait, 8, 70, 71, 75
Delisle, G., 179
Destroit Christian, 177
Dieffuels Hug, 28, 115
Digges Islands, 22 n., 54 n., 98, 99, 129, 148, 166
Digses Eyland, 22, 23, 53, 96, 101, 128 (see also Mansfield Island)

Eclipse of the moon, 34, 118, 176 n.
Ekkertaujok, 20 n., 91, 92, 157
Elfsborg, siege of, xviii
Enhiörningen, cv, 5, 23, 34, 124; guns of, 27, 37, 123, 133, 134, 135
Evans Inlet, 174

Færöe, 7 n., 65
Fair Ness, 165, 174
Fairway Island, 172
Ferröe, 7, 65
Fisher's Strait, 172
Forster, J. R., lxviii n., 117

INDEX

Fox Channel, lxxxv, xciv, 139
Foxe, Luke, cxiv n., 114 n., 118 n., 142, 143, 182
Fretum Christian, 10, 22, 75 (see also Hudson's Strait)
Fretum Hotson, 10 (see also Hudson's Strait)
Fretum Regis, 8, 70, 71, 75
Frobisher, Sir Martin, lxxiv
Frobisher's Bay (or Strait), 9 n., 73, 74

Gabriel Sound, 74, 152, 161
Gerritsz., Hessel, c, 148, 149, 150, 152, 153, 155, 156, 157, 160, 164, 166, 167, 177, 180
Gibbon, Capt., lxxxiv
Gordon, A. R., 113 n.
Gordon Bay, 174
Gordon (or Gourdon), William, cii, cix, 43, 61, 69, 73, 88, 89, 94, 125, 145
Graah, A. W., 74 n., 75, 183
Green Island, 93, 157
Greenland, 151

Hakluyt, R., lxxiii
Hall, James, xxx
Hall's Island, 73
Hansteen, Chr., 72 n.
Haresund, 19, 84, 161, 163
Harsont, 161
Hatton's Headland, 10 n., 75
Hawkeridge, William, lxxxvi
Holberg, L., 1
Holm, G., 68
Homan, J. B., 179 n.
Hope's Advance Bay, 91, 92, 157
Hopes Checked, lxxxii, 144
Hotson Strait, 9, 10 (see also Hudson Strait)
Hubbart's Hope, lxxxii, xcv, 140, 141, 142, 181
Hubert, Josias, lxxxii, 141, 143, 181
Hudson, Henry, lxxviii, 18 n., 77, 157
Hudson's Bay, lxxv, 102
Hudson's Strait, lxxi, 9, 10, 73, 74, 76, 79, 154
Hutchins, Thomas, 135

Icebergs, formation of, 118
Icy Cove, 19 n., 85, 86, 87, 163
Iisefjorde, 9, 74, 152
Iisver, 22, 54, 96, 97, 100, 130, 159
Ilha de Fortune, 152, 155
Isles de Resolution, 137 n.

Jackman's Sound, 15 n., 162
Jaillot, 179
James' Bay, 167, 170, 180
James, Thomas, 142, 182

Jeffery, Th., 182
Jensen, Rasmus, chaplain, cvii, 35, 36, 37, 39, 60
Jeremie, 130, 132, 179
Joris, Carolus, xliv

Karmsund, 6, 65
Karsund, 65
Kildin, xvii, xxiv
King Charles' Cape, 165, 174
King's Foreland, 158
Knight, John, lxxvii
Kohl, Dr., lxxii
Kolde Hug, 53, 127, 173
Koldenes, 97, 164, 165
Kolguew Island, xv

Labrador, 153, 156, 160
Lamprenen, xxi, xlviii, cvi, 5, 15, 17, 24, 50, 104, 111
La Peyrère, xxxvii, xlix, lviii, 83, 117, 120, 175, 178
Lauridsen, P., xxxvii, lvii, xcviii, cviii, 76, 81, 85, 91, 92, 98, 100, 101, 108, 178
Lind, H. D., xiii n., liii n.
Lock's Land, 9 n., 73
Lomblis Strait, 9, 10, 76, 79
Löve, den röde, xviii
Lumley's Inlet, 9 n., 74, 76, 79

Magnetic variation, 8, 9, 40, 54, 71, 122
Major, R. H., xxxi
Manoteousibi, 132, 133
Mansell Island, 102 n.
Mansfield Island, 22 n., 101, 102, 128, 167
Markham, Sir Clements, lxxvii
Mer Christiane, 178
Mer Nouveau, 178
Meta Incognita, 100, 166
Middle Savage Islands, 81
Middleton, C., 183
Mistaken Strait, 77
Munck (see Munk)
Munckenes (see Munkenes)
Munckes Bay, Jens, 51, 125
Munckes Vindterhaffn, Jens, 23, 183
Munk, Erik Nielsen, vii, viii, xiii
Munk, Erik Nielsen, jun., cxvi, 42
Munk, Jens Eriksen, family and childhood, vi-ix; adventures in Brazils, ix-xiii; earliest enterprises, xiii-xiv; voyages to Nova Zemblia, xv-xviii; service in the war with Sweden, xviii-xxi; voyage to Spain and Russia, xxii-xxiii; chases pirates, etc., xxiii, xlvii; interests himself in the whale fishery, xxiv-xxvi;

INDEX. 187

expedition to Hudson's Bay, xxxiii-xxxv; intended second voyage, xxxv-xliv; employment from 1621-1625, xliv-xlvii; service in the thirty-years' war, xlvii-xlix; death, xlix-liv
    Instructions for expedition in 1619, xcvii, 136-146; manuscript, 60-64; map, 146-183
Munk, Niels, vi
Munk, Niels Eriksen, xvii, xxiii
Munkeness, 10, 11, 55, 74, 75, 79, 131, 155, 161, 163
Munk's Cove, 114
Munk's River, 182
Musketo Point, 28 n., 115

Narwhal, cv
Navigatio Septentrionalis, editions and translations of, lv-lxvii, cxviii; manuscript of, 60
Nelson River, 141, 169
Ne Ultra, Button's, lxxxiii
Nevill Bay, 171
New Denmark, 178, 182, 183
Nolk, Anders, xvii, xviii
Nörreland, 24, 106
North Bay, 19 n., 85, 163
Nottingham Island, 98, 99, 100, 130, 166
Nova Dania, 22, 23, 102
Nova Zemblia, xv, xvii
Novum Mare, 22, 102
Novum Mare Christian, 102, 178
Nouveau Danemark, 178
Nyerup, R., lxvii, 64 n.

Old Fort (Churchill), 114
Origanus, David, 71, 119, 145

Petersen, Jan, cix, cxvi, 25, 42, 112
Pilots, Munk's, cix, 3, 20, 89 (see also H. Brock, W. Gordan, J. Petersen, and J. Watson)
Pirates in the North Sea, xxiii
Port Churchill, 23 n., 106, 109, 110, 111, 112, 114, 117, 168
Port de Monc, 179
Port d'hyver de Munck, 177
Port Nelson, 169
Prickett, Abacuck, 18 n.
Prince of Wales Fort, 114
Prince of Wales Island, 97, 158
Promise Island, 172
Ptarmigan, 30 n., 117

Ranken Inlet, 171
Ravn, E., 75, 85, 101, 107
Rensuna (*see* Rinsund)
Resolution Island, 10 n., 76, 77, 154
Richardson, Sir John, 114, 134
Rinsund, 15, 82, 161, 162
Rivière Danoise, 132, 133, 179
Rivière de Bourbon, 179
Rivière de Monc, 132, 179
Rivière du loup marin, 134, 179
Robson, J., 109, 134, 135
Roe's Welcome, lxxxiii, xcv, 172
Rothe, C. P., lxvii
Rundall, Th., lxxxvi
Russian glass, 19, 84
Rype, 30 n., 117

St. Mary's Rock, 23 n., 111
Salisbury Island, 98, 99, 100, 130, 166
Sanson, N., 179
Schenck, Th., 179 n.
Schlegel, J. H., xxxii, li, 64 n.
Seahorse Point, 174
Seale, R. W., 182
Seal River, 179
Severn River, 108
Skudenes, 6, 65
Slange, N., xviii, xix, xx, xxviii, xxxii, l, cvi
Snee Oeland, 21, 9:, 93, 157
Söndfjord, 58 n., 131
Söster, 22, 54, 96, 98, 129
South Bay, 182
Stygge, Maurits, cvii, 11 n., 38, 43, 79
Süd Bay, 183
Sundfjord, 57, 131
Sydernes, 97, 158, 160
Syderö, 7, 65
Synder Bugt, 21, 92, 93

Umfreville, E., 116 n.
Ungava Bay, 20 n., 21 n., 92, 93, 156, 157
Upper Savage Islands, 85

Warwick Foreland, 76
Watson, cii, cix, cxv, 45 n., 73, 86, 89, 105, 125, 169, 172
Weiland, C. F., 183
Weymouth, George, lxxvi, 76
Whalefishery, xxiv, xxvi
Whitbourne, Richard, xcii n.
White Strait, 19 n., 86
Wolstenholme, Sir John, lxxxvii, lxxxix